THE QUEST FOR THE INNER MAN

THE QUEST FOR THE INNER MAN

Transpersonal Psychotherapy and Integral Sadhana

JOSEPH VRINTE

First Published: April 1996

ISBN: 81-208-1502-5

Distributed by

MOTILAL BANARSIDASS
41 U.A. Bungalow Road, Jawahar Nagar, Delhi 110 007
8, Mahalaxmi Chamber, Warden Road, Mumbai 400 026
120 Royapettah High Road, Mylapore, Chennai 600 004
Sanas Plaza, Subhash Nagar, Pune 411 002
16 St. Mark's Road, Bangalore 560 001
8 Camac Street, Calcutta 700 017
Ashok Rajpath, Patna 800 004
Chowk, Varanasi 221 001

PRINTED AT ALL INDIA PRESS
KENNEDY NAGAR, PONDICHERRY 605001, INDIA
PUBLISHED BY SRI MIRA TRUST

THE QUEST FOR THE INNER MAN

TRANSPERSONAL PSYCHOTHERAPY
AND
INTEGRAL SADHANA

Joseph Vrinte

SRI MIRA TRUST
PONDICHERRY, INDIA

First Published: April 1996

ISBN 81-86413-03-0

Published by Sri Mira Trust

Printed at All India Press
Kennedy Nagar, Pondicherry 605001, India

Printed in India

To the Mother, only She knows why.

CONTENTS

PREFACE

In the present work an attempt is made to compare some important ideas of Transpersonal psychotherapy with Sri Aurobindo's integral Yoga with the intention to structure some of the material and to gain more insight into their respective views. Nevertheless, the subject is so wide that it is almost impossible to deal in detail with everything that falls within its scope, and this work is therefore not an exhaustive study of the whole movement of Transpersonal psychotherapy or of the complete works of integral Yoga psychology. It only attempts to explore some points of convergence as well as divergence between the two views without opposing both by an antagonistic *versus*.

In pursuing this purpose a preliminary warning may be in order; the reader has to understand Sri Aurobindo in the context of his vision and spiritual attainments, and this study does not attempt to reduce Sri Aurobindo's psychology to the transpersonal standards and views. Throughout this work we are dealing with two different but often overlapping psychologies. Both views base their psychology on authentic experience, but Sri Aurobindo does not always present his intuitive vision in Western psychological language; he expresses his insights largely in the language of Indian metaphysics based on spiritual intuition, whereas the transpersonal intuitive reflections about the ultimate reality are more based on rational speculations.

Comprising of eight chapters this study commences with a general introduction to psychotherapy, exploring the fundamentals about the nature and aim of psychotherapy. Psychotherapy as an art and science of healing human suffering aims at gaining increased self-knowledge and insight, enabling the individual to evolve new patterns of behaviour which are more supportive for his present development. However, psychotherapy is not restricted to the medical treament of psychological illnesses, it simultaneously aims at the development of the highest human potentials in a psychologically well-integrated individual.

The second chapter offers a comprehensive overview of the current forms of psychotherapy. Transpersonal psychology integrates the mainstream of Western psychotherapeutic insights into the transpersonal approach, and it is therefore essential to briefly explain the central ideas of various psychotherapies in order to understand some of the basic concepts of Transpersonal psychotherapy. Psychotherapy is changing rapidly in its working methods and it is therefore not possible to explore all its ideas and its various techniques. The limited scope of this presentation does not permit the author to attempt an all-comprehensive upto date overview of all the various forms of psychotherapy. In trying to summarize the major fields of psychotherapy there will be some areas that are given insufficient attention or even ignored altogether. With inevitable biasis of the author only those influential theories are selected which clearly illustrate a particular system and which are relevant for this study.

The third chapter attempts to render a critical and constructive account of the transpersonal approach. The author introduces some of the characteristics of spiritual growth in relation to psychotherapy before examining a variety of topics and issues related to transpersonal psychology/psychotherapy. The same chapter also elaborates various techniques used in Transpersonal psychotherapy in order to realise transpersonal potentials, and he concludes this chapter with a comparison between Transpersonal psychotherapy and spiritual discipline.

In the fourth chapter different theories of various leading transpersonal psychologists are briefly disccussed. He critically examines and elucidates the views of A. Maslow, R. Assagioli, K. Wilber, S. Grof and M. Washburn.

Chapter five offers an exposition of the chief characteristics of Sri Aurobindo's integral psychology. Besides presenting some insight into the psychological dimensions of Sri Aurobindo's vision and the aim of his integral Yoga, this chapter also gives a full account of the psycho-spiritual constitution of man. It is through the practice of Yoga that the seeker discovers the extraordinary complexity of his own multi-layered being.

The sixth chapter describes in detail various aspects related to Sri Aurobindo's spiritual practices (sadhana). After introducing at length the foundation of sadhana the author defines the three constituent elements of Yoga in sadhana as well as the three means to the object of sadhana. The terms integration and transformation are given a compresensive explanation as they are the central object of Sri Aurobindo's intergral Yoga.

In the seventh chapter Sri Aurobindo's sadhana is compared with the transpersonal approach. The author relates the various forms of psychotherapy, as discussed in the second chapter, with Sri Aurobindo's integral psychology after which he examines the underlying connections and dissimilarities between Transpersonal psychology and integral Yoga psychology as well as Transpersonal psychotherapy and integral sadhana. He finishes this chapter with various psychological problems inherrent in the process of spiritual development.

The last chapter provides a condensed view of various leading transpersonal psychologists in relation to Sri Aurobindo's visions. He critically evaluates the nature of metaphysics in integral Yoga and Transpersonal psychology, concluding this last chapter with a final confrontation.

This book is pre-eminently intended for all those seekers on the way who seek for unity in a divided art of healing. In the author's personal search into the meaning of human existence, through an introspective process of replacing old boundaries and surveying new ones, he indicates and examines various pros and cons involved on the journey to inward continents and self-discovery. During this process the seeker is bound to find a bewilding set of ideas and techniques in the exploration of the various theories and procedures in psychotherapy and spiritual disciplines. The voyage to spiritual fulfilment through inner exploration of the unknown—in terms of predictability—does hardly create any guarantee of security, and this book does not offer an easy escape route but confronts the reader with the realities of the present human state, placing this state within the context of the transpersonal movement and the integral psychology as envisioned by Sri Aurobindo.

As the reader moves through the various sytems of psychotherapy and integral sadhana he hopefully gains a wider understanding of the two views and a deeper curiosity and appreciation of the complexity of human nature.

Throughout this work I use the gender he rather than the he/she format as this becomes too cumbersome and distracts from smooth reading. However, each and every seeker is viewed as a Being who transcends gender.

I wish to express my sincere appreciation to the many individuals who helped me in this study; to Dr. A. S. Dalal, clinical psychologist of Sri Aurobindo Ashram, Pondicherry, for his initial encouragement to write this work.

I am specially endebted to Dr. R. Jagannath for scrutinizing this manuscript thoroughly, and for drawing my attention to some factual errors in the original work. His detailed comments helped me to refine some ideas as expressed in this work.

I am also very grateful to Dr. Ananda Reddy for taking the trouble of going through the work in manuscript form in the later stages. His critical reading resulted in some clarifying explanations and valuable suggestions.

However, it must be clear that the responsibility of the validity of the interpretation of concepts as presented in this book rests solely with the author.

A special debt of gratitude is reserved for the staff members of Bureau Central; through them I was able to gain some insight into the working methods of Sri Aurobindo's Ashram.

I feel obliged for Ms. Anita Frenkena's library card of the University of Amsterdam. This academic support has helped me immeasurably as it provided me with most of the literature used in this work.

I cannot fail to mention the gracious work of Ms. Latha Govindan who patiently and expeditiously typed the corrections and final draft of this work.

Lastly, I take this opportunity to express my special thanks to the one without whom this work would not exist, the Mother.

Pondicherry 15th February 1996.

The Quest for The Inner Man

CHAPTER I

PSYCHOTHERAPY

1. Introduction

From times immemorial the essence of all therapies was related to spiritual healing. The ancient Greeks used the method of catharsis as a process of purification or cleansing for the recovery of illness. Psychotherapy as an art of healing used to be called 'the cure of souls', a cure for the distressed conscience. In the course of time the study of the human soul was transfered from religion to medicine, the province of the priest was taken over by the psychiatrist. The cure of the souls became the treatment of medical diseases and the care of the mentally disturbed passed on from the theological to the medical realm. Mental illness became a subject of medical classification and was categorized as a disease entity.

Although the roots of psychotherapy can be traced back to antiquity, formal psychotherapy originated in the later part of the nineteenth century with P. Janet and P. Dubois as the first psychotherapists who used rational naturalistic views in the treatment of mental illness. However, the emergence of dynamic psychotherapy as a specialised form of treatment can be accredited to Freud, who completely transformed the practice of mental healing.

In its origin psychotherapy can be seen as an identifiable group of activities clustering around the knowledge of man's psychic apparatus and mental healing. Freud enlivened psychiatry as a dynamic enterprise and brought psychopathology out of the clinic into the consulting room.

The techniques of modern psychotherapeutic systems are often the products of culture, they seem to be predominantly influenced by social processes, circumstances and ideologies. The recent weakening of religions, social/moral laws, and the erosion of traditional authority relations contributed to the development of a new kind of personal identity in which the personal and subjective are paramount. In the developing therapeutic systems the idea of self instead of God became central and this self, with the help of science, has formed a powerful union with matters related to psychological truth and health. The present culture of plenty provided fertile ground for the narcissistic revolution which in turn led to an explosion of character disorders and the need for psychotherapeutic treatment.

Implicitly and explicitly in the work of any psychotherapist there is an underlying theory of personality. Therapeutic methods are often the product of a personality theory. Most of the major theories of personality meaningfully describe a person as he is, and explain psychological distress and its treatment. To be an effective psychotherapist one must work within the context of a cohesive theory of personality. The theoretical framework of psychotherapy often reflects the therapist's personal temperament, character, values, and philosophical assumptions but also the Zeitgeist in which the therapist and his adherents live. A successful therapist therefore develops a theory congruent to his own personality. In a sense psychotherapy is a projective technique that says as much about the therapist's personality as it does about the client's, and often the personality and attitude of the therapist is more important than his adherence to a particular school of thought.

Systems of psychotherapy differ according their dependence on the crucial determinants of behaviour related to a particular personality theory.

Therapy is regarded as an art of healing using any medical method for the relief of any disease. Its aim is limited to the recuperation of health.

The term psychotherapy is used in a general and in a specific way. In a general way, as counseling, it takes place on an informal level with a confidant as the helping assistant, rather than the professional therapist (therapy). Both are viewed as overlapping areas of professional competence, but counseling is more concerned with assisting relatively normal functioning people to achieve their goals more effectively, whereas psychotherapy is more described in terms of alleviating severe problems in life and other more intense psychological processes such as supportive, analytical, and reconstructive measures. It is generally assumed that counseling and psychotherapy are qualitatively the same but differ quantitatively.

In psychotherapy there is a psychotherapist who works according to psychological principles and a client whose personal and/or social integration is inadequately developed.*

Psychotherapy as an art of healing human suffering relieves distress resulting from emotional conflicts or maladaptive behaviour patterns.

However, psychotherapy is not just a means of curing disturbing psychopathological symptoms or the modification of character structure but it is also an art in helping the client to encounter his life situation and in alleviating personal and interpersonal problems. In psychotherapy negative self assumptions as well as distorted views about the client's interpersonal relationships are gradually modified which provides him in the course of time with a new base of confidence for his future development.

Contemporary psychotherapy is not merely concerned with the cure of disease or adjustment processes but it includes change and growth of the individual. Many clients who visit a therapist view their difficulties not as medical problems but rather as symptoms of "a troubled soul". Such clients do not suffer from serious personal anguish but seek self-actualisation of their potentials; they do not seek a therapist for guidance to eliminate their conflicts but to discover themselves and find self-enlightenment.

But such changes are more related towards self-knowledge or social change rather than the transformation of the self; the latter usually develops more gradually outside the therapist's office.

It is difficult to define psychotherapy with any precision. Though definitions of psychotherapy abound, none is completely satisfactory. It is unlikely that any one definition of psychotherapy will ever find universal acceptance. It is therefore impossible, in the present state of theory development, to give an acceptable definition of the term psychotherapy, but any description involves three elements; (a) there

* Throughout this work the term client is consistently addressed as this word avoids the implication of sickness to those who consult a psychotherapist rather than with illness. Whenever the term patient is found in this work, it is only used in case where other writers are quoted.

is an emotional, relational or behavioural dysfunctioning, (b) the treatment is based on psychological principles, (c) and the treatment is implemented by a qualified psychotherapist. All the various definitions also include the importance of the therapeutic relationship, the manifestation of development, and durable change.

Psychotherapy in its broadest sense is defined in the Encyclopaedia Britannica as "the systematic effort of a person or group to relieve distress or disability by influencing the sufferer's mental state, attitudes and behaviour."

J. K. Zeig and M. Munion define psychotherapy as, "a change-oriented process that occurs in the context of a contractual, empowering, and emphatic professional relationship. Its rationale explicitly or implicitly focuses on the personality of the client, the technique of psychotherapy, or both. Durable change is affected on multiple aspects of clients' lives. The process is idiosyncratic and determined by the interaction of the patients' and therapists' preconceived positions."[1]

An eclective definition of psychotherapy would sound like "a systematic helping process that fosters change and development in intrapsychic functioning, interpersonal relationships, and one's capacity to negotiate important life tasks.... Psychotherapy focuses on adapting one's intrapsychic structures, cognitive processes, and behavioral repertoires in a manner that is consistent with one's needs and capacities".[2]

J. Corsini assumes that "all psychotherapies are methods of learning. All psychotherapies are intended to change people: to make them think differently (cognition), to make them feel differently (affection), and to make them act differently (behavior)."[3]

T. Szas denies therapy as a medical treatment, there is no such thing as therapy. Psychotherapy is only the name given to people speaking and listening to each other, it is a conversation rather than a cure and as such it is only a myth. He relates psychotherapy to applied secular ethics, each method of psychotherapy reflects the personality and values of its founder and practitioners. Szas wants to propose a new name for psychotherapy; "iatrologic, the secular cure of souls. Its practitioners ... their activities would constitute, and be classified as, art rather than science."[4]

In psychotherapy the paid professional relationship is undertaken by the client for the purpose of the relief of mental suffering, but also for the purpose of assisting him to make positive changes in attitudes toward self and others, and to find various ways of coping with life situations.

Psychotherapy is a psychologically based treatment process through which a professionally trained psychotherapist uses psychological knowledge to understand, influence and modify the behaviour of psychologically troubled clients.

Therapeutic techniques facilitate the disclosure and resolution of the client's major conflicts within a certain time limit (short or long-term therapy), thus reducing the likelihood of pathological dependencies in any therapeutic endeavour. Psychotherapy moves the individual towards a particular ideal and the techniques used in any form of therapy are only instruments for accomplishing that purpose.

In general, psychotherapy can be defined as the art and science of relieving and healing human suffering, often resulting from emotional conflicts and disturbances, by psychological techniques rather than physical or chemical means. It is essentially a process designed to change the individual in a meaningful way, enabling the person to evolve new patterns of behaviour which are more supportive for his present development. Psychotherapy is a kind of learning process in which the individual is involved as an active participator and includes a constructive personality change as well as the changing of those behaviour patterns that are at present blocking the individual's development. Psychotheapy as a healing process deals with almost every type of mental, emotional, and characterological disturbances. Suffering, feelings of emptiness or meaninglessness are often the first expressions of an encounter with the inner depth experience and in which the individual is confronted with himself and his environment. Before entering therapy the individual is not content with his present existence, there is an inability to cope with life situations or a defective integration. A sense of insecurity, despair, frustration, fear, anxiety, social failure, or other mental strains easily pave the way for seeking guidance of a therapist or a counselor. When the distress or the emotional conflict seriously affects the individual's life psychotherapy becomes a possibility; when the misery is accompanied by an intense sense of confusion regarding the conduct of everyday life or when the client does not respond positively to the crisis he most likely will consult a psychotherapist.

Once the client is healed from psychological suffering he may continue therapy in order to know more about himself and others, and to grow experientially.

2. Crisis

In a crisis, when all is not well with individuals, they encounter themselves as they are and what they can be if they change themselves. The reason for a crisis may be vague without any apparent cause or it may be a sense of unreality and inward emptiness towards life due to a false attunement of human reality which inhibits the free unfolding of the individual's very essence. Most crises originate in the inability of the individual to creatively adjust himself towards life or to assimilate sudden important changes. A psychic crisis manifests itself when psychic sorrow and a strong sense of frustration are no longer controlled. Parts of the individual's inner and outer life have to be reorganised in order to solve the risk of isolation and bitterness.

A life-crisis happens in an absolute, individual and unique way and the so-called psychopathological symptom is often experienced as a very personal drama.

The nature of the problem need not always be interpreted as "illness"; often the problem is more related to one's meaning in life or actualising one's potentials, and psychotherapy is then no longer prescribed as a treatment according to the medical model but rather as an improvement in relation to the growth model.

A crisis causes not only tension and sorrow but also offers a possibility for a new experience of one's identity or for new behaviour patterns. Such a crisis should not be seen as a troublesome circumstance which has to be forgotten immediately, but the individual must be able to come into contact with the crisis as a situation in one's life in which important existential processes are taking place.

Crises often appear as a prelude to a critical examination and transformation of the individual's life style, and if handled in a proper way it may bring out strengths the individual did not realise before the crisis. Experiences that come out of the solution of the crisis constitute an important part of personality development and growth. During a crisis the individual either passively accepts the situation as one's impersonal fate or actively uses the situation as a personal challenge. According to Sheldon Kopp, a crisis arises on account of "the hungry outcry of an unsatisfied soul"[5] due to inner emptiness, and as such a crisis is a time of danger and involves risks, but it also is a time of renewal. One works through pain to joy.

Finally, conflicts may also arise due to moral or religious doubts in the process of growth, or the crisis may be caused by a spiritual awakening. A crisis in integral Yoga is more related to the search for one's integral reality and for the supreme goal of existence in the path of self-discovery.

3. Aim of Psychotherapy

Psychotherapy assumes human suffering and it seems that in the experience of suffering lies the desire to eliminate it. Suffering may be a signal that implies a deeper experience which tries to manifest itself. As such, psychotherapy as a form of treatment can vary between the cure of mental disorders in mentally ill individuals and the acquisition of higher states of consciousness in mentally well-adapted individuals.

Psychotherapy aims at understanding the individual as a whole and helps persons to improve their ways of managing their life through increasing their self-knowledge and insight. Psychotherapy as a voyage of discovery into the various unknown aspects of the self, enables the individual to gain psychological insight into his inadequacy in dealing with life's problems and sense of insecurity; it points at an internal equilibrium by bringing into awareness the underlying deep-seated origins of psychological disturbances. The process is accompanied by the exploration of and venturing into unknown areas and aspects of ourselves. As such, psychotherapy examines self-concepts, removes distortions of this self-concept, and restores psychological health through creating a realistic assessment of self-limitations and potentialities of the individual. The goal of therapy is not only to free the individual from the sense of isolation and estrangement of himself, but also helps the person in adjusting to a rapidly changing society while retaining some individual stability.

Psychotherapy therefore basically exists for the complete personality reorganisation, a reintegration of one's behaviour and awareness in which the individual develops his own problemsolving abilities, aided by the therapist who promotes the natural tendency for healing and accelerates change in a positive direction.

Psychotherapy is not merely "a talking cure", it is also an active relationship in which the client does more than talk; it implies actions and experiences of both the client and the therapist.

The therapist as a counselor brings into awareness the good and healthy behaviour but simultaneously the inadequate and problem causing behaviour-patterns, usually on a supporting level. For a deeper successful therapy he then moves onwards to explore or analyse the origin and development of the underlying conflicts. In this process the therapist utilizes various techniques from his therapeutic methods as a re-educational process in order to effect certain changes, to improve the integration of the personality, and to help the client to move towards a better adaptation. The therapist, with the help of methodical interactions, tries to return to the client something that has been lost and to remove obstacles for maintaining a healthy life rather than trying to juggle away his illness. In the process of self-improvement, through increasing the client's self-knowledge, the therapist functions as a worthwhile guarantee by penetrating deep into the client's world and making these inner contents accessible to reality.

4. Eclecticism

Since the late seventies a decisive shift in opinion has quietly occurred and the elective position has replaced the continued dominance of the major schools of psychotherapy. Therapists are exploring ways of synthesising diverse elements into flexible multifarious orientations. The essence of the eclectic approach is the lack of strict allegiance to any single theoretical system, and the therapist is not constrained by adherence to one approach.

Eclecticism implies the investigation of various schools of thought and the construction of a theory which incorporates different viewpoints into a balanced whole.

Eclecticism has nonetheless been criticised for its absence of a central rationale for therapeutic action. It lacks an organising integrative framework; opposite views are equated, irreconcilable differences are glossed over, and philosophical issues are ignored. A therapist without an over-all philosophical view of life is not able to solve the incompatibilities between the various different theories, and often struggles to integrate in a new way his own unique personalised theoretical position.

Eclectic comprehensive psychotherapy should not be confused with integralism. Integralism is opposed to idealogical rigidity, it tries to meld conflicting schools into a harmonious whole and reconcile divergent points of emphasis into a unified theory. Integralism is a process of synthesising separate ideas and relevant methods to form a basic theoretical coherent model.

Unlike eclecticism, the integrative approach is more committed to achieve a thorough going integration and its results are a true synthesis of those elements that lead to the evolution of new methods rather than a mixture of simple elements from various models. The integrative approach is therefore not a simple sum of prior separate approaches but a framework that is comprehensive, unified, and continuously evolving. To minimize the elicitation of new schools it is essential that contributions from other approaches, including other integrative arrivals, should be thoroughly examined and afterwards incorporated.

Integral therapy in trying to discover a new structure of consciousness does not aim at perfection but at wholeness, in which the individual is conscious of himself, feeling more powerfully related with the depth of his essence and body.

5. Conclusion

Broadly taken, psychotherapy can be described as a mutual therapist/client endeavour to investigate and understand the nature of the latter's mental distress for the purpose of providing relief from his suffering. In its major aim it endeavours to produce changes within the individual which will enable him to maintain a more stable adaptation to oneself and one's world. In the therapeutic process, psychological principles are used to favourably alter intrapsychic functioning and interpersonal patterns, and to strengthen the ego's integrative capacities.

However, psychotherapy need not restrict itself to the healing of psychological illness but may simultaneously aim at the individual's growth, i.e., the attainment of the highest human potentials and maximum mental health. Such therapies focus on the ongoing process and the discovery of a progressive unfolding of ideas, feelings and memories that had been previously unrecognised.

With the emergence of "new" therapies, neurotic problems are gradually replaced by problems in living, emotional distress, and they are no longer used within the medical model but seen in the light of existential problems. The traditional methods of psychotherapy have often added various new approaches to their therapeutic processes, such as the teachings of Eastern disciplines, meditation, self-actualisation, self-awareness, etc, and the boundaries between treatment and growth have become more obscure.

An increasing number of clients enter psychotherapy for the purpose of finding a meaning in their lives, for personal growth or for increasing their creative potentials. The present increased awareness of psychotherapy has had different effects. On the one hand it has led to a greater acceptance of psychotherapy as an instrument for growth or as a treatment modality for mental disorders. On the other hand critical questions have been raised regarding the effectiveness of psychotherapy. It has often been observed that clients who are immensely benefited by psychotherapy frequently relapse and within a few years, after having completed therapy, they become almost as disturbed as they were previously.

Psychotherapy, as a process, is primarily based on the art of relating and the science of understanding behaviour change. There is a trend by various therapists to make psychotherapy an exact science of healing. But within human functioning there are certain symptoms which present themselves as unknowable or unpredictable. As a science psychotherapy can hardly be conclusive as it touches upon existential and moral values as well as religious convictions, and in this way it remains more a "science-fiction". Psychotherapy as a science remains in a paradoxical position as it views mental reality simultaneously as object and subject. In their empirical research work the investigators have ignored inner inconsistencies and self-knowledge of the therapist, and as such their results can only give partial knowledge.

Psychotherapists too often partially translate the reality of the client's life to the construction of their own attached model, which indicates the limitation of their specific methods of assistance for specific problems.

Notes:

1. Zeig, J. K and M. Munion Edt; What is Psychotherapy? Contemporary perspectives, Jossey-Bass Inc Publ, San Fransisco 1990, p. 14.
2. Ibid., p. 244.

3. Wedding, Denny and J. Corsini; Current Psychotherapies, F. E. Peacock Publ Inc, Illinois 1989, p. 5
4. Sasz T; The Myth of Psychotherapy; Mental Healing as Religion, Rethoric and Repression, Oxford University Press, Oxford 1979, p. 208
5. Kopp, Sheldon; All God's Children are lost, but only a few can play the piano, Prentice Hall Press, N-York 1991, p. 7.

CHAPTER II

INTRODUCTION TO VARIOUS THERAPIES

Transpersonal psychotherapy draws from Eastern and Western spiritual disciplines as well as from the insights of psychodynamic and behaviourial psychology. It affirms the role of emotional and interpersonal factors in psychopathology. Transpersonal psychology values the mainstream of Western psychotherapeutic approaches; it does not try to replace them but rather integrate them in a larger perspective beyond the "normal" human capacities and possibilities.

It is therefore essential to briefly elaborate the psychodynamic and behavioural therapies in order to understand some of the basic concepts of Transpersonal psychotherapy.

There is a great variety of therapies for a wide range of psychological disturbances. In his handbook of innovative psychotherapy R. J. Corsini identifies 250 schools of psychotherapy, but more scholarly journals reduce the figure to 12 main orientations.

At present there is no universally recognised way to classify the various different therapies, but in this study Maslow's model of four major theoretical trends, often called "forces" which follow a certain thematic progression, will be elaborated. Among these four forces of therapy, the classical psychoanalytic, cognitive-behavioural, existential-humanistic and transpersonal approaches, major attention is given to the recently developed fourth force in the field of therapy. Each system of therapy explicitly or implicitly sets forth an image of man, the nature of human conflicts and the methods of resolving these conflicts. Out of these theories each system formulates a model of psychotherapy which is usually included in their underlying system. The four fundamental forces have also an intervening influence on their views regarding the relation of beings with their surroundings and through that on the culture as a whole.

As previously mentioned in the preface, the enormous nature of the task does not permit the author to attempt an exclusive review of each of the various types of psychotherapy in this comprehensive work.

In surveying the major fields of psychotherapy certain areas are given insufficient attention which may oversimplify the therapists' views and their contributions.

1. The Psychoanalytical Approach

The Psychodynamic Theory

Psychodynamic therapy is based on the hypothetical postulates of unconscious processes and personality development; it aims at the "insight" of understanding the underlying dynamics through a rational interpretation.

Before Freud's discovery of the theory of unconscious functioning, mental operations and behaviour seemed unknowable and almost mystical. The word unconscious refers to the lack of awareness of the individual's own mental functioning, or the unawareness of all things at a given moment.

Psychodynamic approaches aim at creating an awareness of the latent vast array of unconscious or unknown forces, and of ideas/ thoughts underlying the client's surface behaviour. When clients are able to discover these unconscious processes in their full complexity they gain emotional and cognitive insight which, in turn, liberates psychic energy for better utility in psychological health and for the reconstruction of their personality.

Insight may be described as the ability to look at old experiences from new perspectives, but this insight is valuable only if clients are able to integrate the new information into their present-day life.

The psychodynamic theory represents a metapsychology based on philosophical assumptions as well as a clinical theory with elements of scientific theory.

The psychodynamic theory should not be confused with the psychoanalytic theory. The term psychoanalytic refers specifically to

Freud's theory, whereas the psychodynamic theory (Jung Adler, Rogers, Neo-Freudians, etc) is a broader set of constructs; it relies heavily on the interplay of forces within the mind and utilizes the roots of the psychoanalytic theory as an important foundation.

2. Freud's Psychoanalytical Theory

Freud's psychoanalysis may be considered as a method of investigation of unconscious thoughts and feelings, as a theory of human personality, and as a technique of psychotherapy.

Psychoanalysis is a psychology of the symbolising activity of the mind, and raises questions about the contents of mental states—events symbolised by a mental representation.

Freudian thought can be classified into various postulates: (i) in his concept of psychic determinism, psychic processes are strictly determined by constitutional, developmental, or environmental factors; (ii) his concept of the unconscious plays a predominant part in mental life and functions as a dynamic force. Reason is able to channel the energy (from the instinctual drives) into modes of expression in accord with objective reality; (iii) all behaviour is motivated (motivations are emotional in nature) and goal directed; (iv) he assumed a developmental approach of personality traits and in his dynamic concept of personality, importance is given to infancy and early childhood.

Freud believed that psychological disorders resulted from constitutional factors, early childhood experiences, and precipitating factors in later life. The relative influence of these factors varies.

a. Theory of Personality

Freud's psychoanalytical theory is based on the psychology of intrapsychic conflicts between the various structures of the personality.

Freud viewed personality from six different perspectives; the topographic involves conscious versus unconscious modes of functioning; the structural involves the persistent functional units of the id, ego, and superego; the dynamic, genetic, economic, and adaptive views are not directly related to his psychotherapy and are therefore not elaborated in this chapter.

In Freud's earlier views of personality he classifies the organisation of the psyche in three "locations" or levels of awareness; the conscious with current thoughts and experiences; the pre-conscious, a borderline area of thoughts and feelings the individual is not aware of but with some effort its contents can be summoned by the ordinary process of association; and the unconscious, a storehouse of impulses, passions, instinctual energies, and repressed experiences which are almost inaccessible to the conscious individual.

Freud assumed that mental life represents an unrelenting conflict between the unconscious, biological, instinctual and sexual parts of the mind which are impulsively pressing for discharge, and the conscious parts of the mind which function at a logical realistic and adaptive level. Repressed contents of the unconscious causes various types and degrees of psychopathological disorders.

Subsequently Freud came to recognize certain inconsistencies in his topographical model. Not all unconscious mental contents are instinctual, and conscience operating at both conscious and unconscious levels also plays an important role in psychic conflicts. He therefore reformulated his theory in terms of a structural organisation of mind. This structural theory is more heterogeneous than his topographical theory; by now he attempts to combine biological, empirical, and interpersonal dimensions.

In the structural model mental functions are grouped according to the role they play in conflicts. He classified 3 subdivisions of the psychic apparatus: the id, the ego and the superego, which in a very general sense represents biological needs, psychological principles, and social standards respectively.

The id represents the instinctual urges which are basically sexual and aggressive in origin, but it also comprises repressed ideas, events, and feelings which are excluded from consciousness. The id-functions refer to behaviour which the individual cannot deliberately control.

The superego is classified as the residue of the early history of the individual's moral upbringing. It can be understood to include the tendency to self-criticism (conscience) but also the function of self-observation and the establishment of ego-ideal. The superego-functions are unconsciously performed but open to become conscious.

The ego comprises a group of functions that brings the individual in contact with the external world and mediates between the id and the superego. The ego stands for reason and good sense, it includes the channelling and control of id impulses. The ego also developes purposeful strategies to deal with life's difficulties whether they come from inside or outside. Ego-functions are partly unconscious, (defence mechanisms) partly pre-conscious, and partly conscious.

Though each of these systems has its own functioning the three also interact to govern behaviour. The id seeks pleasure, the ego tests reality, and the superego strives for perfection. Mental health is defined in terms of the success of the ego in protecting the mind from internal dangers. In an integral personality the three components work together as a unified team, but in a psychologically unbalanced personality there are unresolved conflicts between these three.

Freud's theory of personality is based on a number of fundamental principles. There is a dynamic interaction of libidinal* and aggressive impulses. Whenever impulses are involved some mixture of the sexual and aggressive instinctive energies take place. Then there is the deterministic principle in which a connection between current mental experiences and past events can be established, and many of these connections are unconscious. Lastly, in the genetic principle the origins of later conflicts are traced to crucial childhood events.

b. Psychoanalytic Therapy

From his theoretical psychoanalytic principles Freud derived his psychoanalytic therapy. Before explaining the process of psychoanalytic therapy it may be useful to point out that psychoanalysis, as the study and discovery of the unconscious psychic life, when it is applied to psychoanalytic therapy, leaves out the ego and its aberrations. However, Freud's daughter Anna defined psychoanalysis as "to acquire the fullest possible knowledge of all the three institutions [id, ego, superego] of which we [Freudians] believe the psychic personality to be constituted and to learn what are their relations to one another and to the outside world."[1]

Traditional psychoanalytic therapy provides a setting in which the analysant can express thoughts and feelings spontaneously and freely (free association) to a receptive analyst; the analysant gains insight through acting out expressions of his unconscious conflicts and

* Libido is the drive energy which functions as a means of satisfying the sexual need that is experienced as a drive.

through the awareness of the power of the transference relationship. Transference is related to the highly emotional attitude the analysant develops towards the analyst which represents a repetition of past fantasy wishes foisted onto the analyst. In the process of psychotherapy the analysant's free associations are from time to time interrupted and interpreted by the analyst, and gradually the analysant's role of passive reporter is changed into an active observer. Material hitherto unconsciously repressed or consciously suppressed comes to the surface and can now be verbalised and examined.

Psychoanalytic therapy tries to help the client in his critical self-examination and to achieve a resolution of intrapsychic conflicts, i.e., dealing with these conflicts in a more grown-up manner. The psychoanalyst, by making intentional mental states which are incomprehensible for the analysant comprehensible to him, helps the analysant to use his psychic energy more constructively by making him aware of his repressed impulses. The ultimate task of the analyst, by now the therapist, is to make the unconscious conscious through the proverbial talking cure, i.e., free association and analysis. The curative processes as an interrelated series of psychic events within the analysant is accomplished through insight and catharsis (the release of emotions by acting out past experiences). However, the experience of insight into the nature of one's conflicts is not sufficient to bring about a permanent change, it needs to be supplemented by "a working through" process, i.e., the slow and gradual integration of the insight into the analysant's life and it necessarily includes tacit work done by him outside the therapeutic sessions. Though insight enables the analysant to overcome inner conflicts, it is helpful only insofar as such insights are able to change his life situation in a constructive manner.

Freud's analytical psychotherapy, as a whole, involves an intense exploration of repressed traumatic experiences in the realm of the unconscious which prevent normal development of the personality, and endeavours to gain insight into the way these past events influence present behaviour. The therapy focuses on the psychopathological and emotional disturbances of the individual through a reconsctruction of the traumatic past. In this process repressed enegies are released and afterwards used for constructive purposes. The individual can master conflicts by placing them in historical perspective and by understanding his own share in their unnecessary continuance. Thereafter the future can be seen as a period with challenges and possibilities rather than a prolongation of a stifling past.

The widely practiced contemporary psychoanalytic therapy is derived from the psychoanalytical theory but with a modification in the psychoanalytical method. The major changes lie in the greater activity of the therapist, the frequency with which the client is seen, and the duration of treatment. The therapist is more concerned with the events and current problems of everyday life than with analysing the resistance of the client's psychic interior.

F. Alexander established a more flexible form of Freud's psychoanalytic therapy. The therapist, thoroughly understanding the psychoanalytic principles of psychopathology, designs a form of precise treatment that fits the needs of a particular client rather than trying to fit that client to standard analysis.

In this shortened and more directive form of therapy, the therapist uses various techniques in a flexible manner along with dynamic interpretations. In the therapeutic relationship the client is encouraged to express blocked and defended emotions and feelings. The therapeutic progress is based on "corrective emotional experiencing" to counteract the effects of the original trauma rather than making the unconscious conscious.

The goal of this psychoanalytic therapy is to encourage a psychodynamic change, i.e., the improvement in the ego-organisation towards its integration. This may include the resolution of conflicts between the various components of the personality structure, increased ego-strength and the improvement of interpersonal relationships. A successful analysis promotes an increased ego-strength, where the ego is controlling the id and the superego, in order to arrive at a more complete and deeper understanding of oneself. With the development of healthier ego-controls the client is gradually freed from the debilitating anxiety that keeps him from living a fully human life.

c. Defence mechanisms

In Freud's earlier topographical model the principal goal of psychoanalytic therapy was to make the contents of the unconscious conscious. But with the elaboration of the structural theory he felt the need to analyse the functioning of defence mechanisms. By now the major portion of the analytic work is directed toward understanding the client's defences and overcoming resistances.

Defence mechanisms are the ways in which the ego prevents and protects itself from being overwhelmed with anxiety. It refers to aspects of behaviour that may be motivated more by needs to avoid anxiety than by the pursuit of self-fulfilment. Sometimes these defensive maneuvers work well in relieving the anxiety resulting from a conflict, but at other times they may take the form of maladaptive behaviours that are in turn anxiety provoking. According to P. Madison, Freudian defences refer to "unseeable events—to an imaginatively represented interplay of instinctual forces and anti-forces within the person. This interplay results in varied behavioral effects which are observable—resistances, symptoms, dreams, distortions of conscious representation, amnesia, inhibitions, and certain childhood fears."[2]

Freud distinguished several defence mechanisms and each defence attempts to control anxiety by an alteration or distortion of consciousness in a particular way. These defence mechanisms can be either repressive or nonrepressive. The former include reaction-formation, isolation, undoing, denial, projection, amnesia, conversion and displacement, whereas the latter include sublimation, regression and inhibitions. In the nonrepressive defences the substitution of drives is the main mechanism of ego protection and usually the impulse disappears, in contrast to repressive defences which involve a conscious misrepresentation of a drive without the underlying drive being actually changed, i.e., dangerous impulses are not abolished and persist unconsciously.

All the defensive measures of the ego against instinctual impulses are carried out unconsciously, the ego itself knows nothing of the process of defence mechanisms and the client does not witness them in operation. The psychotherapist helps clients to recognize the defensive quality of their behaviour, to reconstruct defences in retrospect, and to explore the underlying needs or wishes they are defending against. Psychoanalysis aims at inducing the client to give up these defences and to replace them by such actions that would correspond to a psychologically mature condition.

These unobservable inner psychic forces produce in therapy the observable effect called resistance. Defences are repetitive automatic means of the ego to ward off anxiety, whereas resistance is a phenomenon in which the client is distracted from pursuing the requirements of the analytic situation. Resistance is the name given to everything in the clients'words and actions that obstruct them in gaining access to their unconscious; but it also illustrates the operation of the general defence mechanism of repression. Resistance serves as a protective mechanism in deeply held beliefs and keeps acute anxiety under control.

Freud classified five manifestations of resistances of which the ego is the source of the first three, namely repression-resistance, transference-resistance, and gain from illness; the fourth resistance is related to the id and the unconscious, and the fifth comes from the superego and seems to originate from a sense of guilt.

In the context of this work it is not relevant to discuss all these five forms of resistances; only one type of ego resistance as well as the resistance of the unconscious need special attention as it will be referred to later on in Sri Aurobindo's integral sadhana.

(A) Ego resistance occupies a prominant place in all psychodynamic approaches, and it lies at the root of the endeavours to explore psychoanalysis. In this form of resistance the client unconsciously withholds or distorts his actions, reactions and experiences due to shame, guilt, embarrassment or emotional upsets. The client manifests such behaviour in order to protect his self-image, (any behaviour that contradicts self-image tends to be forgotten) and to avoid the re-experience of too painful emotional conflicts. This kind of behaviour leaves certain "blank spots" in the client's emotional experiences; this form of ego-resistance as a part of the client's life-style is difficult to detect and if such a resistance is not brought to the client's attention it continues to impede his progress in therapy.

Repression or ego resistance includes a broad variety of avoidance behaviour; the client attempts to escape the contents of his unconscious through forms such as mental reservations, associative avoidance, intellectual opposition or concealed reservation of doubt. During analytical treatment the more forcefully the ego feels itself pressed the more convulsively it clings to these resistances against the therapist's work. The client is unaware of his opposition to the therapist's efforts to change his defensive operations. The ego will go on repressing any instinctual feeling it finds too threatening to express. Somehow clients may conceal from themselves the motives of their own behaviour; they can attribute to external causes behaviour which is in fact intentional and so escape responsibility for it.

Resistance in the therapeutic practice must not be confused with working "against" the therapist but is actually the amount of unconscious psychic energy which the client is able to allow to come to the surface at a particular time. By labelling or interpreting the resistance the therapist is able, with the help of free association, to uncover the facts and feelings associated with the resistance. This interpretation helps clients to accept their own resistances but also helps to gain cognitive insight of its uses and difficulties. Only when the defence is withdrawn and instinctual representatives can make their appearance unhindered in the consciousness, then the client is able to discover the nature of the repressed drives which were producing pathological symptoms. Hence, before the therapist is able to bring into consciousness that which is unconscious, and prior to further analysis, he first uncovers resistances. By now, at a considerable expenditure of effort, the defensive operations can be brought into the consciousness and the therapist will be more able to help clients understand and change their personality.

(B) Resistance of the unconscious is based upon the repetition-compulsion tendency. Even after the ego has decided to relinquish its resistances it still has the difficulty in undoing the repressions, i.e., after the ego resistance has been removed the power of the compulsion to repeat has still to be overcome. Unconscious processes have the innate tendency to reinstate earlier existing conditions. In therapy the "working through" process is related to the reappearance of already interpreted themes in manifestly new guises, and each of them has to be patiently interpreted anew by the therapist.

d. Conclusion

Psychoanalysis is a psychology of the symbolising activity of the mind and raises questions about the contents of mental states or events symbolised by a mental representation.

Critical self-analysis in a psychoanalytical perspective is seen as a process of consciousness which aims at insight; insight into the origin and into the developmental processes of the individual as he experiences himself in interactions with the environment. Freud aimed at the exploration of the unconscious aspects of the psyche, confronting the individual with the abyss within oneself and exposing the same individual to the difficult task of controlling its chaos. His attempts to uncover the unconscious are intended to give the individual some degree of rational control over it and permit a more complete understanding of himself.

Psychoanalysis, though applicable only to a relatively small proportion of the population, can be applied to real life situations unlike experimental psychology. Freud's treatment of deep-seated roots of neurotic behaviour through psychological methods is preferable to the newly pharmacological methods (the neuro-biological approach) which makes the client insensible to conflicts rather than facing and understanding them, and giving them their proper place in a new way of life.

Freud's insistance on the complexity of man with his manifold and conflicting motivations is one of his most distinguished contributions to psychology.

However, it is not clear if psychoanalysis has created a breakthrough to a real psychology of the human being or if it is only a modern philosophical experiment which is still not affirmed by scientific research. The psychoanalytical claim for a scientific stature and for an ethical approbation has been disputed by behaviourism and humanism.

For the behaviourist psychoanalysis is too subjective and unscientific. Freud's concepts are almost entirely mentalistic and cannot be linked to observable behaviour.

For the humanist, psychoanalysis is too objective as the latter conceives human beings as objects that are made up of instinctual and defensive energies only. Such concepts are for the humanist therapist dominant forces in the dehumanisation of human beings.

Freud's main limitation, in his perpetual language of suffering, is his failure to consider interpersonal and sociocultural influences in his analytic theory of intrapsychic conflicts.

In his dualistic approach he tried to bring about a reconciliation between the ego and id. However, this does not solve the larger problem of integrating the split which has come about between the organism as a whole and its environment. Therapy is more than adjustment and Freud's dualistic view of man leaves the individual on one branch of the dualist dilemma. In Freud's psychoanalysis the opposites of the ego and the id are not transcended but compromised.

It seems Freud overemphasises the past and deemphasises the client's personal responsibilities. In his psychic determinism the individual does not act but is moved by aggressive or sexual impulses that are largely unconscious; there is no place for the individual's free will, whereas inner freedom is for the humanist an essential integral aspect of one's living experience.

Commentaries on Freud's complexity of psychoanalytical thought are controversial and varies from severe criticism to extreme praise. According to H. Eysenk, "psychoanalysis must be regarded as a failure. We are left with nothing but imaginary interpretations of pseudo-events, therapeutic failures, illogical and inconsistent theories, erroneous 'insights' of no proven value, and a dictatorial and intolerant group of followers insistent not on truth but on propaganda".[3]

In his anti-psychoanalytic assumptions Eysenck concludes that psychoanalytic therapy does somewhat worse than no therapy at all. But Eysenck in turn makes assumptions with an inadequate degree of objectivity in his objective behavioural approach.

B. Bettelheim in a more commending way discusses the defective and inaccurate translations of Freud's works and he tries to correct erroneous conclusions. Freud was often accused and found guilty of doctrines he never held.

Psychoanalysis does not pretend to create perfectly balanced superhumans who are well integrated with themselves and the universe. Yet it has had an impact on psychology because of its rich and detailed descriptions of psychopathological symptoms and defence mechanisms which continue to elicit response from those psychologists who take man's capacity for self-deception seriously.

Nowadays psychoanalysis as a therapy has many rivals, all claiming the same results as psychoanalysis but faster and less expensive.

e. Neo-Freudians

Neo-Freudians are clearly influenced by Freudian assumptions, they accept the Freudian intrapsychic conflicts and the impact of childhood experiences on adult life. But Freud's biological orientation, apparent in his instinct and libido theory (aggressive and sexual in character) as the ultimate source of all conflicts is rather controversial and produced profound disagreement among various psychoanalysts.

The Neo-Freudian variations on the psychoanalytical theme include overt and covert modifications of theoretical concepts, and of practical methods and applications. They attempted to extend the ego with more adaptive endowments and to expand treatment procedures by altering the range of goals of treatment. They also developed guidelines for short-term psychotherapy, and revised the therapist's role in the treatment by making the client a more direct, active participant. In transcending Freud's focus on inner-individual conflicts they added interpersonal, social, ethical and cultural considerations. In Freud's biologism the source of man's troubles lies within himself, but the Neo-Freudians tend to regard the client's conflicts as a microcosm of social ones; the individual is inconceivable outside the society and suffering must be due to social and environmental factors rather than individual ones. They rejected Freud's biological approach as Freud did not allow any role of sociological or cultural factors in the determination of personality structure. For the Neo-Freudians personality is not so much based on instinctual foundations, but is more related to the influence of society and culture. Biological demands are only seen as secondary in importance to interpersonal relations.

The Neo-Freudians can be roughly classified as Ego-psychologists, Object-Relations psychologists, and Self psychologists.

Ego-psychologists such as E. Erikson, Anna Freud, H. Hartman, H. Sullivan and E. Fromm paid increasing attention to the ego's ability to transcend the impulses of the id, and the impact of the environment on development (interpersonal relations). Their views are less deterministic and mechanistic than Freud's. The ego functions as an independent centre of individual identity and gains strength through mastery of the environment. The ego with its own energies becomes a major force in the development of an adaptive and competent personality.

According to the ego-psychologists there is more involved in the stages of maturation than Freud's hypothetical resolutions of conflicts over sex and aggression; all problems cannot be reduced to repetitions of unconscious childhood conflicts, environmental and cultural factors as well as later developmental stages should also be taken into consideration.

However, the ego analyst may differ from the content of classical analysis, but his therapeutic treatment is similar to the classical analytic process.

The Object-Relations psychologists continued the trend of the ego-psychologists and according to their views the child does not look for gratification of his libido but looks for an object, i.e., a relation with a person. Object-Relations psychologists like Fairbairn and M. Klein focus upon the relationship between the self and objects as the major organising principle in the individual's life. For Freud "others" serve primarily as objects for instinctual gratification, but for Object-Relations theorists "the other" is an authentic individual with needs and wants of his own. The Object-Relations theory provides important links between individual psychology and social systems.

The Self psychologists, such as Kohut and Kernberg, differ from the Object-Relations psychologists in their focus on the internalised relationship between two separate people. They are more concerned with the client's subjective experience of the self rather than the self seeking other relationships. However, the self-in-relation becomes the main concept for both approaches. They both agree that pathology results from early developmental deficits and from early family experiences, rather than Freud's intrapsychic conflicts between id, ego and superego.

The therapeutic relationship gets a more relational quality than in Freud's analysis. The therapist aims at the restoration of early developmental deficits and the restructuring of the client's inner world. The strengthening of the authentic ego is then used for relational purposes.

Neo-Freudians are more optimistic and more eclectic, emphasising the quality of the therapeutic relationship and the function of the rational ego in solving life problems. But the Neo-Freudians, as described above, have had only a relative significance and little influence on psychotherapy as their theories cannot be scientifically assessed and none of them present a systematic account of a new theory.

However, they transformed man who was a non-perfectible concept in Freud's conviction into a personality which is in essence good and free with almost infinite potentials for growth.

3. The Behavioural Approach

The beginning and origin of behaviour therapy can be traced to the work of J. Watson, who maintained that psychologists should use only experimental techniques and not rely on introspection. Behaviourists should study behaviour and not the psyche, which differentiates behaviour therapy from traditional psychotherapy. The behaviourists are sceptical of classifying behavioural problems as mental illnesses but instead they recommend the idea of deviant behaviour, i.e., behavioural or functional disorders.

Watson, criticising subjectivity and mentalism, put forward behaviourism as the objective study of behaviour; all behaviour can be understood as a process of learning. He lays emphasis on the overriding importance of environmental events. Watson did not discuss any technique for improving the individual's behaviour, he completely excluded purpose in the explanation of behaviour and in his extreme position on environmentalism he rejected heredity and instinctive factors.

Historically, behaviour therapy is also rooted in the work of B. F. Skinner's radical behaviourism in which he restricts himself to the study of overt behaviour and environmental conditions that regulate behaviour. Like Watson, he rejects mentalistic concepts, and in his operationalism he maintains that all scientifically acceptable theoretical concepts must be definable in terms of measurements or test procedures. Skinner is popularly associated with operant or instrumental conditioning (the stimulus—response model), and he drew attention towards the importance of the consequences of the response, that is, the reinforcement that follows the response. Positive reinforcement (reward) will encourage continuation of behaviour whereas in negative reinforcement (punishment) the particular behaviour is likely to cease.

But Skinner in his emphasis on direct observable behaviour gives little attention to mental processes and cognition, and his application of conditioning principles to the treatment of clinical problems were rejected as superficial and mechanistic by the clinical psychologists in contrast with the academic experimental psychologists.

Behaviourism mainly strives to give a concrete scientific and methodological shape to psychology. The study of conscious processes and inner life must be ignored because they cannot be studied scientifically. Behaviour is reducible to some physico-chemical processes; there is a definite cause-and-effect determinism in behaviour (stimulus produces response), and there is no intention and free will. Behaviourism views the individual as an object which can be dissected, diagnosed and manipulated. The environment is so controlled that "appropriate contingencies of reinforcement" will automatically produce happiness.

a. Behaviour therapy

Out of the behaviouristic experimentalism grew the traditional conditioning-oriented behaviour therapy. Behaviour therapy brings into contact the scientific method with the psychotherapeutic process and aims at the direct treatment of concrete symptoms.

As a relative newcomer in the psychotherapeutic market, behaviour therapy in the late fifties was defined as the application of modern learning theory to the treatment of clinical problems. There is still no adequate definition of behaviour therapy as the behaviour therapists do not share a set of defining properties. Behaviour therapy, at that time, was seen as the logical extension of behaviourism to complex forms of human activities.

Behaviour therapy has two major characteristics which are also valid for the various approaches in contemporary behaviour therapy; (a) the learning model of human behaviour differs fundamentally from Freud's model of psychoanalytic therapy. The behaviour therapist rejects Freud's concept of abnormal behaviour as a symptom of underlying unconscious conflicts; (b) in modifying maladaptive behaviour it uses experimental techniques and is committed to the scientific method only.

Behaviour therapy assumes that the essential emotional problem lies in something observable and the therapist focuses on the observable source of the emotional problem, thereby separating the problem from the client. The problem and the individual are at different levels, the former becomes objectified whereas the latter stays out of range.

For the behaviour therapist maladaptive behaviour itself is the problem and needs to be changed rather than analysing some underlying disorders or causes.

If maladaptive behaviours are to a considerable degree acquired through learning, then they can also be modified through additional learning. In this way the symptom is the problem and becomes the appropriate target for therapy.

Traditional behaviour therapy emphasises therefore corrective learning experiences in which the client acquires new coping skills. The behaviour therapist is interested in explaining the origin and the maintenance of maladaptive behaviour patterns. If the therapist understands the cause of these patterns he might be able to treat these problems more effectively. The client learns how to break maladaptive habits and how to overcome defeating emotional conflicts. The therapist serves as a source of personal support and tries to investigate behavioural change in the client's natural environment. He assists clients in generating alternative courses of action and helps to analyse the consequences of pursuing various goals. However, the client must be willing to cooperate in the task of making significant changes in real-life behaviour in the real world outside the therapy sessions.

Behaviour therapy, in its approach to psychological disorders, stresses a behavioural analysis of the client's adjustment difficulties, and its psychotherapeutic techniques are used for the direct control and removal of maladaptive behaviours. There are four behavioural techniques of which only a brief description is given.

1. Systematic desensitisation is based on the anxiety hierarchy; the therapist describes a set of threatening situations and trains the client to relax by using various relaxation methods.
2. The aversion technique involves the use of noxious physical stimulation to eliminate unwanted behaviour.
3. The operant conditioning technique implies the systematic manipulation of the consequences of a behaviour so as to modify subsequent behaviour of the same type.
4. In the modeling technique the client witnesses the performance of another person (the model) and learns to modify his unwanted behaviour.

From these techniques it is easy to detect the behaviourist's concern with external behaviour which constitutes the essence of the therapeutic problem. Behavioural man is reducible to stimulus-response connections and infinitely manipulable and controlable by external events in the environment. For the behavioural therapist all problems are construed as pedagogical in nature and alterable only through direct learning of new behavioural associations. The behavioural approaches seek changes through direct conditionings, shaping or training; alternative modes of functioning do not occur as a concomitant of cognitive or emotional insight into one's problems.

The therapeutic relationship between client and therapist may be portrayed as a deliberately structured learning alliance in which the therapist functions as an instrument of direct behavioural influence.

b. Critical estimate of Behaviour therapy

Behaviourism has been severely criticised for its strict technical application of behaviour modification techniques which are primarily based on relief of current symptoms and its substitution. But this symptomatic treatment does not affect the underlying dynamic sources of the symptoms. The therapist often overlooks all of the client's subjective life processes such as concealed thoughts, feelings and symbolism. The psychoanalyst questions the lasting recovery of seriously disturbed clients as a result of behavioural therapy. In its scientific research the behaviour therapist demonstrates merely the superficiality of the behavioural view of humanity.

The behaviourist's emphasis on direct observable behaviour ignores the interaction between the individual and his social environment. In the classical Skinnerian therapy the therapist has almost complete power to control the client rather than helping him to control himself. The behaviour therapist also oversimplifies explanations of the therapeutic transactions between client and therapist. Psychopathology does not solely reside within the individual but also has significant roots in the client's relationship with others and his milieu.

For the humanist, the behaviour therapist misses a human sense of values; at times when people are in a serious crisis related to a sense of significance, the behaviour therapist gives only symptom relief but this does not cure alienation and relief of meaninglessness in life. The behaviour therapist leaves aside the phenomenology of existence at an experiential level, and in this dehumanizing process the therapist does not offer the client a fundamental worth and value as a human being.

Behaviour therapy in its scientific approach will never be able to formulate relatively simple general laws of human behaviour, as human behaviour might prove to be too complex.

Unlike psychodynamic therapies, behavioural therapy is not regarded as necessarily reflective of deeper processes within the psyche. The behaviour therapist in his biological orientation shows due regard for scientific objectivity rather than exploring speculative concepts.

Classical behaviourism began with Watson's application of the empirical scientific method to the study of human behaviour. Such methods ignore the mind, consciousness and subjectivity as they are not clearly observable.

Contemporary behaviour therapy has undergone significant changes in its nature and scope. Corrective learning experiences are no longer associated with only overt behavioural changes but also involve broad changes in cognitive and affective spheres of functioning.

c. Cognitive—Behavioural Therapy

Cognition into Psychology

Muller and Dollard were the first psychologists who contributed to the transition from the classical Watsonian and Skinnerian behaviourist theory to the cognitive behavioural theory. Human thought becomes again a contributing factor of psychotherapy. The seventies witnessed an increased emphasis on cognitive processes and procedures whereas the eighties paid attention to the role of affect in therapeutic change, and biological factors as determinants of mental disorders. Thus cognitive behavioural and emotional channels interact in therapeutic change.

The various approaches in contemporary behaviour therapy include (1) applied behaviour analysis, an extension of Skinner's radical behaviourism. Treatment procedures are based on changing the relationship between overt behaviour and its consequences. (2) the neo-behaviouristic mediational stimulus-response model. The treatment of systematic desensitisation in covert processes follow the laws of learning that govern overt behaviours. (3) Social learning theory of Bandura which is based on a reciprocal interaction of behavioural patterns, cognitive processes and environmental factors. (4) Cognitive-behaviour modification. Cognitive restructuring techniques developed outside the mainstream of behaviour therapy are largely drawn from A. Ellis' and A. Becks' cognitive approaches. Psychological disturbances are not due to experiences themselves but due to the client's interpretation of that experience.

In recent years behaviour therapy has become more cognitive oriented, accepting and using mentalistic concepts, becoming the basis for a more integrated approach to behaviour problems. The interrelatedness of thought and action is now espoused by most behaviour therapists and there is no longer a dichotomy between pure cognitive and pure behavioural interventions.

There is no consensus regarding the origins of cognitive psychotherapy. Some view cognitive approaches as stemming from behaviour therapy whereas others credit A. Ellis and A. Beck as being most influential in the development of cognitive approaches.

In its physicalist reductionism classical behavioural tradition reduces the free and choosing individual or his organistic open system into a reacting mechanical robot. But in cognitive psychology mental determinants become again important influential factors in human behaviour. Acceptance of cognitive factors like imaginations, perceptions, memory, thoughts, expectations and other internal processes make room for entry of mental factors in behaviourism, as these factors bring unity and consistency in the individual's behaviour. Understanding human problem solving behaviour incorporates logical thinking rather than trial-and-error or blind searching. The individual's behaviour is not only controlled by environmental factors but also by internal mental processes.

It is difficult to dwell upon a clear-structured description of the field of modern cognitive psychology, but it deals mostly with concepts such as perception, attention, memory, psycho-linguistics and problem solving abilities (thinking, reasoning). It tries to understand man's cognitive behaviour in terms of the mechanics of his thought processes. Behaviourism only knew reactions to environmental stimuli and only described the outer manifestation of mental processes, ignoring the underlying inner mental mechanisms. Cognitive psychology tries to explore the complex hierarchical structured mechanisms which generate behaviour. The organism gets a more active role and there is place for creative processes.

Cognitive therapy and behavioural therapy are both empirical and problem oriented, but Cognitive therapy applies Skinners' functional analysis to internal experiences, and clients are active participants in their environments.

In cognitive therapy, the therapist and client examine and modify the self-evaluations and cognitions that block effective living. In this process not much attention is given to emotional oriented interventions, as the primary target is the reevaluation of thought and attitudes.

Psychological disorders result from predispositional and situational factors; they can be identified through definite cognitive sets (the expression of various feelings), and/or definite behavioural sets (various physical expressions). Both these contingencies must be considered in the cognitive psychotherapeutic treatment.

In Humanistic psychology cognition is more related to psychological well-being and meaning of life. Cognition, in the psychologies of C. Jung, A. Maslow, and C. Rogers, has the function of obtaining insight and consciousness. In the theory of perception, the concept of perception is replaced by the concept of consiousness, but the latter is related to a direct realistic interpretation and as such consciousness is a behavioural determinant which enables the individual to separate reality from appearances.

In its therapeutic approach importance is given to the inquiry into the development of pathological or destructive mental structures rather than the investigation of mental mechanisms. In his therapeutic approach towards emotional disorders the therapist focuses on the client's conscious mental events instead of unconscious motivations. Psychopathological disorders are related to distorted self-views and distorted views pertaining to the future and the world.

In general the cognitive theory recognizes that there are multiple determinants in psychopathological processes and it therefore integrates other modalities in its approach. This accounts for the rapid development of cognitive-behavioural models.

The cognitive behavioural theories emerged in the early sixties with the growing interest in cognition and the application of cognitive theories to behaviour change. Cognitive-behavioural therapies, in their attempt to change overt behaviour by altering thoughts, emphasise cognitive mechanisms to create behavioural effects, i.e., it incorporates the mediational perspective into the cognitive-behavioural approaches which differentiates them from behavioural therapists. All cognitive-behavioural therapists maintain that cognitive events alter behaviour and behaviour change may be used as an indirect index of cognitive change. The two primary change areas are therefore cognition and behaviour, but to some extent emotional and physiological changes are also used as change indices.

According to K. Dobson "the cognitive-behavioral therapies share a belief that therapeutic change can be effected through an alteration of idiosyncratic, dysfunctional modes of thinking. Additionally, due to the behavioral heritage, many of the cognitive-behavioral methods draw upon behavioral principles and techniques in the conduct of therapy".[4]

The cognitive-behavioural theories recognize the interaction of mediating processes and overt behaviour, and the interactional reciprocity between the individual and the environment in addition to environmental determinism.

The cognitive behavioural therapist combines elements from stimulus-response behaviourism, operant behaviourism, social-learning, Rational-emotive therapy and cognitive development in their methods for behavioural change. However, cognitive awareness of the problem and learning skills by themsclves are not enough to produce change. The client must actually decide to do something, i.e., the task of the cognitive-behavioural therapist is not only related to the integration of the client's thoughts but also to his actions and decisions.

For the cognitive behavioural therapist insight is essential in maintaining change in behaviour, but thought without accompanying action is considered empty.

Present cognitive behaviour models, representing pragmatism, intellectualism and empiricism, are not merely interested in cognition but also in the interaction of all the processes involving thoughts, feelings, and biological and environmental influences.

The cognitive behavioural therapist, stressing the client's rationality and self-responsibility, uses the scientific method with an educational perspective. They attempt to change the client's maladaptive behaviours, improve their functioning in interpersonal relations and restructure the client's cognitive processes in order to reevaluate and correct specific thoughts and behaviours.

Cognitive processes regulate the impact of environmental forces on behaviour, and the cognitive behavioural views on interpersonal relations are the main contributions of the cognitive behavioural model. The client is able to take control of and alter the impact of the environment. The cognitive behavioural therapist does not rely on the therapeutic relationship as a mechanism of change but focuses on the client's own skills and on the interplay of environmental, social, biological and psychological factors.

Nevertheless, its theory does not give attention to the theory of personality and human motivation, and in its empiricism with rational, logical, and objective thinking it rules out intuitive, creative and other subjective modes of thinking. It therefore lacks the full dimensions of human experience and makes the therapy restrictive and mechanistic.

Contemporary cognitive-behavioural therapies are organised into three major divisions.

1. Cognitive-restructuring therapies, like Rational-behaviour therapy, Rational-Emotive therapy and Cognitive therapy, assume that emotional distress is the consequence of maladaptive thoughts. They all stress the importance of challenging irrational thought patterns in order to become aware of emotional disturbances, but the Rational-behaviour therapists advocate other techniques in their achievement toward a healthy emotional balance.
2. Coping-skills therapies represent an integration of Rational-emotive therapy with a social framework. In its goal it trains clients to perceive situational cues more accurately and attempts to provide them with the personal resources to cope independently with future stress situations.
3. Problem solving theories, as a combination of the aforesaid two therapies, stress the importance of an active collaboration between client and therapist. In resolving problem situations, these therapies aim at training the clients to function as their own therapists, i.e., the clients' active role in understanding the complexity of their emotional disorders and applying verifica-

tions in actual problem situations rather than parroting the therapist's rational beliefs.

The various cognitive-behavioural approaches differ in their philosophical orientations and clinical applications but they are all concerned with the effects of social influences and current cognitive activity on overt behaviour.

d. Rational-Emotive therapy

Of the cognitive restructuring therapies A. Ellis' Rational-Emotive Therapy (R.E.T) and A. Beck's Cognitive therapy may be regarded as the most important ones and will be briefly discussed.

A. Ellis' R.E.T originated in the mid fifties when he became aware of the ineffectiveness of psychoanalysis.

Ellis, as a pioneer of the cognitive behavioural theory was initially classified within the existential-humanistic tradition for many years. As pointed out by him, "people are better off when they emphasize human interests rather than those of inanimate objects or of some assumed 'natural order' or of gods".[5] But he continued to emphasise logic, reason, objectivity, behavioural approaches, and action in the process of adjustment to the individual's environment and he is therefore nowadays primarily considered as a cognitive-behaviourist.

R.E.T as a major form of cognitive behavioural therapy stresses cognitive factors in human functioning but does not exclude emotion and behaviour. All three processes are highly interdependent and these overlapping intrapsychic processes are in constant interaction with the individual's environment.

Emotions are cognitive-sensory processes and consist largely of attitudes, beliefs and biases, which can be changed. Though the individual is born with a biological disposition of irrational thinking, the same individual has also a free will and the capacity to learn to think rationally.

For Ellis, emotional disturbance results from people's continuous irrational thinking, their refusal to accept reality and their self-absorption.

R.E.T assumes that beliefs, attitudes or values are central to the personality, and rational or empirically based values lead to healthy emotional functioning, whereas dysfunctional beliefs or attitudes are the cause of emotional upsets. R.E.T maintains that the most efficient way to personality change is to confront clients with their magical philosophies [ought, should, must, etc] on the basis of logico-empirical grounds in order to eliminate disordered thinking. For Ellis, these absolutistic cognitions such as, "must", "should", "ought", "have to", are the central feature of human emotional and behavioural disturbances. These "irrational beliefs" usually obstruct the client's pursuit of his goals and purposes. If the client is able to follow the logico-empirical approach and forego all forms of absolutism it is virtually impossible to be seriously disturbed. As described by Ellis, "Irrational ideas are the basic cause of most emotional disturbances.... If he could become thoroughly released from all these fundamental kinds of illogical thinking, it would be exceptionally difficult for him to become intensely emotionally upset".[6]

The goal of R.E.T is to identify and challenge the irrational beliefs because they are the root cause of emotional disturbances. By substituting unrealistic demands with realistic desires and wishes major changes in behaviour may occur.

The R.E.T therapist in disputing the client's irrational beliefs, stresses the value of learning to be tolerant of oneself and others, and simultaneously indicates a hedonistic philosophy of desiring, wishing, wanting, prefering, etc, as a central feature of psychological health. However, if the client turns these nonabsolute values into dogmas and demands then he will become again psychologically disturbed. According to Ellis, "R.E.T.... invites a long-range hedonistic approach to satisfaction that emphasizes the pleasures and lack of pain of tomorrow as well as the satisfactions of today ... it is merely opposed to frequent, prolonged, or intense negative or self-defeating emotional states".[7] But Ellis does not seek the short range self-defeating hedonism of a childish variety but he is more after a long-range hedonistic philosophy, i.e., the rewarding commitment of postponing present pleasures for future gains.

As mentioned previously the client has the capacity to change his irrational thinking and its self-defeating effects, and the most effective long lasting changes involve the philosophical restructuring of irrational beliefs, as described by Ellis; "The rational therapist makes a forthright unequivocal attack on his [client's] general and specific irrational ideas and tries to induce him to adopt more rational views".[8] Through exerting consistent philosophic pressure on clients to change their thinking and actions, the therapist gives them a specific impetus towards achieving mental health.

In the therapeutic attempt to change the client's irrational beliefs the therapist uses three main therapeutic techniques.

1. The R.E.T-cognitive therapy tries to persuade the client to give up perfectionism and helps him learn to separate rational (non-absolutistic) from irrational (absolutistic) beliefs.
2. The Emotive-evocative therapy uses various means of dramatizing preferences and musts so that clients can clearly distinguish between the two. These means, varying from role-playing, modeling and humor to unconditional acceptance and strong disputing, show the clients' false ideas, how they affect relations with others, and how to replace these irrational ideas with more efficient notions.
3. Behaviour therapy in R.E.T helps the clients to change their dysfunctional symptoms and to change their cognitions.

R.E.T aims at minimising the client's self-defeating outlook, and for Ellis "effective psychotherapy consists of helping clients to clearly see and strongly dispute their conscious and unconscious imperatives, using a number of cognitive, emotive, and behavioral methods, and to thereby make themselves less disturbed and less disturbable".[9]

The R.E.T therapist is not interested in the client's present symptoms in terms of past experiences but, as an educator, in challenging the client's present irrational ideas through a "directive-persuasive-philosophic methodology". For Ellis, Freud's "insight" techniques in the client's problematic behaviour usually does not suffice to enable him to change that behaviour. Insight into the origins of the client's self-defeating behaviour needs to be supplemented by a highly active program of working at the eradication of this behaviour. Ellis' cognitive therapy opposes the stress of the unconscious in psychoanalysis; for the reinstatement of psychological health the deepest roots of the basic problems have to be worked at and removed rather than a mere description of the causes of these processes.

For the R.E.T therapist it is not only desirable to uncover, understand, and accept the client's unrealistic assumptions, but it is also required that the therapist invalidates these assumptions. He insists upon verbal discussion, action, work, effort, and practice.

According to Ellis, "to the usual psychotherapeutic techniques of exploration, ventilation, excavation, and interpretation, the rational therapist adds the more direct techniques of confrontation, confutation, deindoctrination and reëducation".[10]

Although the therapist is fairly stern and not sympathetic, he shows full acceptance and is quite empathic. In the meaningful dialogue the therapist explains and guides the client into the philosophic insights of the self-causation of the clients' disturbed symptoms. Basic personality changes take place only when these insights become attitudinal. However, in the therapist's frequent interpretations and confrontations only the client's beliefs and behaviours are evaluated but never the client as a person, i.e., the client's self.

In a way it appears Ellis is more a hedonistic ethical philosopher than an experienced therapist. He maintains that emotionally disturbed clients are the victims of their own irrational thinking, whereas the behaviour therapist would rather blame irrational environments that stimulate and reinforce irrational thoughts, emotions and behaviours. In using his various therapeutic methods, the client is converted into the R.E.T therapists' questionable philosophy of life rather than being cured of strong emotions. Not all emotions are inherently irrational. Some emotions like alienation and anxiety are part of being human and as such are healthy and authentic.

Ellis in his irrational thinking process gives no consideration to individual differences and leaves out various individual processes such as drive, ego, heredity, the unconscious and temperament. Because R.E.T deals only with limited aspects of the client's functioning it may bring about only superficial change within the individual. It may change symptomatic behaviours but it may not get at the underlying causes.

R.E.T as a cognitive-emotive behaviouristic method of psychotherapy, employing the logico-empirical method of science, encourages the client to surrender absolutes and to acknowledge that nothing is sacred. In teaching the client to practice the philosophy of desiring rather than demanding Ellis espouses a long-range hedonism.

For Ellis, if cognitive restructuring is consistently employed, the humanistic values of tolerance, love, and peace will tend to prevail.

Ellis looks sceptically at transpersonal and mystical terms as he does not believe that the individual can transcend his humanness. According to Ellis "they can become more adept, competent, and intelligent, but they still remain fallible and in no way godly".[11]

e. A. Beck's Cognitive Therapy

The basic premises of Cognitive therapy are similar to Ellis' R.E.T; they differ mainly in the way they are applied.

Cognitive therapy is more related to thought disorders in psychopathology, and like R.E.T it assumes that emotional disorders are the results of unrealistic cognitive appraisals of life events. The client is the architect of his own misfortune and is able to control his own thoughts and actions. Beck's Cognitive therapy like Ellis' R.E.T stresses the importance of behavioural procedures in correcting the dysfunctional cognitions that are assumed to cause emotional distress. The cognitive therapist, focusing on identifying automatic thoughts, encourages the client to examine his mode of thinking and eventually develop new forms of cognition. For Beck the cognitive domain comprises thoughts but also images and in using specific imaginative procedures he tries to modify distorted cognition.

Beck does not consider clients' beliefs as irrational but prefers to consider them as either distorted or dysfunctional thinking patterns.

In its clinical applications it uses like R.E.T the cognitive and behavioural methods which induce alterations in the cognitions and actions of the client. Beck's Cognitive therapy distinguishes overt symptoms from those directed toward changing cognitions; only after symptoms disappear the focus of therapy shifts to underlying cognitions.

In the therapeutic relation Beck emphasises more the Socratic dialogue in contrast to Ellis' direct confrontational approach. The cognitive therapist does not exhort the client to adopt a new set of beliefs but, through dialogue, tries to understand and explore the meanings of the client's automatic thoughts.

f. Conclusion

The original behaviourists claim that environmental conditions and contingencies directly influence behaviour. The behaviour therapists in their approach to psychological disorders are interested in explaining the origin and the maintenance of maladaptive behaviour patterns. If the therapist understands the causes of these patterns then he might be able to treat these problems more effectively. He stresses behavioural analysis of the client's adjustment difficulties and his psychotherapeutic techniques are used for the direct removal of maladaptive behaviours.

Due to the behavioural heritage many of the cognitive behavioural methods draw upon behavioural principles and techniques in the conduct of therapy. As such, the cognitive-behavioural therapist, uses behavioural skills as well as cognitive changes in teaching effective problem solving and self-control skills.

R.E.T, in its cognitive restructuring process, treats psychological disorders through changing the client's distorted cognitions or thoughts and the negative schemas that underlie them. The therapist helps the client to identify and challenge these distorted cognitions and simultaneously guides the client towards psychological health, i.e., self-acceptance and a high level of discomfort tolerance.

The R.E.T therapist is grossly moralistic unlike the behaviour therapist who is strictly psychological.

For the cognitive therapist behaviour is based on the continuous reciprocal interaction of personal determinants (cognitive, affective) and environmental variables (social actions), and like R.E.T the cognitive therapist helps clients to become conscious of maladaptive cognitions and to replace them with more adaptive thought patterns. In Cognitive therapy the modification of cognitions is the principal means but not the end; its aim is to achieve a change on the affective level, whereas in R.E.T the modification of cognitions is the principal end and means.

g. Behaviour Therapy and Its Relation to Psychodynamic Therapy

It is of therapeutic significance that appropriate treatment planning is determined through a correct diagnostic label, an accurate assessment of the relative importance of psychic conflicts, unconscious mental processes as well as conditioned learning and situational factors; not all maladaptive behaviour is necessarily caused by persistent unconscious conflicts, some maladaptive behaviour patterns may be extinguished by simple behavioural interventions or social learning.

The behaviour therapies are more objective and empirical insisting on concrete, external and rational aspects of behaviour, whereas the psychodynamic therapies are more subjective, emphasising abstract, affective and internal aspects of behaviour.

The behaviour therapists pursue more limited therapeutic aims, i.e., symptomatic relief, and the therapist is only concerned with prediction and control of behaviour. The psychoanalytic therapist is more concerned with the presumed underlying conflicts of the complex personality.

The psychoanalyst functions as the vehicle of projected transference reactions, whereas the behaviour therapist operates as a scientific technician playing with stimuli.

Both behaviour and psychodynamic therapies attempt to modify underlying causes of behaviour. One of their differences is related to the concept of cause. Behavioural analysts look for current variables and conditions that control behaviour. In its aim at direct control over symptoms behaviour therapies stand in contrast with psychodynamic therapies. The latter look for unconscious past experiences in current maladaptive behaviour patterns, and fosters change primarily through emotional and cognitive insight.

Despite these differences, at a practical level they both may approach the same goal by a somewhat different pathway.

Both schools share rather similar scientific aims, their theories are based on reductionism and determinism and they both stress the importance of the relationship between the client and the therapist. Common to these approaches seems to be the tolerant acceptance by the therapist and the client's cooperation with him. In both therapies the therapist is preoccupied with the client's anxieties and encourages him to recognize current sources of stress and repetitive patterns of behaviour.

According to Judd Marmor, "all psychotherapy, regardless of the techniques used, is a learning process. Dynamic psychotherapies and behavior therapies simply represent different teaching techniques, and their differences are based in part on differences in their goals and in part on their assumptions about the nature of psychopathology. Certain fundamental elements, however, are present in both approaches".[12]

Both treatments involve a number of specific techniques which vary from "interpretation" to "counterconditioning", and it is mainly in these technical aspects that the two therapeutic approaches differ from eachother. For certain types of clinical problems behavioural therapy may be superior to the psychodynamic method and for others a combination of both therapies may be indicated.

In the final analysis the two approaches can be complementary, the technique of therapy employed depending on the particular aspect of the client's complex psychic functioning. For treatment of his overt symptoms or behaviour patterns behaviour therapy may be advised, whereas for modification of his symbolic distortions of feelings, cognition, affect, motivation, or disturbances in interpersonal adjustment, dynamic psychotherapy may be more suitable.

At the present stage of development both theories have their benefits but neither can explain all clinical events and other approaches are therefore needed.

4. The Humanist-Existential Approach

a. Humanistic psychology

Rapid technological changes, the growing alienation of the individual in a highly industrial society and the threat of nuclear destruction, all prepared the ground for the seeds from which Humanistic psychology, as a third force, grew. Since the gradual replacement of religious and moral traditions by the industrial dehumanisation of life, more and more people are searching within, reflecting upon the meaning of life and discovering a new basis for their values.

Humanistic psychology as an academic "human-potential" movement emerged as a reaction against the reductionistic and pathologizing interpretations of behaviourism and psychoanalysis. These two approaches ignored certain areas of human nature such as values, self-actualisation, self-transcendence, psychological health and the dignity of the individual in therapy and in life.

Humanistic psychology critisises behaviourists for their lack of interest in understanding the wholeness of the human being. In its empirical-analytical approach behaviourism leaves out mental structures, and individuals have no free will, no choice, even no mind!. It considers man as a passive victim of stimuli present in the environment, and the individual is nothing but a machine that consists of chains of conditioned and unconditioned reflexes. But according to the humanist psychologist the individual is master of his own fate rather than a product of environmental forces.

The behaviour therapist stresses the mechanical conception of man, as if man can be explained by a scientific system, ignoring the unique qualities of the person. For the humanist psychologists such a view does not generate an adequate image of man, or a philosophy of life, and does not provide a satisfactory guide to living, to values, and to choices.

Through behavioural techniques man becomes calculated and impersonalised and the humanist psychologist in order to counter alienation stresses the fostering of the fullest exploration of the unique and universal nature of man.

The humanist psychologist disagrees with Freud's pessimistic determinism in which man is considered as the product of instincts and conflicts only; all higher forms of behaviour are seen as acquired and not intrinsic. Man is not a predominantly passive or instinctually regressive recipient of his conflictual drives but he has a kind of self-determination, creativity and authenticity that aims at the ultimate integration of mind, body, and soul of fragmented man.

Humanistic or growth-oriented psychology, in its holistic interpretation of man, focuses on the conscious self and others rather than on unconscious processes or biological aspects of human behaviour; it criticises the psychoanalyst and the behaviourist for their neglect of impulses originating from intrinsic needs for growth and for the fulfilment of innate positive potentials.

The humanist psychologists are concerned about the image of human beings created by traditional psychology. Psychology needs a better image of human beings if it is to be of service to humanity. In its "human" approach it lays sufficient emphasis on the uniqueness of the individual and humanity, the unity of the person, and human goals and values.

Humanistic psychology intends to make the study of man, his nature, and his existential problems the centre of interest of psychology, i.e., in presenting a theoretical model of man as a positive and purposive being it arrives at the "humanisation" of psychology.

Man is viewed as a creative being, controlled by his own values and choices rather than by outside or unconscious forces. The humanist psychologist is not much concerned with biological needs but recognizes the need for human fulfilment, the need for meaning in life, and the individual's responsibility in his own life.

In understanding human personality the humanist psychologist studies the person as an integrated, unique and organised whole. For understanding the person as an integrated whole it is essential to give importance to human existence and the individual's experience regarding one's own identity.

Importance is given to the open-systems theory, i.e., the interaction of the organism with various other systems. Humanist psychologists maintain that growth-motives tend towards higher degrees of organisation in the course of one's life. They see the ultimate goal of life as self-actualisation, the complete fulfilment of human potentials and one's meaningful place in the universe. Failure to realise various potentials are due to the distorting influences in the environment which can be, at least partly, overcome by accepting responsibility for one's own life.

b. Humanistic Psychotherapy

In their therapeutic approach the humanist therapists concentrate on being, expression of feelings, and on the subjective experience (accentuating human properties in relation to the process of self-discovery) rather than on the process of knowing and reflection of thoughts. Intellectual insight does not bring about the needed change in the individual's personality and behaviour.

Humanistic therapies want to avoid the defensive use of rational discussions through accomplishing a direct confrontation between human beings, and to encourage them to express their feelings in a physical way. Such kinds of methods emphasise "doing" instead of "thinking", the individuals are not confronted with their defence mechanisms, neither are unconscious processes interpreted.

Mental illness originates due to lack of contact with the inner experience; getting in touch with and the verbalisation of the inner experiencing process creates emotional stability. The therapist therefore focuses his attention primarily on the experiencing client, theoretical explanations of the manifest behaviours are secondary in comparison with the experiences of the individual.

The humanist therapists are mainly concerned with the individual's present behaviour and direct experiences unaltered by theoretical explanations. They try to expand self-consciousness within the therapeutical relation; feelings and emotions are more important than abstract insights. Growth and maturity as a complete being are more important than isolated problems.

Therapeutic change usually occurs by means of a coherent interpersonal relationship between the client and the therapist. In the "here and now" therapeutic dialogue the therapist serves as a catalyst in whose presence the client comes to realise his capabilites for shaping his own self.

The therapist is not concerned with diagnosis but instead focuses on the client's emotional problems and conflicts regarding values and choices; although the therapist may support, the final decisions and choices rest with the client.

The humanist therapist tends to view man as an inherently active striving and self-potentiating entity, and encourages the client to seek growth-facilitating experiences toward the possibility of self-actualisation.

The essential basis of humanistic psychotherapy is "growth-orientation", and the growth oriented psychotherapies stress the inherent healing capacities and healthy aspects of the individual, i.e., the capacity of the organism to achieve an optimum balance within itself and its environment.

Its techniques aim at the evolvement of the authentic self and its ways of being; by actualising one's own potentialities the individual can live a truly authentic life.

It is evident that this form of therapy needs introspective capacities and is not beneficial for people with serious psychopathological problems.

The humanistic approach, like the other approaches, have been criticised for various reasons. Instead of a difficult slow process on the long road towards personal growth, humanistic psychotherapy offers the individual an instant growth. But this temporary feeling of well-being through emotional catharsis may not be long-lasting enough to bring about self-knowledge or an inner change towards a new direction. The encouragement of emotions, including the improper ones, and spontaniety with instinct dominated individuals who actually need control can be quite dangerous.

Humanistic psychology, encouraging alternative images of man, has failed to develop its ideas with disciplined scholarship. Its methods for studying human reality lack theoretical sophistication. In its unscientific structure and goals it appears to become "strained by its own inner dynamics".[13]

Humanistic psychology lacks a suitable methodology in its investigation of human problems. Its conceptual foundations (logical, linguistic, and epistemological) are vague and need a clear-cut analysis. The terms human, growth, authenticity, person, etc, are vaguely described, and there is no commonly accepted agreement among humanist psychologists regarding the meaning of these ambiguous terms and therefore they need improved theoretical clarification.

According to Schur, the personal growth movement, "if carried very far, could hamper efforts to accomplish meaningful social change. There can be no real self-awareness without social awareness".[14]

The therapist, in continuously exploring the client's feelings, representing an invitation to self-absorption, tends to disregard the social context within which the individual acts.

Self-actualisation need not necessarily take place within the interior of the individually conceived personality, but might also take place in the interaction between people and their social environments, i.e., society as a place for the interplay of collective interests and values.

It appears that humanist psychologists have lacked intellectual discipline and moral sensitivity to provide a carefully worked-out alternative. Therapy in such humanistic approach may become, more or less, a prolonged indulgence in raw experience and wordless action.

c. Conclusion

Present-day humanistic psychology appears to loose its coherent, unified movement and seems to stand more for a heterogeneous assortment of views. Though their intention is to convey positive life-affirming messages, they remain stuck in negative criticism by expressing dissatisfaction with other psychologies.

In its therapeutic contribution, human nature is seen as a quality to be nurtured and allowed to grow, rather than a thing to be reconstructed. This tendency to grow may be compared with Freud's concept of libido, however, for the humanist psychotherapist this growth-tendency need not be tempered like Freud's libidinal instincts but needs to be activated. Freud's compartmentalised, instinct-economical, and pessimistic concept of man stands in sharp contrast with the humanists' holistic and optimistic view of man. The humanist therapists deal with the phenomenological concept of truth and in their therapeutic approach they do not use the positivistic deductive method. They also believe in an existential view of man in which the future oriented being has freedom and choice rather than being the victim of the causal-determined views of the behaviourists or psychoanalysts.

The humanist therapist replaced the power relationship between the client and therapist for an equality of relationship between two partners who are mutually engaged in the search for meaning and understanding. The therapist creates a climate of openness and safety rather than working through the various defence-mechanisms.

d. Phenomenological and Existential Approaches in Humanistic Psychotherapy

The principal sources of inspiration for the humanistic movement have been the phenomenological and existential traditions and their influences within humanistic psychology remain quite distinct.

Phenomenology started with E. Husserl's science of phenomena, i.e., objects as they are experienced in the individual's consciousness. Principally, phenomenology can be called the systematic and full exploration of human consciousness; it has the phenomenological method as a common core and gives an unbiased description of whatever is found in consciousness. Phenomenological psychology explores consciousness in a meaningful structure and function, and refers to phenomenology as a method applied to psychological problems. The exploration of consciousness refers to acts and contents of consciousness as well as to their objects and meanings.

In the course of time various divergent orientations of phenomenology have developed and this diversity makes a single general definition of phenomenology almost impossible.

Phenomenology as a discipline differentiates what is actually being perceived and felt in the current situation and what is residual from the past. It studies not only personal awareness but also the awareness process itself. The phenomenological approaches focus on the expression of the client's and therapist's underlying experience in the therapeutic relationship. The therapist shares a respect for the client's subjective experience and emphasises expanding self-awareness so as to live a more meaningful existence.

Phenomenological psychology must not be confused with humanistic psychology as the former is concerned with the intentional relationship between man and the world, unlike the latter which focuses on individuals.

The phenomenological approach is now often blended with the existential orientation. The borders between phenomenology and existentialism are often blurred, as the two movements frequently conceptually interact and reinforce each other. Both reject reductionistic-mechanistic materialism as well as naive objectivism; they accept man as a living, feeling and concrete human being rather than as an abstraction.

Existentialism as a philosophy of the predicament of man adopts the phenomenological method of the analysis of pure consciousness, and applies this to the analysis of being. The phenomenologists apply their phenomenological method to existential themes such as meaning of life, existential anxiety, and the problem of being in general.

But despite these similar views their intents and purposes are different, the existentialist is more concerned with ontology, the nature of being and existence, including freedom of choice and moral responsibility, whereas the phenomenologist is more concerned with the essence of things, with epistemology and with a description of conscious states. Phenomenological psychology with its emphasis on description and explanation is more related to the scientific approach in psychology, whereas existential psychology dealing with"the living through" process, is more concerned with man's ultimate meaning of life and the spiritual dimension of man.

e. Existential psychotherapy

The basic preoccupation of the existentialist is existence as experienced by man as an individual. Man does not possess existence but he is his existence, and this human existence is a process of becoming and continually changing. However, this notion includes the root of man's existential problems which are mainly related to "the other man" and God. Spiritual growth may liberate the individual from the conventional shackles of society.

The existential psychologists are opposed to the techniques of experimental psychologists where the organism is not allowed to excercise any freedom or choice. They also reject Freud's mechanistic views and restore to the individual a definite search for meaning. The individual is responsible for his own existence and the existential psychologist objects therefore to any kind of external determinism. For the existentialists psychology is mainly concerned with the study of the nature of consciousness and subjective reality such as existential moods or the individual's various personal experiences as they relate to his existence in the world.

The existential approach itself is not a complete therapy but is often referred to as the existential dimension in therapy. Its therapeutic arrangements are not systematised into a coherent school. Existential therapy as a form of dynamic psychotherapy postulates, like psychoanalysis, a dynamic model of the personality structure in which force fulfils an essential role. Human personality is neither based on inner needs and instincts nor on the interpersonal relation with the external world, but on the conflict between the individual and the facts of existence such as death, freedom, loneliness and meaninglessness.

The existential therapist, dealing with the responsibility of intentional choice and becoming, assumes that the individual has the capacity for authenticity, awareness and choice, and that he grows through the exercise of his capacity to create and find a meaning in life.

F. Bugental defines existential therapy as "attempts to disclose to the client the ways in which he keeps himself/herself from the potential fullness of living and to ensure that he or she makes choices that are as aware as possible of these patterns".[15]

For the existential therapist healthy existence need not be related to maximising reinforcements and minimising punishments as the behaviour therapist would suggest, or adapting one's instinctual desires to the demands of the environment as the analytical therapist would suggest, but it is to be authentic and live authentically.

Being human involves the knowledge of being there (in the world) not determined by the past, i.e., the individual is able to live in the present and enter the future with a free choice. This authentic way of being implies a strict individual interpretation of one's own existence. This can be very threatening as the individual is used to deal with life in an inauthentic way where there is no place for one's own choice or meaning of life. Authenticity, as the goal of psychotherapy, involves the client's increased awareness of various aspects of the world and himself that have been previously denied. The existential therapist, being authentic himself, encourages clients to enter into an authentic relationship with the therapist in which they become increasingly aware of themselves as subjects capable of directing their own lives.

Initially the clients are encouraged to freely and honestly express their present experiences, but afterwards the clients' egocentric experiencing is directed to a more authentic dialogue with the therapist. In the authentic encounter between client and therapist the phenomenological method is used by the therapist in an attempt to understand the client's phenomenological world without imposing any preconceptions onto the client's experience. The therapist, focusing on the client's direct experience in the present situation, will encourage the client to consider new alternatives of being and clarify the various choices that he is faced with in therapy, but it is the client who remains responsible for the various alternatives he wants to follow.

The role of the existential therapist is described by J. L. Braaten as "to help their clients to define their own freedom, cultivate their own individuality, accept their own experiencing as the highest authority, to be fully present in the immediacy of the moment, find truth through their own actions, and learn to accept certain limits in life."[16]

On the basis of existential psychology four different psychotherapies came into existence. First there are the existential analysts based on and connected with Heidegger's Daseins analysis. According to M. Boss and Binswanger, psychotherapy aims at analysis of the structure of the client's existence. Though both the psychiatrists remained within the psychoanalytical framework, they incorporated elements from phenomenology and existential philosophy in their approach. The therapist does not direct or correct clients according to some preconceived notions but guides them to become their authentic selves and into the freedom of being able to utilize their own capacities for existence.

The second school is associated with the experiential existential therapists who emphasise the complete exploration of the clients' consciousness and experiences, as they are held to be the cause of their pathology. They use chemotherapy and the Rorschach tests in their research practice.

The third school is related to V. Frankl's Logotherapy which studies the essence of being and the meaning of existence.

The fourth school comprises the Gestalt therapy systematised by F. Perls.

Before briefly explaining the last two forms of existential therapy it may be useful to contrast existential therapy with humanist therapies and add a critical marginal note to existential therapy.

Both approaches aim at explaining human nature by considering the whole organism. In existential humanism men can elevate themselves to the level of God, they are in touch with the infinite though they are ignorant of it. Some of the existential therapists stress these spiritual motives which gives the individual freedom and dignity in life. The humanist therapist expresses similar views, but emphasises the process of self-actualisation rather than the existential process of alienation.

The existential therapist remains occupied with a certain kind of therapeutic nihilism; in his pessimistic view of explaining human nature he is focused on fear, anxiety, sorrow, etc, whereas the humanist therapist is more optimistic in the explanation of human nature and lays much emphasis upon inherent growth potentials toward psychological health.

However, the humanist therapist in guiding clients to become fully functioning persons (self-actualising individuals) is not only confrontated with ill functioning beings, but these clients have also genetic and socio-cultural (interrelational) backgrounds. The same clients have also a personal past which influences their present behaviour and from which they often fear the future. The humanist therapists remain vague regarding these existential views and in their rather naive positivism they remain stuck to the principle of unlimited changeability of the fully functioning person. But without being conscious of these tendencies the individual is not able to transcend them.

The behaviour therapist complains that the existential approach provides little insight into their therapeutic procedures, and the continued emphasis on freedom and authenticity might lead to the desintegration of society.

The psychoanalyst criticises existentialism for its emphasis on the client's responsibility in psychopathological processes, as if the psychotic patients are responsible for what they are driven to!.

Conclusion

Existential therapy does not offer an all comprehensive system but functions more as a mode of reference from which the therapist tries to understand the mental suffering of the client.

The client's fear according to the existentialists originates from existential conflicts that are partly unconscious. Clients use all their energy to tackle this fear with some ineffective defence mechanisms rather than applying this energy for more creative purposes.

In the therapeutic process the therapist focuses on the client's direct experience in the present situation (using Husserl's phenomenological method of "bracketing", entering into the experience itself) so that he is able to become aware of his own self and existence.

This development of the client's authentic awareness enables him to experience responsibility, meaning, and transcendence. As such the existential therapist aims at guiding clients to redefine themselves and their world in order to experience an enlarged sense of being and potency in life.

f. Logotherapy

Logotherapy is usually subsumed under the categories of existential and humanistic psychology as it draws upon unique human qualities.

Logo refers to the Greek word "finding of meaning". In V. Frankl's logotherapy the therapist helps clients to find meaning in their lives by concentrating more on others than on themselves.

Underlying logotherapy is the concept of man as a spiritual being whose existence has an intrinsic meaning which has to be realised. Like Maslow's metapathology, which will be discussed subsequently, Frankl maintains that there is a spiritual dimension to every psychopathological disturbance.

Frankl's philosophical therapy is a therapy of meaning for those confronted with an existential crisis, but he gives simultaneously importance to cognitive and behavioural change and his cognitive-behavioural theories provide an important bridge for existential/humanistic theories.

Logotherapy is a "therapy through meaning" or a meaning-centred therapy. For Frankl, "man can no longer be seen as a being whose basic concern is to satisfy drives and gratify instincts; nor can the human reality be understood merely as the outcome of conditioning processes or conditioned reflexes".[17]

He does not reduce the issue of meaning to mere defence-mechanisms (abreaction of impulses) or reaction-formation (reaction to stimuli), but to a response to the potentiality of nurturing one's will to meaning. For the logotherapist life is never lacking a meaning and when the individual is no longer able to change a situation then the individual is challenged to change himself. Man's most fundamental drive is to understand the meaning of his own existence, i.e., the will to meaning.

This meaning carries two postulates within itself. Firstly, meaning cannot be given by a therapist but has to be found by the clients themselves; the therapist can only show the client that there is meaning in life. Secondly, meaning has an objective element in contrast with instinctive impulses or learned behaviour patterns which deal with subjective profits. The realisation of objective meaning may not serve the individual who fulfils that meaning but does serve the improvement of the given situation itself. However, such meaning-oriented actions do yield steady benefits though these are only subsidiary. If this drive to the will of meaning is not fulfilled it may cause existential frustration, which in turn may result in an escape from freedom and responsibility.

In its therapeutic approach it is quite similar to the classical existential approach, but Frankl's logotherapy is more brief and the logotherapist is more active in confronting the client's existential vacuum of life. The logotherapist emphasises a confrontation with the client's positive and conscious processes as well as the clarification of his future prospects.

In the process of encouraging clients to realise the meaning of their personal existence, Frankl uses two methods which produce rapid behavioural change; dereflection and paradoxical intention.

Dereflection brings about a therapeutic reorganisation of attention; clients are encouraged to ignore obsessions by directing their awareness toward more positive contents of thinking. In paradoxical intention the client is encouraged to do the very thing he fears to happen; i.e., the fear itself is not dealt with but rather the object of fear.

Logotherapy, in studying the essence of being, is concerned with the individual's self; not the self as an ego which is formed through hereditary and environmental influences, but a self as "nous" which, through its own choice, determines its tendency according to hereditary and environmental influences, i.e., how the individual forms himself in his own freedom and responsibility.

Logotherapy aims to activate the stream of inner self-fulfilment through the fulfilment of meaning, and to motivate the client to trust this healing force. Closely related to this inner self-fulfilment is the human capacity for self-transcendence.

Frankl assumes the interrelationship and inseparability of the physical, psychological, and spiritual dimensions within the person, to maintain optimal human functioning. The spiritual dimension contains the individual's self-transcendence, creativity, intuition, faith, and leads the client towards a new meaning of life. For Frankl existence is dependent on self-transcendence, i.e., being human is always being directed to something or someone other than oneself. "Only to the extent that someone is living out this self-transcendence of human existence, is he truly human or does he become his true self."[18]

Self-transcendence reaches out not only for a meaning to fulfil, but also a cause to serve by giving oneself. By virtue of the self-transcendence of human existence man is a being in search of meaning.

g. Gestalt therapy

The German word Gestalt refers to whole or configuration, but the term also implies a unique kind of psychotherapy originated by F. Perls. Perls, a trained psychoanalyst incorporated Goldstein's, Reich's, and Rank's concepts into his phenomenological-existential theory.

Man is considered a total organism functioning as a whole rather than an entity split into separate parts such as mind and body. The organism has the capacity to cope with life and need not repress its instinctual strivings in order to become "civilised". For Perls unaware behaviour is the result of the organism not being in touch with its external environment, and he disagrees with Freud's account regarding unconscious behaviour.

Gestalt tried to replace the Freudian "past" and "why" by the existential, experiential "present" and "how". Gestalt as an existential psychotherapy is based on the process and development of awareness through emotional insight rather than intellectual insight. It has its origin in the humanistic movement and spans a variety of growth and "here and now" therapies like encounter, sensitivity training, Bio-energetica and meditative groups.

Gestalt therapy, like other humanistic psychotherapies, is based on a Gestalt philosophy of life or a way of being. The human being is conceptualised as a bio-psychic unity in which there is no differentiation between a biological need and a psychological wish or desire.

Its philosophical basis is found in existentialism (ontology), phenomenology (epistemology), and holism (axiology).

The holistic viewpoint proceeds from the organic basis of the human being seen as a whole. In Gestalt the whole is greater than a sum of its parts and the organism is endowed with a drive for wholeness. According to Perls "man does not perceive things as unrelated isolates, but organizes them in the perceptual process into meaningful wholes,"[19] and wholeness is the goal of the individual's self-actualising tendency. However, during the process of developmental growth and the individual's interaction with the environment he experiences frustration, conflicts and suffering which result in the split or loss of parts of the self. These conflicts impede the organism's innate striving for completion. Maturity is achieved when the individual is able to integrate his loss into an organised whole, i.e., the integration of authentic self-awareness and contact with others.

The general therapeutic system of Gestalt therapy is centred around three concepts: awareness, contact, and Gestalt formation.

Awareness refers to those experiences which inform the individual about internal and environmental processes, and as a form of personal experience it is in active contact with the individual's environmental field. It motivates the individual to undertake action and provides a sense of the completion of action. Psychopathological interruption of the flow of awareness is often the result of the individuals' distrust of themselves or their environment. According to Perls, "If he [the client] can become truly aware at every instant of himself and his actions on whatever level-fantasy, verbal or physical—he can see how he is producing his difficulties, he can see what his present difficulties are, and he can help himself to solve them in the present, in the here and now".[20]

Awareness of "what is" or being fully conscious leads to spontaneous change and creates the possibility of integrating and separating Gestalts in a meaningful whole. Awareness as a cognitive, sensory, and affective process is accompanied by the process of knowing the individual's control over, choice of, and responsibility for his own behaviour.

Being in contact with individuality and with the organic needs leads to contact with the environment, i.e, the other. In contact each individual must meet the outside world in order to survive, and one's psychological well-being depends on the quality of these contacts. Perls uses M. Buber's philosophical views on the I and Thou relation to explain the concept of contact. The other is approached as Thou, as a person, and not as a means for the I's end.

In Gestalt formation it is important to make a distinction between the organism and the field in which that organism functions. Perls postulates the concept of boundaries between the individual and environment as well as between the split parts within the individual. The contact between the organism and the environment is called "contact-boundary". At this contact boundary all psychological events take place; psychological difficulties arise when the individual's contact boundary with the environment is disturbed.

The organism, for the sake of existence, needs to make contact with the environment, but the individual can also withdraw from this environment to exclude dangerous situations and closing the gestalt rather than contacting the environment and forming new gestalts. This contact with and withdrawal from the environment are the positive and negative aspects of the psychological processes by which the individual lives, they are dialectical opposites, described by Perls as, "the whole organism/environment field is one unit which is dialectically differentiated",[21] i.e., organism/environment, subjective/objective, selfishness/altruism.

A person exists by differentiating self from others and by connecting self with others. This boundary between self and environment must be kept permeable to allow exchanges, but also be firm enough for autonomy. For Perls end-goals are based on the individual's biological needs and the social roles are the means whereby the individual fulfils his end-goals. Healthy beings fulfil their particular end-goal that has emerged into awareness, because Perls assumes that the continuous process of forming gestalts (completeness to needs) is the constant law that maintains the integrity of the organism.

However, if these end-goals are not completed they remain to be experienced as pressing needs, and these unexpressed and unrecognised needs (incomplete gestalts) interfere with the formation of new gestalts. The individual spends only a small amount of energy in completing these natural needs and diverts his attention more to social means as end-goals, replacing his basic natural existence to a pseudosocial existence. Neurosis results from the conflict between the client's and society's needs and demands.

Together with this process of experience on the contact boundary there is another connecting procedure which is classified by Perls as the process of creative adjustment. Mere adjustment to the environment is not sufficient in itself, as the person who only adjusts himself melts with his environment and ceases to exist. Perls maintains that the individual has a capacity for self-regulation that is influenced by self-awareness and contact with the environment. The mature person is aware of his personal and environmental limitations as well as his internal needs. By integrating polarities within the self the individual is able to relegate other needs to the background until completing the gestalt, after which another need can become dominant. In the process of creative adjustment there occurs a combination between the individual's needs, desires and the demands of the environment.

Creativity is a process which replaces old boundaries and surveys new ones, and creative adjustment is only possible if there is a place for new experiences in which previous acquired experiences are integrated. In the Gestalt's view of the healthy personality, the mature person finds wholeness in life by accepting and expressing opposite poles of life. The individual is not preoccupied with social roles and does not adjust to an insane society. However, such healthy individuals run the risk of losing the love and approval of their environment. Being outside the boundaries of society the mature person has to go through a process of alienation, but once clients have discovered the centre of their lives, they themselves take full responsibility for the direction of their lives without blaming the environment. Gestalt therapy ultimately aims at the inner strength of the client. The client is encouraged to take various kinds of risks of being spontaneous and unpredictable in order to gain the freedom to be creative.

In the therapeutic process the Gestalt therapist seeks to redress the imbalance between action and fixity; he is concerned with the encounter between the individual and his environment. The therapist continuously examines how the process of creative adjustment takes place within the client, and how and when the client blocks himself. When the formation of a new gestalt is hampered by an incomplete gestalt, the therapist will draw out this incomplete gestalt in such a way that the client is able to work it out and complete his own organismic process. According to the Gestalt therapist only complete gestalts can be integrated in the organism and therefore he will support (or eventually frustrate) the client to complete all the incomplete gestalts of his life. In this way Gestalt therapy becomes the process in which the client slowly allows himself to be creative rather than being predictable, but this creativity needs courage from the client as well as the therapist.

Within Gestalt therapy there are two therapeutic approaches: the first one focuses mainly on the inner processes of the client in which awareness and emotions are the main subject of treatment, whereas the second one focuses on the way in which the client interacts with his environment and in which the contact dimension is emphasised. Both approaches are limited in their treatment, as in the first one the client is considered too much an individual on his own, and his environment is more or less ignored. In the second approach the contact becomes central and the individual's completion of the experience remains in the background.

The Gestalt therapist paying attention only to various limited aspects of human behaviour has been criticised for various reasons.

In its emphasis on sensory awareness and emotional insight Gestalt therapy neglects the rational insight and the process of assimilation. The release of repressed affects (catharsis) might be purifying but without rational insight there may be other motives which cause subsequently the same accumulation of feelings. To experience a feeling only is to disregard the underlying structure of that feeling, i.e., its underlying wishes, desires, etc. Undifferentiated and undiscriminate feelings heighten the potential for uncontrolled arousal of powerful effects. In Gestalt therapy there is no place to discriminate between emotions and emotional reserve (control of feelings). A true encounter is not a mere self-expression but involves self-transcendence.

Conclusion

In recent years Gestalt therapy is mainly influenced by the humanistic movement and as such there seems to be an exclusive emphasis on personal growth, self-actualisation, and other individual personal experiences. But Gestalt therapy also pays attention to the environment and its influence on the organism.

Gestalt therapy as a phenomenological-existential therapy provides an existential dialogue between the client and the therapist, in which the therapist does not manipulate the client toward some therapeutic goal or cure but encourages the client's self-discovery towards authenticity, responsibility, and growth. The therapist, in providing direct experience, guides clients in active awareness-work towards insight into their own inner contradictions. Once the client becomes aware of previously alienated parts he is able to assimilate or reject them. To live a fully human life, the client's split-up parts have to be reintegrated into the whole person.

Gestalt therapy, unlike verbal or interpretive therapy, is an experiential therapy in which traumas are re-experienced. For Perls the analytic and cathartic procedures of psychoanalysis are insufficient in themselves, "as with purely cathartic discharge there is no transformation of emotion into action, into self-expression and integration.... The patient may 'understand' himself completely, but he is incapable of doing anything himself".[22]

Gestalt therapy is an exploration rather than a direct modification of behaviour. The goal is growth and autonomy through increased awareness. Underlying this therapeutic process is the intent to restore the vitality of the interaction between the client and his environment, and to explore ways in which clients can come out of their unauthentic ways of behaviour.

5. A Critical Estimate of Psychotherapy

Successful psychotherapy cannot guarantee the individual a kind of enjoyable end-state in which all life's obstacles are surmounted, but it can enable the individual to enter paths previously unknown to him.

By redirecting the self-deceptive strategies of the past, the client is able to learn a new stance in the world through risks and hard work. With this increased insight or self-awareness and extended awareness of life possibilities the client is able to achieve various personality changes or alterations in behaviour.

Although the three "forces" have often different and conflicting views regarding human nature and development, and differ regarding the mechanisms of change and the content of psychotherapy, yet each approach agrees on the processes or theory of therapeutic change and offers important perspectives for securing this change within the individual.

In examining various theories and procedures in psychotherapy one is bound to find a truly bewildering set of ideas, techniques and behaviours. The plethora of the theoretical and practical orientations of all schools of psychotherapy often results in confused attitudes and expectations on the part of the clients. Often the client, in search for psychotherapy, may well be in a vulnerable and emotionally aroused state and is therefore unlikely to make balanced judgements about the suitability of the particular form of therapy being offered.

With the existence of more than 250 different kinds of therapies it should be apparent that in its therapeutic efficiency not one approach has found the single true path.

Most brands of psychotherapy rely for their credibility on focusing on one aspect of human functioning and making it central to their system. However, all psychotherapies are severely limited in the degree to which they are capable of modifying man's behaviour or enlarging the client's awareness. It is clear that any psychotherapy, while appropriate for one area of human psychological disturbance is invalid or even harmful in others.

Psychotherapy as a procedure aiming at healing may also aggravate the possibilities of negative changes or effects in the process of healing. An individual who learns during the therapeutic process to behave in a more adaptive way conforming to one's environment may do so at the cost of his creativity. Or the client who is not sufficiently well-integrated and who sheds repressive aspects of his life may only be overwhelmed by anxiety accompanied by a loss of impulse control.

The therapeutic process of insight has its own complications. Insight (as a vehicle of change) in psychotherapy, either intellectual or emotional, is by itself not sufficient to bring about change in the client's life; insight on its own is not enough, it needs to be supplemented by "a working through" process, and acceptance of the client's responsibility for his own conduct. Moreover insight needs to be supplemented by strength, confidence and trust. Genuine change in psychotherapy is accompanied by the development of insight as well as the determination to change and concluded by taking the necessary action.

Achieved intellectual insights may be substituted for other obsessional thoughts or it may impair the individual's self-esteem. Emotional insight can provide catharsis which may produce a certain relief but not necessarily a change.

Excessive awareness of the individual's primitive longings may not always be contributive and even increase the defects in his self-esteem, the main reason for undergoing psychotherapy. For too many people therapy becomes an end in itself, in which the therapeutic experience (the verbalizing insight) fails to change the client's basic life commitments. There is no balance between the individual's inner insight and the constructive utilisation of life energies for an effective change in the client's behaviour. In other words, psychotherapy as an end becomes a way of life rather than a means for change and autonomy.

Conflicting studies in recent years regarding the beneficial aspects of psychotherapy do not always clearly indicate long-lasting benefits. It seems that success of any psychotherapy is often more apparent than real because they establish in many instances only a temporary relief. In the current rage for psychotherapy, without an unsupportive doctrine and in the absence of a mainstream spiritual principle of faith, the therapist often reduces the client's experiences to confirm to his own doctrine. It appears to this author that any superficial positive outcome, without a firm spiritual dimension, would ultimately be fallible and unreliable. Many psychotherapists are realising the limits of a psychotherapy in which the development of the ego is the major and often final goal. If the ultimate human need is directed toward self-transcendence then psychotherapy as an interim device may serve as a bridge to the realisation of this higher human need.

Notes:

1. Freud, Anna; The Ego and the Mechanism of Defence, The Hogarth Press, London 1979, p. 4–5.
2. Madison, P; Freud's Concept of Repression and Defense, its Theoretical and Observational Language, University of Minnesota Press, Minneapolis 1961, p. 14.
3. Eysenk, H; Decline and Fall of the Freudian Empire, Penguin Books Ltd, Middlesex 1985, p. 201–202.
4. Dobson, Keith, S. Edt; Handbook of Cognitive-Behavioural Therapies, Hutchinson, London 1988, p. 29.
5. Bannister, D. Edt; Issues and Approaches in the Psychological Therapies, John Willey and Sons, New-York 1975, p. 168.
6. Ellis, A; Reason and Emotion in Psychotherapy, Lyle Stuart Press, Secausus, New-Jersey 1962, p. 89.
7. Ibid., p. 333.
8. Ibid., p. 94.
9. Zeig, J. K and M. Munion Edt; What is Psychotherapy? Contemporary perspectives, Jossey-Bass Inc Publ, San Fransisco 1990, p. 146–147.
10. Ellis, A; Reason and Emotion in Psychotherapy, Lyle Stuart Press, Secausus, New-Jersey 1962, p. 188.
11. Wedding, Denny and J. Corsini; Current Psychotherapies, F. E. Peacock Publ Inc, Illinois 1989, p. 210.
12. Marmor, J. and S. M. Woods Edt; The Interface Between Psychodynamic and Behavioral Therapies, Plenum Medical Book Comp, New-York 1972, p. 28.
13. A. Maslow; Journal of Humanistic Psychology 1970 No:10, San-Fransisco.
14. Schur, E; The Awareness Trapp; Self-Absorption Instead of Social Change, Quadrangle/The New York Times Book Comp, New-York 1976, p. 193.

15. Zeig, J. K and M. Munion Edt; What is Psychotherapy? Contemporary perspectives, Jossey-Bass Inc Publ, San Fransisco 1990, p. 189.
16. J. L. Braaten;Journal of Mental Hygiene, "The main theories of existentialism from the viewpoint of a psychotherapist". 1961 No:45.
17. Frankl, Victor, E; The Unheard Cry for Meaning, Hodder and Stoughton, London 1979, p. 17.
18. Ibid., p. 35.
19. Perls F; The Gestalt Approach and Eye Witness to Therapy Bentam Books, New-York 1976, p. 3.
20. Ibid., p. 63.
21. Ibid., p. 22.
22. Ibid., p. 111.

CHAPTER III

THE TRANSPERSONAL APPROACH

1. Psychotherapy and Spiritual Growth

Before moving to Transpersonal psychology and its therapeutic inclinations it may be useful to describe some of the characteristics of spiritual growth in relation to psychotherapy in order to get a general idea of the differences between these two approaches, which has its bearing on the discussion of Transpersonal psychotherapy that follows.

Spiritual growth and psychotherapy are both concerned with the essence and nature of man and his well-being.

Psychotherapy, as a treatment of psychological distress or as a way of self-reflection and self-improvement, aims at a break-through of an insight that heals conflicts and by which the individual is reconciled with himself and/or his surroundings. It tries to create a sense of well-being in the common malady of man, his alienation from himself, his fellow creatures and nature. Well-being is related to human potentials, to become what one is in potential, and this requires the partial elevation of the ego.

Psychotherapy, which has developed mostly in this century and which has been changing radically during the last ninety years, tries to base itself on the scientific method; its growth can be seen as a reaction against the influence of materialism on the inner life of the individual.

The therapist, the person who assists in the healing process, does not "save" the individual but only guides him as a teacher into the insight of one's own nature, and in the healing process towards change he is able to show "a model", "a way" and various obstacles on the way.

At present there seems to be a confusing mass of opposing and competitive psychotherapeutic systems; there are differences of opinion regarding the fundamental dynamics of the human personality and the preferences of various psychotherapeutic techniques. The situation seems to become more complicated when techniques of Eastern psychological systems are implemented in the Western approach.

In traditional Western psychotherapeutic movements "spirituality" is not recognized as an authentic aspect of the psyche and spiritual experiences are often considered as pathological symptoms.

Spiritual growth implicates a changing perspective of the Self and reality, and the development of an inner intuitive capacity which exists in every human being.

The term spirituality has been used in a great variety of ways; the Oxford English Dictionary defines it as, "The quality or condition of being spiritual, attachment to or regard for things of the spirit as opposed to material or worldly interests". Spirit here does not refer to the vital principle of man, but to an immaterial or incorporeal being or substance; spirituality refers to a state of being consisting of pure spirit.

The term spirituality signifies the individual's experience of a dimension of power and meaning transcendent to the ordinary sensory reality. These spiritual experiences may be associated with naturalistic mysticism as well as with religious tradition and/or spiritual disciplines.

Spirituality, as distinguished from religion, is more related to authentic mystical experiences whereas religion is more associated with normative practices laid down by a prophet or a religious group.

Spirituality is inspired and sustained by transpersonal experiences, and these experiences are natural manifestations of the deepest domain of the human psyche often revealing the greater depths of life.

In their meeting points psycho-spiritual discipline and psychotherapy could be considered as schools of self-knowledge; by removing ignorance the seeker is able to discover and reunify himself in order to be or become his real self. Self-knowledge is seen as the key to the rediscovery of the seeker's integrity.

Both approaches are concerned with the painful process of making the unconscious conscious; the seeker no longer sees reality as he likes it to be but as it is, and as a result the seeker gains a clearer perception of the world and a greater capacity to understand others, i.e., the self is expanded and the unconscious is able to be constructively integrated within the total personality.

Again, they both assume the existence of hidden potentials and resources, though these are differently perceived by various schools of psychotherapy and the spiritual traditions. An increased self-knowledge gives an ability to integrate these hidden potentials and resources.

Western psychotherapy as well as psycho-spiritual discipline aim to bring about changes in consciousness and both explore the essence and nature of man, his well-being, and the individual's meaning in life.

Both view the suffering of man due to his failure to become whole. This suffering will gradually diminish and disappear in the course of psychotherapy and psycho-spiritual discipline, and be replaced by a taste of openness, self-awareness and inner harmony.

The psyche, as a psychological concept has spiritual needs and by gratifying these needs it moves beyond what psychology offers. A spiritual crisis, however, which may occur during the process needs psychological attention beyond what psycho-spiritual disciplines offer.

The psychotherapist relieves the individual's obstacles and inhibitions in the process of growth and helps to establish a firm base from which the individual can develop later on, through spiritual discipline, an increasing awareness of the divine within. It is again the psychotherapist who reminds the seeker when he drifts too far from his self, escaping in selfish fantasies on the slippery road to the source of one's existence.

Despite these meeting points, the two approaches do not have the same goals, methods or outcomes, and it appears to this author that they are two separate directions that human life can take.

Psycho-spiritual discipline tends to show the way to a kind of inner harmony and relief of tension and as such may have psychotherapeutic effects and benefits, but it is not a psychotherapy in a strict sense. Spiritual growth is concerned with metaphysical, moral, cosmological, and psychological truth, whereas psychotherapy is more concerned with the growth of emotional and mental processes and healing the peculiarly disturbed individual; the latter encourages a sense of mastery over oneself and one's dynamic conditions of life, whereas the former fosters a sense of freedom from attachments and surrender to the Divine. Spiritual growth involves the whole person and is, unlike psychotherapy, less occupied with painful psychopathological symptoms and its improvement.

Clients in psychotherapy seek guidance for the relief of their psychological distress. The psychotherapist relieves obstacles and inhibitions in the process of growth and helps the client to overcome intrapsychic conflicts. Psychotherapy seeks to improve the ordinary self to be more efficient, more enjoyable and have less conflicts. The seeker of spiritual growth, on the other hand, uses detachment from the external physical world in order to get what he seeks; to be reunited with the universal Spirit. The seekers sacrifice their egos for serving purposes beyond themselves, i.e., the universal Self.

The main difference lies in the usage of the term "psyche". Psychotherapy uses psyche or mind more or less as a clinical entity, whereas psycho-spiritual discipline deals with something far more extensive than a person and its connected psychological problems. Being unaware of the distinction between soul and spirit, the Western psychotherapist confuses psychotherapy with spiritual discipline.

Those who undertake the struggle to overcome the obstacles to spiritual realisation are yearning for the divine beyond recognizable psychological motivations such as duties or satisfactions of religious, intellectual, moral and social life. Psychotherapy, on the contrary, is concerned with acquiring ego-strength, independence, self-esteem, and meaningful relationships which have been identified as components of psychological health. As such psychotherapy is a way of life, in which the client is motivated towards the therapist's goal unlike the authentic spiritual traditions in which the search for spiritual illumination is undertaken for its own sake.

Psycho-spiritual disciplines recognize the limitations of rationality within the personality. Intellectual knowledge cannot solve the final questions of life, it often prevents the development of intuitive spiritual experiences and subdues "man's creative mastery of self". In contrast to rational Western psychotherapy which seeks "causes" and attempts "adjustment", the spiritual approach emphasises inner liberation for the attainment of reunion with the universal Spirit and as such cannot be identified with psychotherapy.

Actually, spiritual development is concerned with other realms of existence, with the fulfilment of man's increasing awareness of levels of excellence and awareness of existence as part of a cosmic design. Disciplined spiritual practices seek spiritual realisation in which the seeker's consciousness rises above the material realm and where the ego is transcended.

Traditional psychotherapy betrays uncertainty in exploring and understanding the higher levels of the human personality. In its excessive probings into the chaotic unconscious or superficial surface consciousness psychotherapy has ignored the existence of higher planes of the being. By understanding unconscious mechanisms as the cause of mental disorders, only the ignorance of the lower nature of the being is dispelled. But by analysing the sources of conflicts it does not furnish the individual with a love for truth and psychotherapy as such can not come to grips with the ultimate spiritual problems of life; it does not provide any spiritual principles for future guidance.

Psychotherapy is primarily concerned with the art of healing psychological disturbances through behaviour modification, resolution of psychodynamic conflicts, and personal growth. It can be effective in resolving stubborn psychological blockages, freeing the self for growth. As such psychotherapy can be considered as a good preparation for psycho-spiritual disciplines which deal with the higher realms of being. In psycho-spiritual disciplines the transpersonal realm (higher states of consciousness) is supposed to be whole in itself and need not be healed by any therapeutic process.

Psycho-spiritual growth is more an art of living in tune with the Infinite. It tries to get directly in touch with our inmost experiences through psycho-spiritual insight, without relying on the external structures of the mind. If the psychotherapeutical methods supplement their intellectual and emotional insights with the illuminative power of spiritual insight, then they are able to reach the divine forces within man.

However, in the relation between conventional psychotherapy and the process of spiritual development various transpersonal psychologists do not make a distinction between psychotherapy and the spiritual search for self-realisation on the transpersonal level. According to Grof, "biographically oriented analysis and transpersonal experiences are two complementary aspects of the process of the systematical self-realisation".[1] For Grof the psychotherapeutical process is not a treament of a disease but an adventurous self-realisation and self-discovery. The therapist helps the client by means of creating a stimulating situation for self-realisation.

In her journey to integral wholeness, the integration of the physical, emotional, mental and spiritual aspects of well-being, F. Vaughan also views psychotherapy and spirituality as complementary and interdependent aspects of human development. She indicates that the desire for authentic transcendence cannot be satisfied by psychological growth-strategies alone, but need to be supplemented by spiritual disciplines. Wholeness is based on both the personal and the transpersonal realms of the self.

Actually, spiritual growth does not offer a therapy in the usual sense of the word, though it is able to enlarge the effectiveness of psychotherapy as both emphasise self-development.

The difference lies in their concept of the self. Psychotherapy considers the self as an object (ego) which is limited to the body, whereas in spiritual disciplines the self is interpreted as pure subjective consciousness, a unifying principle which exists within itself. Spiritual growth requires a harmony between the two selves from which further development occurs later on. The individual in his spiritual practice is not expected to be completely free from ego tendencies, but these tendencies are gradually controlled as increasing identification with the universal or transcendental Self makes them lose their power and influence.

It can therefore be said that psychotherapy as a process of mental exploration, has its value as a technique of treatment in which the individual is guided to master a certain level of stability and objectivity. A similar view is described by A. J. Deikman: "In psychotherapy, you [the therapist] are basically working to help the client clarify the motivations that underlie behavior that is frustrating and restricting him or her at the level of interpersonal relationships and also with regards to their work efficiency and creativity...... Now all kinds of behaviors might be improved in the course of spiritual development, but only as a secondary by-product of something that really has a different focus. Indeed, spiritual development may require a certain degree of health to have things go well. Thus I could see psychotherapy as providing a very important foundation from which someone might gain access to larger dimensions of reality.... Psychotherapy and spiritual development are two different levels of the same continuum, but they do not substitute for each other. They work synergistically with each other".[2]

However, by approaching the spiritual experience from a psychotherapeutic viewpoint, the therapist often looses the essence of the spiritual experience, the latter cannot be understood merely by our human thoughts and feelings. Psychotherapy can therefore not take the place of spiritual growth, as no permanent solution can be found in the process of inner growth unless the entire personality is completely spiritualised. Spiritual insight can enlarge psychotherapy, if the latter is prepared to extend the scientific definition of reality including the non-material or spiritual dimensions of human experience and a new vision for tomorrow's humanity.

2. Transpersonal Psychology

The intolerable pressures of technology which threaten to dehumanize society move many a person towards the spiritual approach in mental healing.

Humanistic psychology opposes the materialistic and positivist views regarding the reduction of the individual and the universe to an impersonal mechanism. As an addition to the emotive-instinctual model of psychoanalysis and the empirical physicalists model of behaviour it reintroduced mind to psychology. The basic goal in Humanistic psychology is self-actualisation in a growth-oriented humanistic position, but in its holistic approach it tends to ignore the spiritual dimension of the whole personality. Transpersonal psychology affirms all that humanistic psychology stands for, but adds the dimensions of soul and spirit, and the higher destiny of man.

Transpersonal psychology as a movement has been acknowledged only in the past 25 years as a subject for scientific investigation; the transpersonal realm is not the exclusive domain of priests, yogis or mystics but also of scientists; it is an open system undergoing a continuous development. In this development it brings together the ancient wisdom of all the great spiritual systems of the world and the pragmatism of Western science. It maintains that life around us is only an outer form of spiritual processes which form the basis of reality, and the higher spiritual urges/drives are therefore indispensable for optimum health.

The emergence of the transpersonal realm in psychology was heralded by Maslow's presentation of "The Farther Reaches of

Human Nature". He found that the basic underlying assumptions of the humanistic orientation did not adequately conform to the individual's inner personal world and the place of man in the universe. He considered "Humanistic, 'Third Force Psychology' to be transitional, a preparation for a still higher 'Fourth psychology', transpersonal, transhuman, and centered in the cosmos rather than in human needs and interests, going beyond humanness, identity and self-actualisation".[3]

While Humanistic psychology emphasises human experience itself as the prime reality, the transpersonal view inquires into the study of higher and more positive states of consciousness and the enlargement of the concept of self-actualisation. Transpersonal psychology is concerned with the study of the wider relatedness between the individual's psychological and spiritual dimensions and universal life principles, as well as the study of transpersonal experiences and their correlates. In extending the frontiers of understanding human nature and human potentialities, the transpersonal experiences are seen as an optimal form of intentionality rather than a flight from reality, and as such they are integrated within a larger understanding of the human psyche.

The Latin prefix trans is associated with several meanings such as "connecting", "through" or "beyond", whereas the Latin root of the word persona is related to theatrical mask. Personality can be understood as a set of masks the individual wears to hide his identity in order to gain approval or avoid pain.

The term transpersonal applies to "a state of being or consciousness beyond individuality, beyond the development of the individual person into something which is more inclusive than the individual person".[4]

It directs attention to that area which is beyond the normal experience of phenomena and which is above the ordinary personality, i.e., the human soul with its spiritual dimensions.

However, an important interpretation of the term transpersonal in Transpersonal psychology is that the transcendent is expressed through the personal.

In Transpersonal psychology the ego is given less importance and may ultimately be seen as a hindrance to transpersonal realisation. The transpersonal experience goes beyond self-actualisation to self-transcendence; the integration of the physical, vital, mental and spiritual aspects of the being. In a holistic approach to psychological health the spiritual dimensions of the person are affirmed as a vital aspect of human potentials, and the transpersonal enquiry aims at unifying man's spiritual and psychological perspectives. In the individual's search for meaning he encounters a latent dimension within himself, a reservoir of higher powers; by conscious efforts and guidance through appropriate techniques and tools this spiritual dimension is able to become active.

In the first issue of the Journal of Transpersonal Psychology Sutich defined Transpersonal psychology as "the title given to an emerging force in the psychology field by a group of psychologists and professional men and women from other fields who are interested in those ultimate human capacities and potentialities that have no systematic place in positivistic or behavioristic theory ("first force"), classical psychoanalytic theory ("second force"), or humanistic psychology ("third force"). The emerging Transpersonal Psychology ("fourth force") is concerned specifically with the empirical, scientific study of, and responsible implementation of the findings relevant to, becoming, individual and species-wide metaneeds, ultimate values, unitive consciousness, peak-experiences, B-values, ecstacy, mystical experiences, awe, being, self-actualization, essence, bliss, wonder, ultimate meaning, transcendence of self, spirit, oneness, cosmic awareness, individual and species-wide synergy, maximal interpersonal encounter, sacralization of everyday life, transcendental phenomena, cosmic self-humor and playfulness; maximal sensory awareness, responsiveness and expression; and related concepts, experiences and activities".[5]

In one of the latest Journals of Transpersonal Psychology D. H. Lajoie and S. I. Shapiro provide a systematic survey of the various definitions of Transpersonal psychology during the first twenty-three years of its existence with the intention to generate a precise, contemporary definition of Transpersonal psychology. In their chronological list of 40 citations only those definitions will be discussed which are relevant to this study.

E. Hoffman bases his definition on A. Maslow's vision and defines Transpersonal psychology as "an approach founded and introduced within humanistic psychology by Abraham Maslow in the 1960's, which seeks to incorporate human spirituality into a comprehensive model of human nature and its potential. Also known as the Fourth Force".

R. Walsh and F. Vaughan define Transpersonal psychology as "the study of optimum psychological health and well-being. It recognizes the potential for experiencing a broad range of states of consciousness, in some of which identity may extend beyond the usual limits of ego and personality". In the introduction of Paths Beyond Ego they add a comprehensive approach to a transpersonal vision. They advocate "an eclective, integrative quest that includes personal and transpersonal, ancient and modern, East and West, knowledge and wisdom, art and philosophy, science and religion, introspection and contemplation".

S. Grof defines the transpersonal orientation as "a model of the human psyche that recognizes the importance of the spiritual or cosmic dimensions and the potential for conscious evolution".

In Washburn's definition, Transpersonal psychology makes a study of "human nature and development that proceeds on the assumption that human beings possess potentialities that surpass the limits of the normally developed ego. It is an enquiry that presupposes that the ego, as ordinarily constituted, can be transcended, and that a higher, transegoic plane or stage of life is possible".

Finally, K. Wilber in his definition emphasises "a psychological presentation of the perennial philosophy of the great Chain of Being, fully up-dated and grounded in modern research and scientific developments. It fully acknowledges and incorporates the findings of modern psychiatry, behaviorism, and developmental psychology, and then adds, where necessary, the further insights and experiences of the existential and spiritual dimensions of the human being".[6]

In their final analysis D. H. Lajoie and S. Shapiro found that the most frequently used themes in the different definitions of Transpersonal psychology were related to:

States of consciousness
Highest or ultimate potentials
Beyond ego or personal self
Transcendence
Spiritual.

With these themes and the compilation of all the previous definitions they offer the following contemporary definition of transpersonal psychology; "Transpersonal psychology is concerned with the study of humanity's highest potential, and with the recognition, understanding, and realization of unitive, spiritual, and transcendent states of consciousness".[7]

The concept of beyond the ego is not included in this definition because "its meaning has been interpreted in different ways both with classical spiritual traditions and within modern transpersonal psychology".[8]

All these definitions do not tie the disciplines to any particular religion, philosophy, specific doctrine, worldview or metaphysics.

From these definitions it becomes clear that Transpersonal psychology is not just a spiritual psychology, but a synthesis of psychological and spiritual approaches to the psyche. Nevertheless Transpersonal psychology assumes that human development ultimately aims at a spiritual fulfilment and human nature can therefore be fully understood only from the spiritual perspective.

The term Transpersonal psychology is still developing and its definition will continue to change and evolve.

As mentioned before, the very term "transpersonal" implies going beyond personality, for personality is only one facet of the Self, and Transpersonal psychology seeks to apprehend identity with the total self, the highest potential in human beings. In the possibility of growth towards wholeness, beyond exclusive identification with the body or ego, the individual achieves a more inclusive state of awareness, in which his personality is not abandoned or destroyed but its limitations and restrictions are transcended. Personality is no longer the source of our identity but the instrument by which the individual expresses that identity in the world. Enlightened qualities of being can be discovered not by getting rid of personality but by refining it and by converting obstacles into stepping stones on the path of spiritual development. In this extension of identity the individual moves beyond individuality.

Transpersonal psychology assumes that man's highest potential lies in the spiritual experience, and the fulfilment of spiritual experiences in human development. It does not seek to impose a new belief system or a new metaphysics but attempts to expand the field of psychological inquiry, and to integrate ancient wisdom and modern science. Western scientific approaches and spiritual disciplines are seen as complementary, if science is used for gaining access to inner wisdom. Earlier scientific approaches failed to deal adequately with human experiences of the spiritual realm, i.e., higher entities, ultimate purpose, God, love, etc, either ruling out its validity or labelling it "pathological". But the transpersonal psychologist insists that the various human experiences within the field of spiritual psychology are not incompatible with the essence of science, on condition that science includes subjective experiences as part of its subject matter.

The feeling that Western psychology up to now has been culture-bound and limited by multitudes of implicit assumptions that make up the consensus reality of the Western world, and its failure to deal adequately with human experiences related to spirituality, higher entities, etc, has been satisfactorily met by the emergence of Transpersonal psychology. It considers the human psyche as an open and transcendental system of consciousness; it emphasises not so much human behaviour itself, but the study of transcendental and spiritual experiences, and man's higher functions so as to become able to grasp the unifying and universal elements which are characteristic of all cultures.

3. Transpersonal Psychotherapy

Transpersonal psychotherapy takes Spirit as the basis of reality and in its therapeutical approach it concentrates on the restoration of the lost contact with the spiritual Self. It is characterised by the acceptance of the spiritual and cosmic dimensions of the personality and the possibility for the development of consciousness. For the transpersonal psychotherapist the ordinary concept of self and the everyday average consciousness are only limited facets of a more complex nature and his principal task is to help the client to differentiate between the ego-self and the transpersonal self.

The transpersonal psychotherapist examines the negative influence of psychological conflicts on spiritual development, and the positive influence of spiritual practices on intrapersonal and interpersonal conflicts. The therapist in exploring the client's dark areas of the psyche guides him towards an integration of rejected aspects of the self into a larger image of wholeness. In this way the therapist attempts "to bridge the long-neglected and often difficult gap between emotional development on the one hand and spiritual maturation on the other—the instinctual and the sublime, the personal and the transpersonal"[9]

However, the therapist does not provide the client with clear-cut solutions or predetermined goals to resolve his personal problems, but enables the person to open up to inner resources or inner healing potentials. As such the therapist assists the client in the process of disidentification from and transcendence of psychodynamic issues. During this process the transpersonal therapist brings into awareness the client's unknown latent capacities for transpersonal experiences which are supposed to have a healing potential and are therefore valuable remedies in the course of self-healing. Nevertheless, the healing effects of these experiences are often only temporary and the therapist therefore does not aim at treating these experiences as ends in themselves but integrating them effectively as meaningful aspects into the client's daily life.

To be effective, the therapist's own commitment to spiritual growth is of utmost importance in his willingness to join the client in a mutual search for healing power. "A transpersonal context in therapy is determined entirely by the beliefs, values and intentions of the therapist".[10]

The therapist may utilize the therapeutic relationship to enlarge his own spiritual growth through consciously serving the client.

Transpersonal psychotherapy tries to achieve its goal by paying attention to non-realised human potentials and through the expansion of consciousness. In the course of therapy, when the individual becomes gradually aware of the transpersonal dimension of being, his behaviour tends to change, and unsoluble problems at the ego-level are often transcended. A client may experience problems, but the same client is more than his problem. There is a light within each individual, an essence free of all conditioned elements of personal problems and which can be experienced by each of us.

In its therapeutic approach it stresses active transformation through direct experience rather than rational insight. In the process of transformation of the personality it encourages the individual to penetrate into his transpersonal realm; it is like a journey into the unknown where the individual constantly encounters new elements of the deeper levels of his being.

Transpersonal psychotherapy holds that misery is not inherent in the human condition and it aims at the liberation of the root cause of misery: the disidentification of the ego and the discovery of one's own true nature. In this inward developmental process it emphasises the importance of one's own responsibility in one's relations and in the world; all life experiences are part of a learning process and transpersonal psychotherapy helps to integrate these experiences into the context of the individual's life.

The individual seeking help from a transpersonal therapist is expected to have a considerable amount of mental stability or a reasonable degree of self-integration, so that the same individual is able to disseminate unconscious elements into the conscious and thereafter expand his consciousness.

Transpersonal psychotherapy has built upon contributions of traditional psychotherapies—psychoanalytical, behavioural and humanistic—and includes many of their views, goals and techniques, but it places them in a larger and more expanded context. In addition to the goals of traditional psychotherapies Transpersonal psychotherapy aims at the disindentification and transcendence of these issues. It is not so much concerned with psychopathological symptoms and does not aim at the relief of daily compulsions, but in contrast it moves the client towards a wider field of human capacities and self-transcendence.

Transpersonal psychotherapy in its clinical practice emphasises the validity and healing potentials of transpersonal experiences and as such goes beyond the traditional therapeutic goals. Its ultimate goal is related to the individual's fullest development as a psychological and spiritual being. From this perspective it becomes clear that Transpersonal psychotherapy does not differ so much from traditional psychotherapy in its methods or techniques but more in its contents and scope. The full realisation of the transpersonal experience implies the transcendence of ego-defenses, unlike the traditional dictum of attempting to strengthen the ego.

Transpersonal psychotherapy profoundly contributes to healing processes or "wholeness-making" as described by S. Grof: "those who have experienced states of cosmic unity have an entire new attitude toward the psychotherapeutic process.... The therapeutical potential of the experiences that have a spiritual quality far surpasses anything available in connection with manipulations focusing on biographical material. Any conceptual system and technique of psychotherapy that does not utilize the perinatal and transpersonal domains of the psyche not only offers a superficial and incomplete image of human beings but deprives itself and its clients of powerful mechanisms of healing and personality transformation".[11]

F. Vaughan suggests, "on the inward arc of human development healing remains incomplete unless the human aspiration for transcendence is taken into account".[12]

Transpersonal therapy aims at the development of the awareness of the transpersonal self and questions beliefs about the nature of the self and reality. For F. Vaughan Transpersonal psychotherapy "includes traditional areas and concerns, adding to these an interest in facilitating growth and awareness beyond traditionally recognized levels of health. The importance of modifying consciousness and the validity of transcendental experience and identity is affirmed".[13]

She relates the transpersonal dimension of human potentials to the integration of the transpersonal experience which will lead to self-realisation and transcendence.

T. Weide describes Transpersonal psychotherapy as, "on the one hand, the employment of transpersonal energies during 'regular' psychotherapy, and, on the other hand, as the utilization of 'standard' psychological knowledge for transpersonal purposes".[14]

A. Sutich defines Transpersonal therapy as, "the psychological processes related to the realization (i.e. making real) of states such as 'illumination', 'mystical union', 'transcendence', and 'cosmic unity'. It is also concerned with the psychological conditions or psychodynamic processes which directly or indirectly form barriers to these transpersonal realizations".[15]

These definitions affirm the importance and validity of the transcendent experience and identity. Though the individual transcends the psychodynamic level and enters into the transpersonal realm, unifying spiritual and psychological perspectives, these explorations remain confined to the highest reaches of human nature and its developmental process. Transpersonal therapy deals with the experience of an extension of identity beyond the usual limits of the ego, beyond space and time but it remains confined to the term 'humanness', as it does not recognize any transpersonal self-substance beyond the limits of human consciousness. In this way transpersonal therapists seem to limit themselves to the evocation of highest *human* potentials, the full realisation of *human* possibilities.

K. Wilber relates the various levels of the "spectrum of consciousness" with the major fields of Western psychotherapy, assigning a particular school of therapy to each major level of the spectrum and he is concerned with the pathologies which occur at any of these levels.

For Wilber, transpersonal therapy aims at the level of "Unity consciousness", but he comes into linguistic difficulties when he explores the highest level of the spectrum—the Brahman and Atman consciousness. The term 'therapy' can be used in this level only as a concession to language.

Actually a medical approach to 'healing' within a transpersonal perspective sounds paradoxical and it may be argued that the very phrase "Transpersonal psychotherapy" is a contradiction in terms. The transpersonal field has no finite limits, it is already whole within itself and needs no clinical healing as in psychotherapy. Transpersonal therapy is therefore more associated with a method of self-perfectioning, a healing process of psycho-spiritual illness rather than a method of medical treatment.

4. Psycho-spiritual Practices in Transpersonal Psychotherapy

In addition to the psychodynamic and behavioural techniques, Transpersonal psychotherapy uses various forms of yoga, meditation, trance work, imagery, and other spiritual practices as techniques. These various techniques are used in Transpersonal psychotherapy to assist clients to open the spiritual dimension and to realise transpersonal potentials. However, the reader should keep in mind that "these techniques are less important than the therapist's respect for the transformative power of transpersonal experiences".[16]

This wide range of techniques for the various aspects of the personality—physical (body), vital (emotions), mental (mind), and spiritual—are drawn from various Eastern disciplines and Western psychology.

The physical level includes diet and various forms of bodywork. These techniques aim at psycho-physical relaxation, self-mastery as well as the release of habitual patterns of tension.

The vital level includes the release of emotional blocks relieving repressed thoughts and feelings from the past enabling the client to live fully and freely in the present. The reduction of destructive emotions does not take place through repression, but through clear awareness and consciously relinquishing them and simultaneously cultivating positive emotions.

At the mental level the therapist may use the rational-emotive or existential-humanistic approach.

Imaginative techniques are based on visualisations through conscious use of images, i.e., to get in touch with the contents of the unconscious and transmit it to the conscious mind. The imaginative activity of the mind, unlike dreaming, is a product of the waking state.

Imagination is closely linked with intuition, because intuition appears in the conscious mind not in its abstract pure form but assumes the shape of images. As a form of introspection it enables the individual to penetrate into the inner and deeper layers of the psyche. Through eliciting unconscious images and bringing them to the conscious level the individual is able to integrate his personality at a higher level.

Dreams, as radical departures from everyday reality, monitor the inner life of the psyche. They often provide a key to mental health as they reveal truth about subjective inner experiences, and draw attention to unconscious factors that are usually ignored or consciously denied. "As mirrors of the psyche they rearrange and impose order on experience, calling attention to what we already know intuitively".[17]

Dreams can be a profound source of insight and a useful guidance on the spiritual path. They are able to offer the dreamer a key avenue for self-exploration as well as a path to an expanded universal wisdom. As such dreams become a valuable technique for revealing transpersonal material.

For Freud dreams are the royal road to the unconscious which refers to the dreamer's struggle with unresolved residues of the past.

Dream analysis, the reductive method of dream interpretation, relieved many people from mental distress. But for the transpersonal therapist the unconscious is too complex in its contents to reduce it only to disguised wish fulfilments such as primitive sexual impulses and self-assertion, Freud's central theme in all dreams.

C. Jung regards dreams as an expression of man's inner life which contains messages of healing, inspiration and intuitive wisdom. They serve a compensatory function that helps to restore balance to the psyche. He disagreed with Freud's interpretations of the symbolic dream contents as cryptic statements about biological functions, for Jung they were references to complex transcendental realities. In his view dreams have an integrative function and refer to the unknown side of the individual (the collective unconscious). The growth-enhancing potential of the dream moves the individual to higher levels of personality integration.

Actually, dreams when viewed in the context of the life of the dreamer can be interpreted from any level, from the emotive-instinctual to the existential or spiritual level. The more consciously developed individual will respond to higher levels of interpretation.

Meditation: Historically meditation has been an essential element in nearly all contemplative spiritual traditions.

As a way of self-discovery meditation reveals the true facts of existence, but it is also a way of learning to still the disturbances of the individual's outer and inner life. In exploring the inner world meditation is helpful in increasing tranquility, understanding, creativity and in reducing mental tension and anxiety.

D. Fontana in "the meditator's hand book" describes meditation as "the movement from the rational, linear, logical world into the world of intuition, where truth presents itself in flashes of insight and causes profound changes in the way we respond to experience."[18]

Meditative practices can be classified into two major types, the concentrative and the contemplative meditation. In concentrative meditation the mind remains focused upon the object of concentration and is held there steadily, while insight develops of its own accord. Examples of concentrative meditation are Patanjali's raja yoga and pschyo-spiritual practices of various religious traditions. In contemplative or receptive meditation the meditator gains insight through observing the shifting contents of his awareness as an unmoving witness. It is the practice of sustained nonselective awareness, whatever emerges in the mind is observed crisply but without being acted upon or reacted to. Important forms of contemplative meditation are insight meditation of Buddhism (Vipassana) or Zen meditation.

Meditation when practiced regularly disengages the ego's attention from external involvements and interiorizes awareness. In this way repressed inner subjective stimuli of the unconscious come to the foreground of the ego consciousness. However, in the course of sustained practice meditation arrests ego-activities and ultimately transcends the ego. In overcoming the limitation of the ego, the latter is not fragmented but left intact to function in the world when it is appropriate for the ego to do so.

In Transpersonal psychotherapy meditation is used as a technique only after the ego has gained a certain strength and is able to become an impediment to further spiritual advancement. Those clients who lack ego-strength are dissolving precisely what needs to be strengthened. The ego, to be able to encounter unwelcome repressed material needs to be firmly established in order to overcome this confrontation with the personal submerged unconscious. In J. Engler's words, "you have to be somebody before you can be nobody".[19]

The ego must be able to function and maintain its place in the world before it can abandon it.

Facing the individual's unconscious contents can be a dramatic affair and need not always be in the direction of spiritual growth. In cases where the ego needs to be fortified first, traditional psychotherapy might be quite helpful as a preparatory stage in dealing with the conscious integrative functions of the ego.

Traditionally meditation is employed as an essential practice for advanced psycho-spiritual development. In recent times meditation is also used by Western psychotherapists for reducing specific psychological or psychophysiological disorders, as well as by healthy nonclinical individuals for a heightened sense of psychological well-being. Meditation, when used as a clinical intervention for self regulation and self exploration, or as a possible adjunct of psychotherapy often extracts the contents of the meditation technique from its original context. Those who use meditation in this way may obtain increased tranquility and enjoyment, but without a noticeable gain in wisdom and these meditators still carry the burden of unresolved conflicts. Meditation certainly has psychotherapeutic potentials; however, if meditation is used in a clinical model only, then the various psychopathological symptoms disappear for some time but the more deep-rooted underlying issues are not dealt with and the cure may be only temporary.

Meditation used as a technique for self-transformation is usually accompanied by changes of identity backed up with a major reorientation in life; the means for attaining psychological health is related to non-attachment, calmness, control, purification, and the reduction of aversion and ignorance. The meditator by turning his attention away from bodily striving is able to control aggressive and sexual impulses, and in these altered states of consciousness the seeker is able to bypass his neurotic tendencies. But to break neurotic symptoms requires more than meditation, it demands not only the discipline to control the unruly self, but also a coherent system of truth and belief. To eliminate meditation of its metaphysical setting , reducing it to a mere psychological self-help device, may easily lead to the omittance of the spritual roots of its tradition.

Meditation alone can certainly have notable positive effects, but when the client lacks a concern for spiritual fulfilment then meditative therapy remains only a strictly symptomatic cure.

5. The Ego in Transpersonal Psychotherapy

The transpersonal therapist aims at the holistic understanding of human nature and development, based on the assumption that human beings possess the potential to surpass the limits of the ego, transcending into a higher transegoic plane.

According to F. Vaughan; "Transpersonal psychotherapy is not so much concerned with the attainment of ego achievements but rather with the capacity for self-transcendence as an integral part of transpersonal self-realisation".[20]

In Western therapy the development of the ego, as an essential stage of human growth and stability receives all attention; the ego is indispensable for mental health. The positive aspects of the ego are utilised for overcoming psychological disturbances, and a well-developed ego is often equated with psychological health.

The function of the ego can be broadly classified as the principle of separate individuation, the principle of action (I want) and the principle of continuity (I am the same like yesterday). It has an integrative function regarding opposing forces, f. e, non-interference versus control. A minimum sense of ego identity is regarded essential for psychological health. However, this psychological health requires simultaneously a contrary reaction of the ego: the release of the I, a trans-ego state within the realm of the individual's actual experience, which is characterised by the surrender to another person or

God (unification). By purifying and illumining the self-assertive possessive ego can it be in accord with the ultimate truth.

The ego functions as an instrument for this world, but it is not able to go beyond this world into the Kingdom of God. Only by the victory over the limitations of the egocentric self, when the ego breaks its boundaries and unites with the cosmic Self, it becomes a fit instrument for the real Self.

Transpersonal psychotherapy presumes that the seeker has already achieved a certain degree of adult maturity and strength as an individual. Without prior resolution of developmental tasks such as social adjustment, personal identity, and interpersonal relationships, these matters may overlap the deeper aims of psycho-spiritual discipline. Nevertheless the ego is merely a tool of great importance within its own frame of reference; it becomes a hindrance when misapplied and therefore has to be kept in perspective.

Transcending the ego should not be confused with mere loss of ego-strength. In excelling the ego, the individual stops over-valuating the needs of the inflated ego. However, the latter is not dissolved but remains intact with all its essential strengths and weaknesses, i.e., not the loss or destruction of the ego but rather seeing through the ego, surpassing itself. In giving up the desire for egocentric gratification the individual is not being deprived of desires but learns to acknowledge them without being driven by their gratification. Once the process of disidentification with the ego has started, the individual is aware that the ego-functions are still available if he needs to deal with worldly matters, but by now the same individual has better things to do, i.e., re-establishing an intimate relationship with one's true self, one's spiritual essence. In this way ego transcendence does not mean the loss of one's ego-oriented rules of social behaviour but the individual sees through them, accepting responsibility for every willed action.

The transpersonal therapist would advise the forthcoming spiritual practitioners to work through personal psychodynamic issues first, (childhood traumas and other unresolved emotional matters) in order to clarify and purify underlying psychological problems before the a spiritual awakening takes place. This view is brilliantly described by Wilber: "Most neurotics suffer not because of lack of ego transcendence, but from the prior lack of ego-esteem, and therapy must be, first and foremost, the facilitator of strong ego-esteem, and then—but only then—the facilitator of ego-transcendence".[21]

Only a strong psychological grounding, a mature level of ego organisation, allows the practitioner to enter into those spiritual practices which aim at the manifestation of mature psycho-spiritual development, i.e., transcending various personality structures as well as the development of awareness to deal with the powerful energies in the transegoic realm.

As mentioned previously while discussing ego-transcendence during meditation, when the ego has not yet come to terms with its less respectable instincts then it becomes possessed by the strongly repressed unconscious. There is always the danger of disorder when the position of the ego is called in question. But when the ego is first tamed before it is transcended, the invasion of the conscious by unconscious contents will be smoothly integrated. By now, when the tamed ego surpasses itself there is no such invasion of the conscious by primordial repressed contents but there is instead mystical insight.

Before entering into the discussion of the different theories of various transpersonal psychologists it is useful to compare Transpersonal psychotherapy with spiritual discipline because there is a considerable congruence as well as conflict between the two approaches.

Traditional psychotherapy is concerned with the cultivation of ego-strength; however, mere changes in the ego may temporarily diminish one's sense of discontentment but such surface modifications have no effect on the underlying cause of suffering. In Transpersonal psychotherapy and spiritual discipline the root cause of suffering is related to the impoverishment of the spiritual dimension of life. Spiritual discipline as well as Transpersonal psychotherapy are both concerned with the process of expanding awareness that underlies psycho-spiritual growth, and both include conceptual models of evolution emphasising the attainment of more advanced states of consciousness. Both approaches require therefore a certain degree of psychological maturity and health so that unavoidable difficulties on the slippery path of spiritual development can be overcome without being overwhelmed.

In the advanced stages of contemplative development, both methods aim at the removal of barriers which obstruct the seeker's spiritual growth rather than the sole recovery from psychological unbalances. In the process of exploration of the spiritual dimension both approaches respect the seeker's own developing awareness of transcendent being through the unfoldment of the inner and higher realms of being.

In Transpersonal psychotherapy the therapist guides clients in the process of integration of their transpersonal experiences into their daily lives and stimulates clients to behave in congruence with their spiritual beliefs. These transcendent experiences in Transpersonal psychotherapy may be associated with religious traditions and spiritual disciplines but also with Maslow's farther reaches of human nature. At the highest levels of consciousness the individual experiences a transpersonal unity of consciousness with others, but one does not lose his personal identity.

However, in Transpersonal psychotherapy, interested in the psychological interpretation of spiritual and mystical experiences, man remains at the centre of life, there is no divine purpose to which men can give themselves.

Spiritual discipline, on the contrary, involves a person's experience of a dimension of meaning transcendent to the world of sensory reality and contributes to an understanding of the meaning and purpose of spiritual life. It expands contemplative psychological inquiry beyond the farther reaches of human nature. In spiritual disciplines man serves the Divine beyond the ordinary world of appearances. The seeker gradually becomes aware of higher and more subtle energies which transform the whole meaning of ordinary life.

In "the ultimate concern" the transpersonal and spiritual approach are not mutually exclusive but complementary and interdependent aspects in the journey to wholeness. Self-transcendence cannot be achieved by mere spiritual concerns and practices only but could, in addition, be supplemented by psychological growth strategies and interpretations. As such Transpersonal psychotherapy may be considered as a valuable form of support for the initiation towards inner growth and a preparation before entering the authentic spiritual discipline.

Notes:

1. Grof, S; Beyond the Brain: Birth, Death and Transcendence in Psychotherapy, State University of N-York Press, New-York 1985, p. 262.

2. Tart. C. and A. Deikman; Journal of Transpersonal Psychology Vol. 23, NO:1, 1991, p. 39.
3. Maslow, A; Towards a Psychology of Being, Van Nostrand Rein hold Comp, New-York, 2nd ed 1968, p. III-IV.
4. A. Sutich; "The Emergence of the Transpersonal orientation", Journal of Transpersonal Psychology, Vol 1, No:1, 1976, p. 16.
5. Ibid., p. 15–16.
6. Lajoie. D. H. and S. Shapiro;Journal of Transpersonal Psychology, Vol. 24, No:1, 1992.
7. Ibid., p. 91.
8. Ibid., p. 95.
9. Zeig, J. K and M. Munion Edt; What is Psychotherapy? Contemporary perspectives, Jossey-Bass Inc Publ, San Fransisco1990. A. B. Chinen "Transpersonal Psychotherapy", p. 204.
10. Walsh R, and F. Vaughan, Edt; Beyond Ego: Transpersonal Dimen sions in Psychology, Jeremy Tharcher Inc, Los Angeles 1980, p. 183.
11. Grof, S; Beyond the Brain: Birth, Death and Transcendence in Psychotherapy, State University of N-York Press, New-York 1985, p. 369.
12. Vaughan F; The Inward Arc; Healing and Wholeness in Psychoherapy and Spirituality, Shambhala Publ, Boston 1985, p. 9.
13. Walsh R, and F. Vaughan, Edt; Beyond Ego: Transpersonal Dimensions in Psychology, Jeremy Tharcher Inc, Los Angeles 1980, p. 16.
14. N. Weide; "Varieties of Transpersonal Therapy", Journal of Transpersonal Psychology, Vol. 5, No:1, 1973, p. 7.
15. A. Sutich; "Transpersonal Psychotherapy. History and Definition". In S. Boorstein Edt; Transpersonal Psychotherapy, Science and Behaviour Books, Stanford 1991, p. 9.
16. Zeig, J. K and M. Munion Edt; What is Psychotherapy? Contemporary perspectives, Jossey-Bass Inc Publ, San Fransisco1990. A. B. Chinen "Transpersonal Psychotherapy", p. 203.
17. Vaughan F; The Inward Arc; Healing and Wholeness in Psychotherapy and Spirituality, Shambhala Publ, Boston 1985, p. 167.
18. Fontana, D; The Meditator's Handbook, Element Books Ltd, Rockport 1992, p. 30.
19. Wilber, Ken and J, Engler, D. P. Brown; Transformation of Con-sciousness, Shambhala, Boston 1986, p. 24.
20. F. Vaughan; "Transpersonal perspectives in psychotherapy", Journal of Humanistic Psychology, San Fransisco, 1977.
21. Walsh, R, and F. Vaughan, Edt; Paths Beyond Ego, Jeremy Tharcher, Los Angeles 1993, p. 129.

CHAPTER IV

VARIOUS LEADING TRANSPERSONAL PSYCHOLOGISTS

Transpersonal psychologists represent the beginning of a systematic comparative psychotherapy which tries to unite the various schools in one thought. To understand the transpersonal psychotherapist one has to know the therapist's views and ideas which are related to his work.

This chapter examines some of the leading transpersonal psychologists' referential frameworks, several of their limited hypotheses and it explores a variety of new issues related to the transpersonal realm of human nature. An exhaustive treatment of each transpersonal theory is beyond the limited purpose of this chapter. For a complete understanding of their views the reader is recommended to study their original works.

The following presentation is more of an indicative nature, only the salient ideas are described as a basis for a critical evaluation discussed in the last section of this work.

1. A. Maslow's Metapsychology

Maslow did not contribute much to the practical aspects of Transpersonal psychology and he is not specifically engaged in any form of therapy. However, many of his concepts are used by various transpersonal therapists and his influence remains very important. He developed the nucleus of Transpersonal psychology in which new ideas could be developed in the near future.

In the process of depersonalisation in life the human potentials are directed towards nuclear annihilation and environmental suicide rather than the realisation of spiritual values, and it was Maslow who was concerned with the divine qualities of the human being.

Maslow did not offer a definite elaborated psychological theory based on facts but presented the reader a unique vision of human nature, which was the intuitive product of his inner experiences. His theory is founded upon the holistic-dynamic view in which the individual is seen as an organised, integral and dynamic system. Isolated behaviour is considered unimportant unless it is related to the central purposes of the organism. Behaviour is an expression of the total organism and not a loose collection of separated functionings.

In his attempt to develop a comprehensive theory of human motivation based on the hierarchy of needs Maslow tried to integrate into a single theoretical structure the partial truths of Freud, Jung, Adler, Goldstein and Fromm. His motivational theory is based on the idea that behaviour is controlled through a limited number of developing fundamental needs, from the lower basic needs such as physiological and safety needs, the need for love and self-esteem, to the higher needs of self-actualisation, which operate in a fixed sequence; through these various needs the individual is motivated.

These universal needs arrange themselves in a hierarchy of prepotency, for the individual is not driven by all the needs at the same time. A satisfied need no longer motivates behaviour and as the lower needs are put to rest they will inevitably be supplanted by higher needs, and as a consequence higher needs emerge only when the lower ones are gratified. Gratification of the lower basic needs comes from the environment around the individual, in contrast to the higher needs which are more autonomous and related to the deeper self within the individual.

Maslow would like each individual to find out what he is really like inside, both as a member of the human species and as a particular individual.

To Maslow the "inner nature" belongs to the realm of Being and this inner being is a biological autonomous individuality, including the person's temperament, capacities and reactions but simultaneously a way of experiencing biological brotherhood with all human beings.

Maslow's model of the hierarchy of needs is based on the existence of a certain directional tendency towards growth and development. This tendency for growth in the direction of a full psychic development led Maslow to the study of self-actualising individuals.

Unfortunately, growth upwards in the hierarchy of needs is limited and is generally obstructed in such a way that most individuals remain somewhere half-way up the hierarchy; the fully developed personality is reached only by a few. It needs courage to grow, as growth does not have only rewards and pleasures but is often accompanied by intrinsic pain. In order to develop, the individual needs to give up an easier, less effortful life in exchange for a more responsible, more difficult one.

One of the major internal obstructions mentioned by Maslow is connected with the ego's defence mechanism. Identifying excluded or unacceptable ideas or emotions is a painful process. But once they have been identified and if, with courage, they can be given up, then the repression is replaced by a recovery of one's inner essence, one's real self.

In his latest work, "The Farther Reaches of Human Nature", he discusses a new defence mechanism which he described as "the Jonah Complex"; the evasion of growth due to "fear of one's greatness or running away from one's best talents". The individual tends to be ambivalent regarding his highest possibilities. On the one hand godlike possibilities are enjoyed whereas on the other hand the individual shivers with fear before those very same possibilities. According to Maslow "probably all the Freudian defence mechanisms are available and used against the highest within ourselves just as they are mobilized against the lowest within ourselves".[1]

Despite these hindrances on the slippery path towards growth, the consequences of growth-choices are better from the viewpoint of the individual's own biological values; in other words, the individual who is aware of the possibility of choosing between regression and growth will always refuse regression and choose growth.

An important consequence of the process of psychological growth is the concept of psychological health. According to Maslow, "Healthy people have sufficiently gratified their basic needs ... so that they are motivated primarily by trends to self-actualization. (defined as ongoing actualization of potentials)".[2] Later he replaced the concept of psychological health by the concept of being "fully human", as not all people move towards self-actualisation when their basic needs are gratified.

Maslow, using the term self-actualisation to refer to the best and most psychologically healthy examples of human species, investigated these models to get the clearest picture of capabilities of human nature. Self-actualising people have the urge to make real or actual what they already potentially are; they are not seeking gratification of the basic needs, but are striving for a self-perfecting life, for full development of the potentialities of the organism.

By studying self-actualisers Maslow discovered another aspect of psychological health which he introduced as the "Peak-experience". In his work on self-actualisation he was trying to go beyond normal psychology to a more complete vision of human nature, but with his studies on the peak-experience Maslow was seeking to go beyond human nature to a more complete understanding of reality as a whole. Peak-experiences, or secularised mystical experiences are described by Maslow as "the best moments of the human being ... experiences of ecstacy, rapture, bliss, of the greatest joy".[3] When he presented the characteristics of the peak-experience, he differentiated two kinds of peakers. In the first there is the cosmic consciousness in which the whole of the cosmos is perceived and everything in it is seen in relationship with everything else, including the perceiver. The relationship is a fusion of the I with the universal but not a transcendence of the ego. In the other kind of peak-experience there is a consciousness in which the world and the ego are totally forgotten; there is no fusion but a transcendence of the ego into the beyond.

Maslow dissociated the general concept of the peak-experience from the religious mystical and supernatural area, and replaced the term "mystic experience" by "peak-experience", which does not belong to priests, saints or yogis only but is available to all mankind and therefore open to human investigation. By giving an empirical foundation for this concept of the peak experience and the idea of transcendence, Maslow showed that religious experience can be approached rationally; by rejecting religious supernaturalism he created a kind of natural mysticism, dispensing with such ideas as a personal God and divine creator.

However, it seems to this author that Maslow when trying to accept the "God-like" experience, but keeping shy from "God", does so due to his crude concept of God, a God standing outside of the cosmos (as creator). It is this fight against the untenable dogma of an extra-cosmic God which leads Maslow into confusion. In naturalising religion he subsumes religion under natural science, explaining the supernatural in natural terms. It seems that the transpersonal movement still follows Maslow's naturalistic ideas, they explore the deeper realms of the spiritual experience but deny God as the source of such experiences. Transpersonal psychology does not deal with those spiritual experiences which call for a divine origin. According to Maslow ultimate values are found by observing the best of mankind rather than moving to God, but here he mistakes his peak-experiences, "the happiest moments of life", for the real spiritual experience where the individual moves beyond the transpersonal domain towards God or the Divine.

In "The Farther Reaches of Human Nature", which deals with his latest views, Maslow moves into the realm of the transpersonal and the development of higher states of consciousness. In "A Theory of Metamotivation" he speaks of inborn higher metaneeds, in which the self-actualiser has transcended striving or desiring and is now enriching his life through expansion of horizons. These metaneeds are as inherent as lower needs and they too must be gratified if the fullest growth is to be achieved.

Obstructed metaneeds may produce "metapathology", Maslow's term for spiritual illness which is related to the psycho-spiritual crisis of the individual; they are psychological disturbances which arise if the individual's spiritual cravings (metaneeds) are not satisfied. Maslow defined metapathology as the "the illnesses resulting from deprivation of intrinsic values (metaneeds)".[4] The self-actualising person needs metaneeds in order to achieve full humanness and to avoid illness. Metapathologies are vaguely described by theologists and philosophers under the law of spiritual shortcomings, whereas psychologists and scientists describe them as psychological or biological illnesses. But for Maslow these spiritual illnesses are related to the deprivation of metaneed gratification; they are the root cause of all human suffering in which the individual is alienated from his own true self or spiritual essence. Failure to recognize transpersonal needs may underlie much of contemporary individual, social, and global pathology.

These metaneeds, like the peak-experience, are considered by Maslow as falling within the realm of human nature rather than belonging to a different realm. The higher aspirations of mankind thus become accessible to scientific study. These ultimates lie within human nature and one need not look to a non-human, or non-natural source to understand them.

In a final modification to his account of self-actualising people, Maslow divides them into two kinds of self-actualisers, transcending and non-transcending. The latter are psychologically healthy people but have no experiences of transcendence. Such people live in the world and achieve fulfilment within it; they tend to be doers rather than meditators. The transcenders are more metamotivated and find it easier to transcend the ego, to go beyond self-actualisation. They are more godlike, innovators of the new and perceivers of unitive consciousness.

Transcendence as mystical experience is related to the mystic fusion with another person or with the whole cosmos. This is a special phenomenological state in which the distinction between self and not-self has been transcended and where the individual becomes an enlarged self in which the universal values are incorporated.

For Maslow the whole process of transcendence is based on the concept of integration; the higher is built upon, rests upon but includes the lower. However, it also means to become divine or godlike, to go beyond the merely human but by this Maslow does not mean the Spiritual self, nothing supernatural. The "metahuman" or "becoming divine" is part of the potential of human nature and therefore remains a natural human characteristic.

It is in the farther reaches of human nature that the ego-oriented ways of experiencing are gradually replaced by an impersonal cosmic experience where the individual self is, at least partly, dissolved into the cosmos. The transpersonal experience therefore goes beyond self-actualisation to self-transcendence, the highest level of human consciousness.

On the basis of these improved views of self-actualising people Maslow developed a new concept which he called the "Plateau-Experience". The peak-experiences were just passive emotional, transient, ecstatic bursts, which were not always illuminative or cognitive. The plateau-experience is a more stable and more lasting type of unitive experience representing a new and more profound way of viewing and experiencing the world.

The cognitive elements become greater and greater as the emotional intensity dies out. The plateau-experience is also far more voluntary than the peak-experience; one can learn to see in this unitive way almost at will, albeit by long and hard work. However, to take up residence on the high plateau of unitive consciousness seems to require a lifelong effort. But Maslow seems unclear when he maintains that the plateau-experience includes a transcendence of ordinary humanness. Here he confuses extraordinary humanness and the metahuman; he goes beyond ordinary humanness but does not transcend the extraordinary. He could not do so, as he had to stick to his research methodology. In the phenomenological state there remains a subtle duality between the witness and the witnessed and Maslow was not able to transcend this subtle differentiation.

Critical Estimate

Maslow's visionary ideas about his Being-psychology remain involved in his vitalistic biological approach which gives insufficient significance to the spiritual dimension of human development. He considers the spiritual life of the individual to be part of the human essence but is unclear when he also describes it as the highest part of the individual's biological instinctoid nature. Spiritual experience as a transcendent experience does not necessarily need to be considered a prolongation of the instinctoid, biopsychical characteristics of human nature.

As a pioneer, Maslow was interested in exploring new issues and new fields in psychology, formulating significant questions but rarely coming up with final answers. However, his theories were based on hypotheses presented for testing rather than for final belief and meant to generate future research.

As an original thinker his strength lies in his concern for the higher areas and positive dimensions of human functioning and human experience.

Maslow placed the transcendent experience, the transcending of average humanity at the centre of his psychology, giving the individual meaning and purpose within himself. He visualised human nature as typified by naturally self-transcending, psychologically healthy people who seek for wider horizons, for the remote rather than the near and easily-graspable. Maslow's transcendent experience does not require a metaphysical shift or belief in a divine order but can be explained within the area of human nature without recourse to what he called "theistic superstitions".

2. R. Assagioli's Psychosynthesis

Psychosynthesis is a method of psychological self improvement and an approach to the development of creative human potentials; its aim is based on the unfolding of the individual's true spiritual nature.

Psychosynthesis originated in depth psychology and is a kind of psychotherapy with a transpersonal connection. In its approach to the integration of the totality of human nature it emphasises not only personal growth through intuition, creative insight, etc, but it also explores the spiritual dimension of the personality (the transpersonal realm). Assagioli defines Psychosynthesis as, "a method of treatment for psychological disturbances, of integral education and self-realisation; it may also be considered as the individual expression of a wider principle, of a general law of inter-individual and cosmic synthesis".[5]

In Psychosynthesis all the different parts of the personality, physical—mental—spiritual, are analysed and united again in a new harmonious way to form an integrated whole. The reconstruction of the personality is initially focused around the personal self, "I", but the awareness of the personal self, however, leads to an open contact with the spiritual Self, the connection with the divine. According to S. Bartoli in the preface of Transpersonal Development, "Psychosynthesis is able to make use of all the potential of this 'planet-man' who represents a microcosm in a continuous state of development", and in the words of Assagioli himself, "transpersonal psychosynthesis creates a harmonious framework which will favour assimilation and integration of the new spiritual energies with the existing, so-called 'normal' aspects of the personality".[6]

Psychosynthetic techniques are not only used to strengthen underdeveloped functions and for the transformation of psychological energies, but also for the arousal of latent potentialities and the activation of superconscious energies.

The essence of personal psychosynthesis is related to the release of energies of the total being and as a consequence to fulfill the possibility of actualising human potentials; mature self-actualisation includes the higher reaches of human experience, the individual's true essence, a transpersonal Self. This deepest essence of Being, the organising principle of life is the latent potential within each individual and belongs to the area of human experience. However, the transpersonal realm is that area of the human psyche which transcends personal existence. This transpersonal field of human experience refers to the range beyond the personal dimension, but this beyond is intrinsic to human experience.

Man's spiritual being is the source of psychological health; the realisation of this source, the individual's most authentic identity, is essential in psychosynthesis.

Assagioli defines spirituality as "all the states of awareness, all the functions and activities which have as common denominator the possessing of values higher than the average, values such as ethical, the aesthetic, the heroic, the humanitarian and the altruistic, but all these experiences are connected with awareness of the contents of the superconscious, which may or may not include the experience of the Self".[7]

In an attempt to accurately define the meaning of the word "Spirit", Assagioli makes a distinction between "what is in essence its ultimate reality, and what are its various manifestations.... In itself the Spirit is the Supreme Reality when looked at in transcendent terms.... The Spirit, then, transcends every restriction of time and space, every material limitation.... In man, the term 'spiritual' can be attributed to everything that compels him to transcend his selfish exclusivism, his fears, his inertia and his love of pleasure ... everything that induces him to recognize a greater, superior reality, social or ideal in nature, and to become one with it, extending the limits of his own personality".[8]

Spiritual psychosynthesis becomes an integrated form of spirituality, which includes the whole man, and which extends itself to social life. It is concerned with life's problems from a higher synthetic point of view. According to Assagioli, in the study of the final stage of spiritual deyelopment, "there are those few who have transcended normal humanity and now stand at the threshold of the superhuman, spiritual stage".[9] [the highest stage of inner development].

Unfortunately Assagioli nowhere describes the stage beyond this threshold of humanity. It seems Assagioli replaces the spiritual reality of the Divine Being by the spiritual Reality of man, though in an article, "The spiritual elements in our personality", written in 1932, he refers to the higher transcendent spiritual Reality as the Divine Being, adding confusion to the nature of the spiritual Self.

The Transpersonal Self in Psychosynthesis

The personal self, the I, is a spark of the transpersonal Self. This I emerges into the light of the transpersonal Self and draws its energy from it. The spiritual Self is the origin of light and love, and is not concerned with the stream of thoughts, feelings or physical conditions unlike the personal I. However, there are not two separate I's within the individual. In reality the Self is one, only at the personality level the self is that part of the higher Self that can be assimilated, at a certain moment, through the waking consciousness; this higher Self is a reflection of the transpersonal Self and afterwards it may succeed in uniting with its origin. The transpersonal Self is the central Reality of pure Being; though individual it is connected with the universal and the larger whole of human existence. It is an ontological reality, it never changes in its essence, is immortal and in contact with the transcendent reality. It constantly radiates its qualities into the Superconscious but it transcends superconscious experiences, like illuminative flashes of intuitive insights and expanded states of awareness.

Assagioli meaningfully differentiates self-actualisation from self-realisation and relates the former to Maslow's concept of psychological growth and maturation, and the awakening of latent potentialities of the human being, whereas the latter is the experience and consciousness of the united spiritual centre; it is not the realisation of the personal, conscious 'I' but the psychic growth of the Self through the development of latent possibilities.

The Various Levels of Consciousness

In the psychological construction of the human being Assagioli recognizes the lower, middle, and higher unconscious (superconscious), the field of consciousness, the conscious self or I, the higher Self (true Self) and the collective unconscious.

The Unconscious

Psychosynthetic treatment includes a psychoanalytical phase as the starting point to eliminate resistances. Through the methods of psychoanalysis the individual explores vast regions of the lower unconscious which dominate him. The forces of the lower unconscious correspond to Freud's unconscious primitive urges, instincts and fundamental drives, as well as elementary psychological activities which direct the life and the body and various psychopathological manifestations; they are all retained in the lower unconscious by defense mechanisms and resistances.

The unconscious is formed of psychological elements identical to our waking consciousness. According to Assagioli, "to know ourselves is not enough to make an inventory of the elements that form our conscious being. An extensive exploration of the vast regions of our unconscious must also be undertaken ... in order to discover dark forces that ensnare and menace us".[10]

To find the spiritual Self the individual has to traverse the unconscious, an area where negative tendencies are trying to prevent the passage towards the superconscious level. However, the unconscious is not only an area of suppressed and repressed material but is also a source of creative potentials and wisdom.

The Superconscious

Assagioli's term of the superconscious indicates the transpersonal area of the psyche. It is the instrument through which the Self expresses itself. It is not above the individual but hidden, and the personality is connected with it when the consciousness is raised into new experiences; the transpersonal realm will now manifest itself through its spiritual energy by sudden flashes of insight. The inflow of superconscious energies may be compared with Maslow's Peak-experience; it is accompanied by a clarity of vision, high aspirations, ecstasy and transpersonal illuminations. According to Assagioli, "in the Superconscious we receive higher intuitions and higher aspirations in artistic, philosophical or scientific areas".[11]

As our notion of the Self grows, the field of consciousness increases accordingly so that it becomes more aware of superconscious matter. Maslow's transcending self-actualisers are in contact with these superconscious contents.

Assagioli's model of human personality resembles the Jungian model, both pay attention to the collective elements of the psyche as well as the spiritual dimension of the personality. Like Jung, Assagioli maintains that the collective unconscious is common to all living beings, each individual carries within himself personal as well as collective unconscious material, due to the active interchange between the individual and a collective field of all other beings. But Jung seems obsessed with the collective unconscious and his Self is not a living experience, part of the personality, but merely an archetype and an inverifiable idea. Jung's cosmic consciousness is identical with the collective unconscious and he does not distinguish it from the superconscious.

Assagioli, however, meaningfully distinguishes the collective unconscious from the transpersonal realm. He makes a distinction between the prepersonal (primitive contents) and the transpersonal (superconscious contents) of the collective unconscious. The superconscious realm expresses itself in the individual's higher evolved impulses such as aesthetic, ethical and religious experiences, artistic inspiration, altruistic love, states of intuitive and mystical consciousness, and spiritual insight.

These impulses are all factual and real in the pragmatic sense as they produce changes in the inner as well as the outer world. They have a transforming character and can be influenced by psycho-spiritual practices. Beyond the superconscious activity lies the Spirit (Self).

Psychosynthesis as Therapy

Psychosynthesis, as a conscious reconstruction of the personality aims at the reorganisation of the individual elements of the psyche toward a harmoneous inner unity of the "whole" personality. As a way of looking at reality it tries to liberate the deeper—often unconscious—meaning from the familiar data. Each occurrence in such reality is considered as a possibility for the development of an enlarged reality with a new manifestation of inner potentialities. In this synthetic experience the inner and outer world are united in a natural way and this growth-producing process is characterised by the integral experience of unity and diversity. Its aim is best described by Assagioli thus: "Psychosynthesis works toward the integration of the personality, the recognition and actualization of the energies of the superconscious, and the realization of the self—first the personal self, the center of identity around which the personality becomes integrated and then the Transpersonal Self, that deepest center of consciousness and will in which individuality and universality blend".[12]

As a therapy psychosynthesis encourages exploration of the interior parts of the being; it tries to unravel and unlock the transpersonal realm, as the awareness of the superconscious content is a prerequisite of psychological health.

However, for the psychosynthetic therapist, transcendent states of consciousness in the transpersonal realm do not guarantee a psychologically balanced functioning. Before exploring the transpersonal realm the personality should be well integrated, there should be control over and ability to use the normal human energies, as without these preparations the superconscious experience can lead to serious mental disturbances. The realisation of the self can cause ego inflation, i.e., when the individual's divinity remains attached to the personal ego then the realisation of the Self may lead towards the ego's psychotic delusion of magnitude; or "the bursting in of superconscious elements, particularly if they are sudden and very intense, can disturb the former balance of the ordinary personality, producing various reactions, over-excitement or a sense of disorientation".[13]

The initial motivation for the individual to seek counseling is the freedom from pain which is related to a particular problem or it may be of an existential nature. Nevertheless, beyond the immediate motivation there exists a hidden intention which usually reflects a deeper need. The therapy starts therefore with a methodical and empirical exploration of the unconscious in order to reach the roots of underlying psychological disturbances and to release previously repressed psychological energy. For Assagioli, the realisation of the I as a centre of identity is therefore of equal importance as an essential tool for psychological health. This I is here no longer a centre of conflicts (subpersonality conflicts) but the centre of true humanness. It becomes clear that the therapeutic work of psychosynthesis concentrates at the initial stage on unconscious processes, but in contrast to other therapies, it is rather reserved in the interference of the unconscious; on the one hand because it emphasises the conscious parts of the personality, and on the other hand too deep an involvement in the unconscious may cause certain dangers, i.e., instead of the tendency towards unity in multiplicity the Self is overwhelmed by the unconscious with disastrous effects. When the unconscious contents cause obstruction for personal growth then the therapist tries to restore the communication with the hidden powers within the unconscious, but in such a way that the individual himself can apply these powers for his own welfare rather than being used by them. Similar views are held by Jung in the confrontation with the "Shadow", the unconscious powers of the individual's inner life. These powers, often destructive, need to be revealed to the conscious first and recognised before they can be transformed into creativity and wholeness.

But Assagioli warns us again and again to the dangers of going too deep into the unconscious. It is easy to give conscious recognition to the basic characteristics of ones' personality, but "recognizing this aspect of our personality does not mean allowing ourselves to be ruled by it. It means getting ready for it to be transformed".[14]

He advises the individual to start seeking an experience of the higher realities and then cautiously explore the region of the unconscious.

Assagioli, like Sri Aurobindo, does not want the individual to repress or suppress the lower energies but bring them under control with a calm firmness. When the individual's awareness has broadened itself, redirecting the hidden unconscious forces into constructive channels, then higher potentialities can be explored. In this way psychosynthesis moves from the existential experience towards the transpersonal realm. The rebuilding of personality takes place through an expansion of the normal consciousness into the unifying principle of the true Self, the synthesising spiritual Centre. Once the unifying centre is found psychosynthesis can be achieved; a new united personality can be built around this Self.

Psychosynthesis itself can therefore be divided into "personal" and "spiritual", the former aiming at development and perfection of the personality, and the latter as the harmonious co-ordination and unification with the Self, i.e., in psychological terms the union of the personality with the spiritual Self. Actually, Assagioli's personal and spiritual psychosynthesis are almost identical to Maslow's non-transcending and transcending actualisers respectively. In the growth of the personal dimension, self-actualisation does not take place only through the harmonisation of all the aspects of the personality, but also through the gradual emergence of the I (the Self). Through the process of disidentification of the personal I the individual is able to achieve a more inclusive state of awareness and identification with the transpersonal Self. The I is not abandoned or destroyed but its limitations and self-centred tendencies are transcended. Both the personal and the spiritual dimensions are distinct but not separate and need to be developed simultaneously and in balance, before progressive unification of the personal and spiritual dimensions takes place, i.e., the realisation of the transpersonal Self.

Function of the therapist: in the psychoanalytical phase the therapist plays an active role in uncovering the client's unconscious processes which are threatening further endeavors for growth. Once the various elements of the client's personality are known and understood the therapist guides the client to remodel (transform) the interior personality through a process of disidentification and control. By now the client is ready to discover and realise spiritual potentials and enter into the transpersonal realm. The therapist slowly withdraws himself and the dialogue between client and therapist is replaced by an inner dialogue in which the client gradually identifies himself with the Self.

Psychosynthesis as a transpersonal or spiritual therapy may be better named "counselling in action," (Diana Whitmore) rather than a therapy.

Synthesis, Integration, Transformation

In Integration each function must be made a whole before it can be synthesised with other parts and psychosynthesis therefore tries to raise the energy of the less developed parts. A weaker function is elevated to the level of a stronger one. In the supreme synthesis all parts come together and realise the whole which includes all yet transcends each individual part. Synthesis arranges itself through a higher principle and brings the two antipoles (thesis and anti-thesis) into a higher scale, while it additionally unites them into a more elevating reality.

Transformation in psychosynthesis is used for human betterment, to make human life more purposeful. True relationship with the various multiple personalities is possible by recognizing and accepting the larger needs of all sub-personalities concerned. In doing so the individual releases energy which was previously used for suppression. Here transformation is based on the principle of gratification of the lower needs of each subpersonality. According to Will Parfitt, "we can only transform subpersonalities when we connect with and fulfil their basic needs".[15] After the gratification of their basic needs (the making conscious of the suppressed aspects of our lower unconscious), energy is set free for the emergence of underlying qualities and with this emergence a transformation takes place in which the subpersonality can be changed.

However, transforming a negative psychological pattern involves more than eliminating dysfunctional behaviour, a profound change implies the growth from a negative symptom to a positive solution. It is not clear from Assagioli's writings what he exactly means by the term transformation. Is it the gratification, or the control through moral purification, of the lower aspects of the personality? It seems that the individual has to gratify the various needs first before he is able to control them.

In Assagioli's process of transformation, the higher levels do not cancel the preceding ones but include them. But how does unity at all levels take place? Through control of the narrow passions of our small individual personality and the wise use of universal forces. "Obedience to these moral principles is the only way in which we can truly become free".[16] In this way, transformation of the personality, through active purification of selfish attitudes, is a longtime process by which the Spirit is allowed to operate on the individual. It seems that Assagioli uses transformation more in the Freudian terms of sublimation, as the release of accumulated energies for constructive purposes.

Conclusion

The main contribution of Assagioli, but also Maslow, Jung, etc, is their respect and interest for the spiritual dimension of the psyche and human existence; their endeavour to introduce the transpersonal experience as a justified subject matter of research in the field of psychology. Assagioli approached psychological disturbances not merely as a symptom of psychopathology but rather as a crisis of spiritual awakening. His therapeutical approach is based on the integration of the material of the lower unconscious with the contents of the superconscious.

The functions of the spiritual realm, such as religious experiences, ecstasy, intuition or insight, are facts and real in a pragmatic sense, and these experiences lend themselves to observation and experiments.

However, Assagioli, like other transpersonal psychologists, is not a metaphysician but an empirical scientist of the spiritual dimension of personality. He does not include within his conceptual system a metaphysical analysis of the spiritual Self, and remains neutral towards metaphysical explorations, towards the Mystery of the Supreme Reality as this lies outside the confines of psychology. For Assagioli, "Psychosynthesis does not own nor attempt to give a metaphysical nor a theological explanation of the great Mystery, it leads to the door, but stops there".[17] As such, Psychosynthesis is directed towards man and it stops there. It cannot be considered as the complete aim of life; it does provide only a limited working conception of life nor is it fully capable of serving as a personal philosophy.

Nevertheless its psychological techniques can be considered as a means towards the transformation of the bio-mental life into a spiritual life.

3. Ken Wilber's Transformation of Consciousness

K. Wilber, one of the foremost thinkers in Transpersonal psychology, in his detailed interpretations of human consciousness and the evolution of human nature sets forth a pluridimensional concept of human nature, which is composed of many levels.

In his "Spectrum of Consciousness" Wilber unravels a universal doctrine on the nature of man and reality, based on a synthesis of Eastern and Western approaches to psychology, which he calls "Perennial Psychology". The main concept of the "Spectrum of Consciousness" is based on his insight into a multi-leveled manifestation or expression of a single consciousness within the human personality; the spectrum of consciousness is a pluridimensional approach to human identity, each level of the spectrum being marked by a different sense of individual identity.

Wilber selects five major levels, beginning with the Level of Mind, man's innermost consciousness which is identical with the absolute and ultimate reality of the Universe. This "Brahman" level is infinite and eternal; it is not so much an 'altered' state of consciousness but rather the only true state of consciousness. According to Wilber, "Reality is a level of consciousness ... Reality is what is revealed from the non-dual level of consciousness that we have termed Mind. The observer is the observed".[18]

Next follows the Transpersonal Level, which represents that area of the spectrum where the individual is not conscious of his identity with the All, but is also not totally confined within the boundaries of the individual organism. On the third level of the spectrum, the Existential Level, the individual is identified with his total psychophysical organism as distinct from the environment, whereas on the fourth level, the Ego Level, he is identified with his ego or self-image, in which intellectual processes predominate. On the fifth level, the Shadow Level, the individual is identified with an inaccurate self-image.

Each level of the spectrum represents an increasingly narrowed sphere of identity, but since the Level of Mind is the only reality, the various other levels of consciousness are products of dualism, which Wilber compares with maya or illusion. Through successive dualisms the various levels of the spectrum of consciousness evolve, although in an illusory fashion since the reality of each level is always nothing but the Mind. According to Wilber, "Each dualism is accompanied by a repression and a projection; a dualism represses its non-dual or 'unitary' character, and projects that process as two apparently antagonistic opposites".[19]

Wilber extends these concepts to the various schools of Western psychotherapy and Eastern disciplines, each addressing problems on different levels of the spectrum. He distinguishes three broad ranges of overall psycho-spiritual development-prepersonal, personal and transpersonal-each divided into three stages. For Wilber "the different stages of development are vulnerable to qualitatively distinct psychopathologies". The various forms of Western psychotherapy are concerned with different levels of the spectrum and each approach is correct in so far as it addresses its own level.

At the top of the spectrum are the Ego-Level therapies where the individual's self-image is distorted due to a split between the conscious and unconscious processes of the psyche. Psychotherapies such as psychoanalysis, object-relations therapy, and behaviour therapy reinstate the individual's accurate self-image by expanding his sense of identity to all facets of the psyche.

Existential-Level therapies are primarily concerned with Maslow's so called self-actualisation process, the actualisation of being fully human. "The Existential-level therapies are concerned with the total psychophysical organism and the crises it may face as well as the incredible potentials it may display".[20]

Biosocial-Band therapies, the upper limits of the Existential Level, represent the cultural and social patterns, and its influences on the organism. These therapies such as inter-personal therapy, transactional analysis, and family therapy, are concerned with the social context of pathology.

Transpersonal-Band therapies represent supra-individual consciousness, like C. Jung's collective unconscious or R. Assagioli's transpersonal self. The individual is no longer exclusively identified with his separate self-sense and "there is a suspension of all dualisms (except some form of primary dualism)". Therapies at this level deal with spiritual crises.

At the bottom of the spectrum are the Level-of-Mind Therapies (spiritual practices) where the individual goes into his innermost consciousness which is identical with the ultimate reality. Therapies at this level such as Vedanta, Taoism, and Christian mysticism aim at healing the primary dualism, after which the individual awakens to and enters into the world of cosmic consciousness. However, he does admit that at this level the term "therapy" is used only as a concession to language and as such it has no relevance to psychotherapy.

Wilber assumes that to the extent an individual can remove his exclusive attachments of the Ego and Existential levels, the ascent of the transpersonal and Mind levels is facilitated. He compares the spontaneous ascent, which is potentially inherent in everyone, with Maslow's hierarchy of needs; as soon as one level is cleared the next level spontaneously emerges.

He concludes that therapeutic measures on the Ego and Existential levels may facilitate the descent to the Transpersonal and Level-of-Mind therapies, but this descent to the Transpersonal and Mind levels need not always require Ego and Existential therapies, the former levels may reduce the work to be done on the latter levels but this need not be mandatory.

Wilber maintains that Eastern spiritual disciplines are mostly concerned with the Level-of-Mind therapies, pathology at this level stems from ignorance of Mind. Western psychotherapy seeks the roots of psychopathology more in the Ego and Existential therapies. For Wilber each therapy on its own level is correct and taken together they form a complementary approach within the spectrum.

However, Wilber's therapeutic model based on the spectrum of consciousness has its weak points. R. Coan rightly questions

Wilber's speculations regarding the appropriateness of different forms of therapy for different levels in the spectrum. Wilber's scheme does not pay sufficient attention to individual variations in levels of awareness, and the pattern of psychopathological or psycho-spiritual splits cannot be healed on a standard sequence of procedures, as these patterns vary from one individual to another.

In his "Atman project" Wilber uses the same holistic approach to the different orders of personality and human development. The lowest realm of development involves biological functions and processes, and these are divided into five stages similar to the three lower levels of the spectrum of consciousness. With the intermediate realms the individual enters the transpersonal. The Subtle sphere consists of a lower level, the astral and paranormal realm, and a higher level, the religious intuition, symbolical visions or the perception of divine light or sounds. Beyond this higher Subtle level lies the Causal region; its lower level forms the culminating point of the divine consciousness, whereas in its higher level all forms are fully transcended and united with the Formless Consciousness. The Ultimate Realm finally culminates in an integration of the gross, subtle and causal levels, and at this level Consciousness fully awakens in its original state. This is the ultimate Unity toward which all evolution, human as well as cosmic, seems to point.

Psychological development proceeds through a triple process, from disidentification towards transcendence and on to integration. As a higher-order structure emerges in consciousness, the self identifies its being with that structure; but as evolution proceeds, the next higher order then emerges and the self disidentifies from the lower structure and shifts its identification to the higher structure. Because the self is differentiated from the lower structure, it transcends that structure and becomes capable of acting on that lower structure from the higher level. In this way all the preceding levels can be integrated into consciousness. As this process of transcendence and integration continues one arrives at the ultimate Unity itself.

Wilber stresses the transformative aspect of evolution by which each stage of evolution transforms the previous level instead of negating it. He distinguishes transformation from 'translation', by dividing consciousness into a "deep structure" which contains all the potentialities and limitations of that level, and a "surface structure", a particular manifestation of the deep structure. Wilber relates the movement of a surface structure to translation and the movement of a deep structure to transformation. A transformation helps to create new types of translations and these translations help to maintain that transformation. Each transformation upwards marks the emergence of a higher level, and evolution seems to be a series of such transformations or changes in deep structure.

In the "Transformation of Consciousness" Wilber deals with certain fundamental patterns in ontogenic development. Using the model of psychological development he distinguishes two general structures of the psyche; (a) The basic structures (for example, cognitive development) are relatively autonomous units, which remain in existence in the course of development and in which the higher includes the lower. (b) The transition or replacement structures (for example, moral or self-development) are phase-specific and temporary structures that tend to be more or less entirely replaced by subsequent phases of development. Higher stages do not include but replace lower ones. Each basic structure supports various transitional structures or self-stages, and Wilber obviously refers to the same distinction as described previously, between transformation and translation. There exists a continuous correlation between the basic and transitional stages.

But Wilber adds a third component to the spectrum model of development, the self or self-structure which functions as the link between basic and transitional structures. As a basic structure begins to emerge, the self may identify with this basic structure; but in the growth process , in the ascent of the hierarchy of the basic structural development, the self must negate its exclusive identification with that particular level in order to ascend to the next higher basic level. The lower transitional stage is negated but the lower basic structure will be integrated in the new level. In explaining the fundamental differences between basic structures and transitional structures, Wilber assumes two fundamentally different types of human growth, though the two are nonetheless intimately related, the former serving as a developmental substrate for the latter. But the particular types of transition structures are generated primarily by the self-system acting on the substrate of the basic structure.

In the development of human consciousness Wilber draws the transpersonal realm within the personal domain, but such inclusion may cause a dangerous situation. The 'I' is only a channel of the transpersonal, the personal gives only form to the transpersonal, but in Wilber's view the 'I' assimilates the transpersonal enlargement and as a consequence this same 'I' may blow-up.

In discussing the nine major levels of the basic structure Wilber compares these levels with Sri Aurobindo's model of the hierarchy of minds.

A critical elaboration of this comparison will be given in the concluding chapter of this work.

4. S. Grof's Holotrope Therapy

Though there are some small differences between the ideas of Wilber and Grof their main ideas regarding the expansion of existing models of the psyche show remarkable similarities and therefore Grof's development will be only briefly discussed.

Grof's conceptual frame as described and used in his writings remains a model and is not a proper description of reality; it is in fact a collection of insights coming from those people who have in various ways developed a frame-work in which different psychic experiences and related disturbances can be interpreted.

In his transpersonal approach Grof uses the holographic model which implies the transcendence of the usual distinction between the part and the whole, defined by Grof as, "The holographic model is no longer confined to the limited logic of traditional thought, the part ceases to be just a fragment of the whole but, under certain circumstances, reflects and contains the whole".[21] Matter and consciousness are both aspects of the same undivided whole; they are intimately interwoven and not two separate entities.

Like Wilber, Grof is of the opinion that there is a need for the 'Spectrum model' in the therapeutic systems. According to Grof, "there was not one western psychotherapeutic system fit for the description of certain symptoms which occurred in the advanced therapeutical stages or on the higher psychedelic levels. For that old and eastern spiritual philosophies were needed, like Vedanta, various Yoga systems, Mahayana buddhism, taoism or sufism".[22] It is not possible to describe the whole spectrum of the human experience with the help of one psychological system. According to Wilber, the various psychotherapeutic trends did not originate primarily through difference in methodology but because they concentrated themselves on different levels of the spectrum of consciousness. Each Western psychotherapeutic system focuses its attention on a certain level of consciousness but it tries to broaden its own approach and apply this on the whole spectrum (the entire human psyche), whereas this is only suitable for certain levels. Each therapy is limited by its beliefs about human nature and its self concept, and as long as each therapeutic system focuses on its own level then they are all 'correct'.

Grof tries in his holographic integration, as Wilber does in his spectrum model, to bring about a combination of the views of Freud, Adler, Jung and Reich but also important aspects of Gestalt, Existentialism, and many others. An integrated future psychology will use the supplementing insights of each of the different psychological schools.

Grof's model is mainly based on experiential psychotherapy in the form of psychedelic sessions and "holotropic Breathwork". In the therapeutic process he emphasises the release of long-repressed emotional traumas, (in confronting old traumas and working through them the client gets rid of these problems) and the release of accumulated energies "to transform psychosomatic symptoms into a stream of dynamic experiences". The therapy is based on a combination of techniques such as holotropic breathwork (accelerated breathing patterns), sound technology (evocative music), certain forms of concentrated body work, and a non-prejudiced approach towards an extensive cartography of the psyche.

These tension relieving techniques, mainly based on Janov's primal therapy, are supposed to induce pleasant feelings and even ecstatic transcendental experiences. The powerful healing and transformative effects in controlled intentional hyperventilation are described by Grof thus: "continued hyperventilation leads to increasing relaxation, sense of expansion and well-being, and visions of light. The individual can be flooded with feelings of love, mystical connection to other people, nature, entire cosmos, and God. Experiences of this kind are extremely healing...."[23]

During the therapeutical process the individual encounters four levels of changing consciousness.

1. The Abstract level is connected with the sense organs. The sense oriented experiences have almost no meaning for the process of self-realisation, moreover they form obstacles which have to be faced before the individual is able to enter the unconscious. Grof reckons special forms of intensive aesthetical experiences to the first level of the changed perception.
2. On the next level, the biographical or the individual unconscious, all unresolved conflicts or repressed traumatic memories are able to come to the conscious and become the content of an experience. Most traditional psychotherapeutic approaches (psychoanalytical, existential and humanistic therapies) limit themselves to this level of the psyche.
3. The perinatal level is related to the memories and traumas of biological birth. The rebirthing therapy takes place through re-examining biological birth and an indepth confrontation with death.

   An experiential encounter with birth is often accompanied by an intensive existential crisis which can be resolved only by referring to the intrinsic spiritual dimensions of the psyche. The unconscious perinatal level is an important link between traditional psychology and transpersonal psychology. This model offers new insights into the dynamic structure of all sorts of psychopathological systems. Perinatal experiences do not only contain emotional and psychosomatic aspects, but also important philosophical, spiritual and religious aspects, and are therefore able to bring about a radical transformation of the personality. Jung's and O. Rank's therapy work on this level of the psyche.
4. The transcendental level or the transpersonal realm, the farther reaches of the human psyche, reaches beyond the limits of the individual's ego and body. This level represents a direct connection between the individual psyche, the collective unconscious and the universe at large.

   The transpersonal consciousness is infinite, beyond time and space and is independent of the individual's physical senses although it is used by them, as described by the great mystics of all great religions.

In Grof's 'Holotropic mind', he describes three experiential regions within the transpersonal realm.

a. An expansion of consciousness within the everyday concept of time and space, it includes transpersonal extension of consciousness to other people—all humanity—to the totality of life, and the experience of cosmic unity.
b. An expansion of consciousness beyond the everyday concept of time and space, it includes racial and collective experiences beyond ancestral memories, past life experiences and the experience of cosmic consciousness, i.e., the individual's identification with the creative principle of the universe.
c. Transpersonal experiences with 'psychoid' characteristics. The psychoid phenomena indicate the existence of connections between individual consciousness and the world of matter, they are not independent existences but can enter into an expressive interaction.

   These psychoid phenomena can be divided into three basic categories. The first category contains "inner experiences that are synchronistic with events in the material world—synchronicities, in the Jungian sense".[24] The second category represents the coincidence of various external events that are meaningfully connected with inner experiences, i.e., physical manifestations that accompany transpersonal states of consciousness that seem to violate the accepted laws of nature, as the act of levitation. It also includes astral realms and auras. In the third category mental activity is used to deliberately manipulate consensus reality and includes psychokinesis and Yogic siddhis.

Grof, like other transpersonal therapists tries to create a new scientific approach for self-realisation and therapy, in which there is sufficient space for the mystical dimensions of existence and higher spiritual values.

Wilber emphasises the linear character of the developmental consciousness, but according to Grof, "the psyche is multidimensional and holographic, a description with the help of a linear model yields to unavoidable inaccuracies and deformations".[25] His new psychology re-establishes the spiritual experience as the innate capacity of the soul, and through his techniques the mystical becomes easily attainable for many, but also capable for misuse and escape from the world. His therapeutical concepts are not based on self-control but rather in a let-go attitude. To open the gate into the unconscious he uses, among others, the method of hyperventilation, and the release of obstacles may take place through a tolerant acceptance of them.

By insisting on ecstasy Grof runs the risk of displacing the path "through" ecstasy by a path "to" ecstasy. Such ecstatic experiences remain limited to the holotropic sessions and may easily become the new opiate of the mass. The need for instant gratification in this instant therapy is probably as valuable as all other miracle cures which disregard insight and explanation.

5. M. Washburn's Transpersonal Theory of Human Development

As mentioned previously Washburn defines Transpersonal psychology as, "the study of human nature and development that proceeds on the assumption that human beings possess potentialities that surpass the limits of the normally developed ego. It is an inquiry that presupposes that the ego, as ordinarily constituted, can be transcended and that a higher, transegoic plane or stage of life is possible"[26]. Transpersonal psychology is not only concerned with concepts such as ego, unconscious and integration, but it is also involved with religious ideas such as transcendence, transformation and spiritual realisation. However, Transpersonal psychology is not just a psychology of religion or spiritual psychology but a synthesis of spiritual and psychological approaches to the psyche. These two perspectives are not on a par, "rather it [Transpersonal psychology] accords a higher status to the spiritual standpoint ... spirituality should play the leading role in a unified science of humankind".[27] Spiritual experiences are humanity's highest potentials and spiritual fulfilment is the ultimate aim of humanity.

Unfortunately, in extending the frontiers of understanding human nature and human potentials, Washburn, like other transpersonal psychologists, remains preoccupied with the concept of "human" instead of the "divine".

In his "Ego and the Dynamic ground" he compares Wilber's structural—hierarchical transpersonal paradigm with his own dynamic—dialectical paradigm which is closely geared to the former. But there are some basic differences regarding the conception of the psychic constitution and its underlying triphasic transpersonal perspective of human development (the pre-egoic, egoic and transegoic).

According to Washburn, "The dynamic—dialectical paradigm is based on a bipolar conception of the psyche, and it sees triphasic development as proceeding by way of a dialectical interplay between the two psychic poles.... According to the bipolar conception, the ego is the seat of one of the two psychic poles, the Dynamic Ground the seat of the other. The dialectical interplay governing triphasic development is thus most fundamentally an interplay between the ego and the Dynamic Ground. The [Wilber's] structural—hierarchical paradigm, in contrast, sees triphasic development as proceeding by way of a tier-by-tier movement through the ascending structural levels".[28]

The Dynamic Ground is the seat of dynamism, creative vision and the source from which originates spiritual possibilities. The Dynamic Ground as Spirit, being the ultimate and primordial Self is the sovereign power of the psyche, whereas the ego is a subordinate power or the lesser self of the psyche. Due to repression the ego splits itself from the Dynamic Ground and assumes the posture of an exclusive supreme self of the psyche. But the ego suffers from its loss with the true Self and its return to the Dynamic Ground involves a regression, but "a regression in the service of transcendence". However, the power of the Ground challenges the supremacy of the ego's claim which causes internal conflicts. When the ego has finally overcome its resistance, a transition from regression to regeneration occurs in which the power of the Ground manifests itself as a higher spirit. Finally in the transegoic stage the regenerative process leads to a complete integration, a union of ego and Spirit where the ego becomes the instrument of the higher sovereign Spirit.

With these features of the dynamic dialectical paradigm Washburn aims at the improvement of Wilber's linear movement. Washburn's paradigm, though drawing information from traditional psycho-spiritual sources, falls well within the classical psychodynamic tradition; development follows a spiral course and takes place when interpolar conflicts are resolved. Wilber's paradigm is more rooted in structurally oriented psychology; development follows a linear course of ascent and descent and takes place in terms of full mastery of basic life abilities.

Integration

For Washburn integration is based on the process of negation (repression of nonegoic potentialities), return (regression in the service of transcendence), and higher integration (synthesis of perfected humanness).

In bipolar integration the two poles of the psyche interact in a complete unified way, but this integration is not a unity of equals; the ego, though being rerooted in the dynamic Ground, surrenders itself to Spirit and accedes to the authority of the greater Self.

In the rebirth in spirit, the ego personality is spiritualised and simultaneously spirit is personalised; this process culminates in an integrated or perfected humanness. Spirit, being the inner core of integrated life, and personality, Spirit's means for outer expression, are both necessary for complete humanness, in which spirit is the primarily and most truly essential. Integration for Washburn leads to the culminating stage of human existence where human nature is finally perfected; the end of human development and the complete actualisation of one's intrinsic nature, i.e., "the end of becoming human and the beginning of being a complete human being".[29]

Integration remains a matter of being fully human within the range of native human possibilities. For Washburn integration is the unification of the totality of human resources, anything which is omitted makes the integration incomplete.

Though he denies the superhuman Washburn admits extraordinary experiences among integrated persons and although human, they must also be considered divine, i.e., divinity as a human possibility. These remarkable experiences take place mostly in the prophetic vision, in saintly compassion and in mystical illumination. However, it is the divine power itself that elects the times and places when it will reveal itself to the ego, and this is statistically extremely rare.

Transformation of the Ego

For Washburn the ego functions as an instrument of the dynamic Ground. "It is a distinct existent but not a self-subsistent one —a semi-entity rather than a true substance".[30] This ego-self is real and needs to be transformed, unlike Wilber's ego-self which is an illusion and exists only as a developmental epiphenomenon.

In terms of psycho-spiritual development, Washburn's lower self of the ego-subject and the higher self of Spirit are united as one, whereas Wilber's illusive egoic self is dispelled. In psycho-spiritual development the ego initially differentiates itself from the Ground (pre-egoic state) through the ego's repressive dissociation from the Ground. This original shift from non-egoic to egoic dominance occurs due to alienation and this psychic split is differently treated in different ways in the various psychodynamic therapies.

The mental ego, though contained by original repression, is irresistibly drawn to the power of the Ground. The moment when original repression is broken, then the ego confronts itself with the power of the Ground. The ego eventually realises its inferior position and reverses its stance toward the power of the Ground. Through removal of the ego's own impediments and its surrender to the divine power (the spontaneous movement of spiritual force) the ego becomes one with the pure spiritual force. The power of the Ground no longer occurs as an opposing force but rather as a benevolent force. In this transegoic stage the nonegoic pole is sovereign but the egoic pole remains nonetheless subject and is rooted in the Ground where it serves the power of the Ground, i.e., "the ego becomes the instrument of sovereign spirit".

When the ego is at one with the Ground then according to Washburn "the power of the Ground is able to disclose itself fully and with complete fidelity to its intrinsic nature, not just as the holy but as the grace of the divine life".[31] For Washburn the power of the Ground has a distinctive self-nature which is fully evident in the free expression of the power as spirit.

It is not a theoretical postulate or explanatory construct but a fundamental reality of the soul. "As a psychic energy, it amplifies experiences across all dimensions and, as spirit, it effects dramatic transformations of the ego and of subjective life generally".[32] However, Washburn becomes unclear when he wants to subject the power of the Ground to strict scientific study. He realises that empirical science is not able to empirically verify the power of the Dynamic Ground, and he therefore wants to prove its existence only in a subjective and introspective sense; but these methods are not the manipulative rational and analytic methods used in scientific study.

When he moves to the ultimate ontological status of this power he, unfortunately, acknowledges that this status is beyond human cognitive capacity to know. He affirms the dynamic reality of the power of the Ground, its divine nature but "it cannot be affirmed (or denied) that it also is something that exists independently of the psyche.... Spirit may have its ultimate origin in a metaphysical source lying completely beyond the soul. However, the ego can have no experience, and therefore no knowledge, of the power of the Ground as it may (or may not) exist beyond these boundaries".[33]

Washburn avoids general metaphysical statements as their speculative contents conflict with his scientific inclinations.

Washburn assigns a much larger place to the ego in his Dynamic Ground as compared with Sri Aurobindo's annihilation of the ego in the process of transformation. Washburn's ego is retained in his trans-egoic phase; in their relation the ego and the Dynamic Ground need not interact in an antagonistic dualistic fashion, but can in principle work in harmonious union. However, as will be explained later on, for Sri Aurobindo, as long as the ego is not replaced by the true being there remains a subtle duality and complete transformation of the lower parts of the being remains impossible.

6. Critical Evaluation of the Various Transpersonal Psychotherapists

By including the spiritual development in the therapeutical level, transpersonal psychology reintroduced spirituality in the present materialistic society. Transpersonal psychology moves some distance towards a new synthesis, it reacts against the restrictive nature of modern psychology and it turns often to the oriental heritage for inspiration. The transpersonal psychotherapist, unlike the traditional psychotherapist, is not merely concerned with the individual as such, but the latter is seen against his cosmic background. The transpersonal psychotherapist offers a dynamic growth process toward self-transcendence and tries to bring the individual closer to his true self. He acknowledges the potentials of the higher consciousness, the transpersonal realm, and tries to activate or re-awake those transpersonal potentials which are already present in the human mind. The transpersonal psychotherapist prepares the individual for the necessary healthy psychological conditions pertaining to the development of spiritual life, i.e., the integration of the deeper spiritual Self and the superficial ego. According to E. Underhill, "More than the passion for the Absolute is needed to make a Mystic. They must be combined with an appropriate psychological make-up".[34]

Psychotherapeutical methods are primarily psychological, they utilize the positive aspects of the ego for improving psychological growth, but ultimately they lead to the spiritual dimension which is concerned with the profounder depths of man. Transpersonal psychology considers spirituality as much a core of man's total Self as his bio-psychological nature and the transpersonal psychotherapist is able to improve the individual's capacity to respond to this spiritual dimension in a trustworthy manner.

Spiritual experiences and insights have a therapeutic value in so far as they are capable of establishing an integrated personality. These experiences, soothing troubled emotions, stabilizing the will and bringing insight, can be extraordinarily functional and effective in the development of positive psychological health. However, the transpersonal psychotherapist in his analysis must not confuse the meaning of spirituality with the spiritual way, as the authentic elements of the spiritual way falls outside the frontiers of therapy.

Psychologizing some of the conceptions and related techniques of the spiritual disciplines may divest them of their spiritual values, and by misunderstanding or misinterpretation may easily lead to real dangers.

According to H. Cox, (a christian religious thinker who was at that time not familiar with the transpersonal movement) when the Western psychologists today begin to feel disillusioned with the limits of science or reason they often look to the Orient for a new basis of the science of the soul. However, he warns them for the dangerous aspects of the 'present love affair with the Orient'. "The danger lies in the enormous power psychological ways of thinking now wield in our culture, a power so vast that the current psychologizing of Eastern contemplative disciplines-unless it is preceded by a thorough revolution in Western psychology itself-could rob these disciplines of their spiritual substance. It could pervert them into Western mental health gimmicks and thereby prevent them from introducing the sharply alternative vision of life they are capable of bringing to us.... The merger of Western psychology and Eastern spirituality ... would not cure the soullessness of psychology but would distort the Oriental teachings into something they are not".[35]

Western psychological adaptations of spiritual disciplines need to involve a thorough commitment to "the long-standing" spiritual tradition, rather than aiming at practical results or "pragmatic bliss". Spiritual discipline is not to be used as a short term search for an easy solution for one's day to day problems. For the transpersonal psychologist the primary necessity is not a piecemeal solution to the individual's and society's problems, but the reconstruction of the primary mode of human consciousness, complemented by the individual's rational and analytical reconstruction of the nature of his world.

All the transpersonal psychologists, as discussed in this chapter, view the various spiritual disciplines in the context of their own thought; it seems that they are unable to step outside the preconceptions of their traditional intellectual capacities.

Notes:

1. Maslow, A; The Farther Reaches of Human Nature, The Viking Press, New-York 1971, p. 301.
2. Maslow, A; Towards a Psychology of Being, Van Nostrand Reinhold Comp, New-York, 2nd ed 1968, p. 25.
3. Maslow, A; The Farther Reaches of Human Nature, The Viking Press, New-York 1971, p. 105.
4. Ibid., p. 299.
5. Assagioli, R; Psychosynthesis, The Viking Press Inc, New-york 1971, p. 30.
6. Assagioli, R; Transpersonal Development: The Dimension Beyond Psychosynthesis, Aquarian/Thorsons, London 1993, p. 130.
7. Assagioli, R; Psychosynthesis, The Viking Press Inc, New-york 1971, p. 38.
8. Assagioli, R; Transpersonal Development: The Dimension Beyond Psychosynthesis, Aquarian/Thorsons, London 1993, p. 196.
9. Ibid., p. 107.
10. Assagioli, R; Psychosynthesis, The Viking Press Inc, New-york 1971, p. 21.
11. Ibid., p. 3.
12. J. Ferman and J. Vargini in Boorstein, S. Edt; Transpersonal Psychotherapy, Science and Behaviour Books, Stanford 1991, p. 93.

13. Assagioli, R; Transpersonal Development: The Dimension Beyond Psychosynthesis, Aquarian/Thorsons, London 1993, p. 28.
14. Ibid., p. 91.
15. Parfitt, W; The Elements of Psychosynthesis, Element Books, Longmead 1990, p. 26.
16. Assagioli, R; Transpersonal Development: The Dimension Beyond Psychosynthesis, Aquarian/Thorsons, London 1993, p. 161.
17. Assagioli, R; Psychosynthesis, The Viking Press Inc, New-york 1971, p. 6.
18. Wilber, Ken; Spectrum of Consciousness, Theosophical Publishing House, Illinois 1982, p. 53.
19. Ibid., p. 119.
20. K. Wilber; "Psychologia Perennis" in Walsh R, and F. Vaughan, Edt; Beyond Ego: Transpersonal Dimensions in Psychology, Jeremy Tharcher Inc, Los Angeles 1980, p. 80–81.
21. Grof, S; The Holotropic Mind, Harper Collins, San Fransisco 1993, p. 10.
22. Grof, S; Beyond the Brain: Birth, Death and Transcendence in Psychotherapy, State University of N-York Press, New-York 1985, p. 66.
23. Grof, S; The adventure of self-discovery, Sunny Press, Albany 1988, p. 171.
24. Grof, S; The Holotropic Mind, Harper Collins, San Fransisco 1993, p. 175.
25. Grof, S; Beyond the Brain: Birth, Death and Transcendence in Psychotherapy, State University of N-York Press, New-York 1985, p. 71.
26. Washburn, M; the Ego and the Dynamic Ground; A Transpersonal Theory of Human Development, State University of New York Press, Albany 1988, p. V.
27. Ibiq ., p. 1.
28. Ibid., p. 10.
29. Ibid., p. 215.
30. Ibid., p. 15.
31. Ibid., p. 118.
32. Ibid., p. 119.
33. Ibid., p. 120.
34. Underhill, E; Mysticism, Methum and Co Ltd, London 1911, p. 108.
35. Cox, H; Turning East. The promise and peril of the new orientalism, Penguin Books Ltd, London 1977, p. 75.

CHAPTER V

INTRODUCTION TO INTEGRAL YOGA PSYCHOLOGY

According to Sri Aurobindo, psychology as a science of consciousness studies the various parts of our being. Consciousness is described in Webster's New International dictionary as "the totality in psychology of sensations, perceptions, ideas, attitudes, and feelings of which an individual is aware at any given time, or awareness of an inward psychological or spiritual fact". In this description Consciousness refers to the totality of the impressions, thoughts and feelings which make up the individual's conscious being. In this way consciousness is related to a subject to which it belongs as a property. However, this definition describes states and phenomena of consciousness but not consciousness itself. For Sri Aurobindo consciousness is not related to a subject or with the psychological functions of the mind. It is a primordial self-illuminative occurrence of Sat-chit-ananda (Being-consciousness-bliss), of which the Atman is a partial manifestation. Consciousness, as a reality inherent in existence, is not only a power of awareness but it is also a dynamic and creative energy.

Sri Aurobindo defines consciousness as "the fundamental thing in existence—it is the energy, the motion, the movement of consciousness that creates the universe and all that is in it—not only the macrocosm but the microcosm is nothing but consciousness arranging itself".[1] Consciousness indicates therefore a self-aware force of existence as well as an illuminative state of self-awareness.

The observable consciousness is only a little visible part of our being; below and behind are depths to which the surface nature has no visible access. Regarding this view Sri Aurobindo writes, "Even the movements of this little surface nature cannot be understood nor its true law discovered until we know all that is below or behind and supplies it—and know too all that is around it and above".[2]

Superficial psychology explores only the individual's superficial mentality and the laws of one's physical life, but it does not lead the seeker to the mysterious depth of subjective existence. Psychology is a means by which the individual arrives at the knowledge of the workings of Nature and life, and, as the individual goes deeper, of the workings of God through Nature and life. Psychology as such progresses from the study of mind and the soul to the perception of the true soul in all beings. As a subjective science it should be studied within oneself. Man, as a mental being, instead of dwelling upon his surface nature, must become aware of the deep hidden self, the real reality of his being and make the growth of the soul the highest good. In looking behind the obscure surface of one's egoistic being, the seeker finds the real man whose whole existence needs another explanation than the working of the natural elements and another goal than mere egoistic satisfaction. The seeker in his search discovers his unity with the rest of the world and his unity with the Divine. In integral Yoga psychology the seeker moves beyond the superficial man and tries to discover the workings of the whole nature of the real man, i.e., to arrive at a psycho-physical knowledge with a spiritual foundation.

For Sri Aurobindo, psychology as a science limits itself to psycho-physical phenomena, it gives only truth of processes, but it leaves out the ultimate nature of mind and consciousness. Matters about the ultimate Reality, or metaphysical problems are left untouched. Only when psychology becomes a new science and turns its face towards the Divine, then it will be able to deal directly with forces of the Mind and arrive at what is beyond Mind. Sri Aurobindo wants the individual to rediscover his integral spiritual consciousness, for it links the highest to the lowest through all the mediating terms and achieves an indivisible whole.

This integral consciousness does not abolish the universe or the individual existence, it takes them up and transforms them by revealing to them their true significance and unites them with the Divine Reality and the Divine Nature.

Man in his everlasting growth towards the whole and in his urge for self-transcendence always reaches out to a greater truth which expresses itself in various ways—social, cultural, psychological and spiritual. For Sri Aurobindo psychology as a science of consciousness means more than the study of the individual's egoistic individuality. The psychologist will soon discover that man's whole existence stands in need of an explanation beyond the natural elements; to know himself one must find out the real man, the true spiritual individual. The observable consciousness is only the surface part of the being; below, behind and above are depths and widths which supply the movements of this little surface nature, but of which the seeker has no knowledge. Because we do not know ourselves we are unable to develop the hidden possibilities of our mental capacities. According to Sri Aurobindo, "Man, the mental being, once aware that there is this deep, great and hidden self, the real reality of his being, must necessarily seek to enter into it, to become conscious in it, to make there his centre instead of dwelling on the surface, to win and apply its diviner law and supreme nature and capacity, to make himself one with it so that he shall become the Real instead of the Apparent Man".[3]

Man's highest aspiration is to attain an integral self-perfection in which he can fully cooperate with the divine's creative adventure in the formation of a divine life. Divine life here means the manifestation of the latent divinity in man, as well as the reconstruction of the individual's outer being and environment by the transforming power of the Divine.

Sri Aurobindo's integral psychology is a means by which the seeker arrives at the knowledge of the workings of God through Nature and through life. It is founded upon the emergence of a new centre of consciousness which is capable of manifesting successively the Divine upon earth. In man as a body-mind-spirit continuum, the integral self-realisation unfolds itself in the realisation of the universal and transcendental Self through the method of widening, deepening and heightening one's awareness. It is by going into the spiritual realm that the individual gains knowledge of the Self and of the Universe. The deeper Self seen as the source of consciousness is not inconscient in its nature but is essentially superconscient.

According to Sri Aurobindo the human soul is only potentially the eternal companion of the Divine. For real freedom it needs to be awakened and pass from potentiality to actuality. He intends to lead the spiritual seeker into higher life, living consciously in the Divine and acting from that consciousness, i.e., union between the Divine and man.

He does not only guide the seeker in solving temporal psychological problems in a mundane existence, but he also tries to find out ways and means by which the individual and humanity could improve spiritually, and hence he guides in the exploration of the divinity within each seeker. Spiritual progress as an ongoing dynamic process is described as a double process, a process in which the Divine descends in man while man ascends into the Divine. There is a link that connects the finite man with the Infinite Self. The descent is characterised by the manifestation of the Divine in the human form and nature while the ascent is described as man rising into the Divine nature and consciousness. In this way the Divine takes upon itself the human nature with all its outer obstacles and makes it the instrument of the Divine essence.

The word Yoga literally means union, but Yoga as used by Patanjali does not mean the spiritual union of the individual soul with the Universal Soul. Patanjali uses Yoga as a practical system of spiritual effort, a psychological technique to control body, senses and conscious as well as unconscious processes in order to attain perfection.

Sri Aurobindo defines Yoga as "a methodised effort towards self-perfection by the expression of the potentialities latent in the being and a union of the human individual with the universal and transcendent Existence we see partially expressed in man and in the Cosmos".[4]

Yoga is not founded on a fixed set of religious or spiritual ideas but is more related to inner spiritual experiences. It means the union of the human consciousness with something transcendent, something divine. For Sri Aurobindo the contact of human consciousness with the divine is the very essence of Yoga. The individual transcends his present level of human consciousness and rises into a higher and wider mode of consciousness. The egoistic consciousness is exchanged for a cosmic consciousness and the individual is united with some deeper consciousness within, in which one is aware of one's own inner being and the real truth of existence. However, Yoga means not only union (its goal) but it also means the process or method by which that union is achieved. Its methods are psychological processes which aim at a change of consciousness through a series of self-purifications, a conquest of desires, the release from the hold of blinding passions, and a progressive surrender of the ego to the Beyond-ego. Sri Aurobindo's Yoga does not deal with superficial psychological motives or with surface manipulations of the mental realm; it aims at a spiritual change of consciousness, a refounding of Life and a growth of the spirit in Nature, i. e, human existence functions as a means of reaching the Divine. According to Sri Aurobindo, "Yoga is nothing but practical psychology".[5] The synthesis of Yoga reunites God and Nature in a perfected human life, and therefore, "All life is yoga".

Corresponding to the three principal powers of the individual, —will, knowledge, love, —there are three yogas; yoga of works (Karma yoga), yoga of knowledge, (Jnana yoga), and yoga of love and devotion (Bhakti yoga). Karma yoga envisages union with the Will, turning man's will Godwards through a dynamic surrender of all actions of one's nature. Jnana yoga takes its stand upon the individual's mind and seeks to turn his consciousness towards the Divine. Bhakti yoga seeks a divine fulfilment of the emotional being of man; the emotions of the heart of man are turned towards the Divine.

Integral Yoga takes up the essence of these three yogas, but differs in its aim underlying its comprehensiveness. Sri Aurobindo's integral union aims at the integrality of the Divine, the fulfilment of the individual's divine destiny upon earth. It is a union with the Divine in life rather than a union with the Supreme in some heaven beyond. Its object is therefore not only related to the divine realisation of the individual, but also to bring down the supramental consciousness into earth-nature, i.e., the dynamic descent of the superconscient into the waking consciousness instead of merely ascending into some supreme Absolute. According to Sri Aurobindo, "our Yoga is nothing less than to break up the whole formation of our past and present which makes up the ordinary material and mental man and to create a new centre of vision and a new universe of activities in ourselves which shall constitute a divine humanity or a superhuman nature".[6]

As such there exists a wide gap between Yoga and science. Science proceeds from an objective Ultimate which explains all subjective phenomena, but Yoga proceeds from the opposite view, the ultimate Truth is spiritual and subjective and in that light objective phenomena must be viewed.

"One can't see the soul under a microscope"; in Yoga the seeker passes beyond the domain of rational inquiry, and its methods and experiences go according to a law of their own.

Only when science enters into the ways of the Divine and its processes it is able to discover and understand the workings of the Divine Consciousness.

Spirituality for Sri Aurobindo is not a mere process of transcendental self-realisation but more a process of spiritual self-manifestation, the free participation in the creative joy of the Spirit. To participate in this creative joy of the Spirit involves the interrelation of the upward movement of human aspiration with the downward movement of the Divine Grace. Both movements are inseparable aspects in the complete change of being and transformation of terrestrial existence. The meaning of spirituality is related to the infinite, self-existent consciousness of the Spirit. Often mental, aesthetic or vital processes are misnamed as "spirituality", but they lack the essential character of the higher and new consciousness.

The spiritual dimension of the Being feels the presence of the infinite and the finite, and discovers the eternal unity in all divisions and differences. This same spiritual dimension does not exclude any essential human activity but lifts it all up out of its imperfection and transforms it. The true spiritual aim regards life, mind, and body not as ends in themselves sufficient for their own satisfaction, but as instruments of the soul; a soul incarnated for a divine fulfilment upon earth. It reveals to man the divinity in every part of his being, the kingdom of God which dwells within but also a kingdom of the Divine Spirit upon earth, the Divine in the universe. In the words of Sri Aurobindo: "A spirituality that would take up into itself man's rationalism, aestheticism, ethicism, vitalism, corporeality, his aspiration towards knowledge, his attraction towards beauty, his need of love, his urge towards perfection, his demand for power and fullness of life and being, a spirituality that would reveal to these ill-accorded forces their divine sense and reconcile them all to each other"...[7]. For Sri Aurobindo spirituality includes these human formulas. They are of value to mind and life and as such preparatory movements to the awakening of the Spirit or soul. Spirituality reveals to these half-lighted forces their divine source and reconciles them all to each other; they become instruments of the light and power of the divine being and divine Nature.

Spirituality does not aim to solve the problems humanity is facing at the present moment, but it creates a new foundation of our being and our life. Only an inner spiritual change is able to offer a solution to the present problems of life; to discover the spiritual being within and to help others towards the same is one's real service to mankind. At the same time Sri Aurobindo believes that "the spiritual man has not stood back altogether from the life of humanity; for the sense of unity with all beings, the stress of a universal love and compassion, the will to spend the energies for the good of all creatures, are central to the dynamic outflowering of the spirit".[8]

Spirituality illumines the inner being and transcends the mind; it is able to uplift by the inner influence the outward nature of the individual. For Sri Aurobindo spirituality "is in its very nature a thing subjective and not mechanical; it is nothing if it is not lived inwardly and if the outward life does not flow out of this inward living".[9]

The spiritual life is not something that can be easily formulated in a rigid definition, "it is an immense kingdom potentially larger than the other kingdoms below it, with a hundred provinces, a thousand types, stages, forms, paths, variations of the spiritual ideal, degrees of spiritual advancement".[10]

However, there is no essential difference between the spiritual life in the East and the West, they only differ in their names, forms or their emphasis on one special aim or another, but the spiritual urge is the same everywhere.

Sri Aurobindo's integral sadhana gets meaning only when viewed against this background, a background where the individual becomes divine in consciousness and lives inwardly as well as outwardly the divine life.

Before giving an elaborate description of Sri Aurobindo's integral sadhana it will be useful to give some detailed information regarding the aim of integral Yoga so as to distinguish it from other yoga-systems, and the psychological make-up of the being so as to enable the reader to place his concept of sadhana in a wider context.

1. Aim of Sri Aurobindo's Integral Yoga

Integral Yoga, as a passage from an outer phenomenal mental, vital and material life-existence to an inner existence, is the way of complete God-realisation; a complete transformation of consciousness on each plane of the being corresponding to a complete transformation of life. This character of integral Yoga is described by Sri Aurobindo thus: "Our mind, will, heart, life, body, and inner and inmost existence, our superconscious and subconscious, as well as our conscious parts must all be thus given, must all become a means, a field of this realisation and transformation and participate in the illumination and change from human into a divine consciousness and nature".[11]

Integral Yoga's aim is to rise and enter into a higher divine consciousness and to manifest this higher consciousness upon earth. This includes a change of consciousness as well as a change of life. The old yogas demanded a complete renunciation of wordly life, but integral Yoga aims at a new transformed life. Life becomes a field of experience and self-training in which the seeker gets free from ordinary desires and attachments in the mind, life and body, i.e., the ordinary life is dealt with from a new inner attitude. In the new life all connections must be founded on a spiritual intimacy other than any of one's present connections, which implies a transition from ego-centredness to God centredness.

The mind, life and body are not merely used as a ladder to rise to higher peaks but they are also used as instruments to bring down below the glories of the highest. This integral divine transformation distinguishes it from all other systems of Eastern spiritual discipline. In his purview Sri Aurobindo includes the spiritual and material world with the intention to establish the Divine consciousness in the individual and earthly life. Its aim is not only a personal liberation but also a liberation in and of Nature—not simply from Nature, i.e., to work out the Will of the Divine in the world and the fulfilment of the divine humanity in ourselves and others.

Integral Yoga has for its end more than the ordinary aims of humanity, its aim is to live in the Divine, in God and not in mere egoism, but simultaneously not apart from Nature and mundane existence.

The true object of integral Yoga is of two kinds; a growth of the spirit in Nature, and a spiritual change of consciousness. This full object of yoga can only be accomplished when the conscious yoga in man becomes outwardly co-existent and connected with life; "All life is yoga". In the ignorance of the dividing mind the individual is cut off from his transcendental source and regards himself as a separate being among other countless separate beings. By identifying the separate individuality with the true universal or transcendent Self the seeker is no longer limited by the little ego but is in union with the supreme Self, which is one's own true being and the real truth of existence. This union of the individual's instrumental being and soul must be expressed by a change of one's imperfect nature into the very likeness of the Divine Nature.

The entire definition of the aim of integral Yoga is described by Sri Aurobindo as "the conversion of the human soul into the divine soul and of natural life into divine living".[12]

The term "integral" refers to Sri Aurobindo's stress on the development of all aspects of the human being, the body, mind and soul to their highest potential. None of these is to be developed to the exclusion of the others, for integral Yoga implies the binding together of all these various parts by the power of the Self or the indwelling Divine. Integral Yoga does not reject the physical, vital and mental realms, they are indispensable instruments for the divine ascent and descent. They have to be controlled, purified and transformed rather than destroyed. As the seeker progresses, he is able to combine the bodily life, mental existence and the spiritual being, resolve their discords into a harmonious movement, perfect the material and mental existence as the instruments of a divine self-expression and so create in himself the perfect Man. According to Sri Aurobindo, "the principle of this yoga is not perfection of the human nature as it is but a psychic and spiritual transformation of all the parts of the being through the action of an inner consciousness and then of a higher consciousness which works on them, throws out their old movements or changes them into the image of its own and so transmutes lower into higher nature".[13]

Integral Yoga is Sri Aurobindo's name for his synthesis of yoga-methods; it complements all partial approaches by integrating the entire being of man through a synthesis of Karma, Jnana and Bhakti yoga. In the words of Sri Aurobindo, "By knowledge we seek unity with the Divine in his conscious being; by works we seek also unity with the Divine in his conscious being, not statically, but dynamically, through conscious union with the divine Will; but by love we seek unity with him in all the delight of his being".[14]

It is clear by now that the aim of integral Yoga is not only freedom from the bondage of human nature but its perfect control with a view to transform, spiritualise and divinise it. This can only be achieved by the intervention of a supracosmic consciousness-force, which Sri Aurobindo calls the Supermind or Supramental. Only the Supermind has the integrative power to bring about this comprehensive and all-inclusive transformation of the individual's life, mind and body.

Sri Aurobindo's dynamic view of yoga is an effort towards the realisation of the potentialities of human personality, and the union of the human individual with the Divine, which ultimately leads to the manifestation of the Divine on earth.

The goal of integral Yoga is more difficult to reach than any other; it is only for those who have the capacity to face every risk, even the risk of failure. The seeker must not enter this path unless he is sure of his readiness to go through to the end. Only if there is a strong will within and a great steadiness to face all difficulties then this spiritual path can be followed. The path of Sri Aurobindo's Yoga is steep and does not seek to avoid regions of darkness; only patience, perseverance and an integral surrender can ensure the goal to be realised. One who has not the courage to face patiently life and its difficulties will never be able to go through the still greater inner difficulties of the sadhana. Difficulties are to be met in the right spirit, and if the seeker does not come out stronger then there must be some defects within oneself, some impurity or weakness which has to be traced and corrected. Some have to overcome the difficulties of their nature first, others have a splendid beginning but face all the difficulties afterwards.

According to Sri Aurobindo, integral Yoga "is a difficult Yoga to follow and not many can really meet the demands it makes on the nature ... it is a slow and difficult process; the road is long and it is hard to establish even the necessary basis. The old existing nature resists and obstructs and difficulties rise one after another and repeatedly till they are overcome".[15] The difficult and complex way of integral Yoga is therefore not a path for anyone to follow but only for those who accept to seek its aim, and for those who's inner strength is supplemented by the true aid of the Guru.

The seeker ought not to plunge into this path without a fairly long period of preparation and purification. This period of preparation enables the seeker to arrive at the proper inner psychological conditions to face the spiritual battles and sufferings. "Sri Aurobindo himself does not care to accept many into his path and rejects many more than he accepts".[16] This yoga can only be done to the end by those who are ready to abolish their ego, and cannot be done if there are the demands and instincts of the lower parts of human nature, i.e., the old past habits of the mental, vital and physical formations.

The path of integral Yoga is not a short cut to the Divine, spiritual victory needs the struggle and labour to reach the heights; his Yoga is "'bitter like poison in the beginning' because of the difficulty and struggle, 'but in the end sweet as nectar' because of the joy of realisation, the peace of liberation".[17]

But integral Yoga is much more of the nature of a battle than others for other reasons than an individual battle. As a continuation of one's own heavy load, the seeker bears a great part of the world's burden too. After the individual has won his own personal battle he has still to conquer the collective battle because his enlarged inner existence contains the being of others. Ordinary Yoga emphasises usually only one single aim and is therefore less exposed to relapses in the spiritual progress, but the aim of integral Yoga is so complex and many-sided that we cannot expect any smooth, uninterrupted progress.

This long battle with ourselves and with opposing forces around us may seem interminable, but they are only temporary difficulties which can be overcome by faith in the Divine. Sri Aurobindo maintains that "so long as a man has that faith, ... I will say that even if his nature is full of obstacles and crammed with denials and difficulties, and even if he has many years of struggle, he is marked out for success in the spiritual life".[18] The Divine does not throw aside all difficulties and sufferings but it carries the seeker through them and out of them. The spiritual optimist, trusting the inner guidance does not escape the difficulties but is able to meet them without pain and despondency. When this faith is not there the seeker has to undergo a hard and difficult discipline to overcome constant fluctuations, disappointments and failures. After a certain point, in the more advanced stages of Yoga, the periodical violent storms and attacks of depression, which almost all sadhaks have to face, tend to diminish in force and duration, provided that they are not allowed to grow chronic by any kind of mental encouragement. The effort demanded of the sadhak is that of aspiration, rejection and surrender, the rest comes of itself by the Divine Grace. A present incapacity is only a temporary difficulty as for the seeker of the integral Yoga perfection is already latent in the being, "man carries the seed of the divine life in himself, in his own spirit".

2. Organisation of the Being

The Psycho-Spiritual Construction of Man

Sri Aurobindo refers to many different planes or parts of the being within the structure of the individual personality.

In the organisation of the being and its parts three systems are simultaneously active;

a) a surface system, made up of the physical, vital and mental levels of consciousness which constitute the outer being.
b) a concentric or depth sytem, consisting of the inner being and the innermost or psychic being.
c) a vertical system, an ascending and descending series of super-imposed levels, extending from below the surface mind (the inconscient and subconscient) to far above the reasoning mind (Higher mind, Illumined mind, Intuitive mind, Overmind and Supermind).

Man as known to us is not the real man or not the complete man in his true perspective. According to Sri Aurobindo, "Men do not know themselves and have not learned to distinguish the different parts of their being; for these are usually lumped together by them as mind, because it is through a mentalised perceptiton and understanding that they know or feel them; therefore they do not understand their own states and actions, or, if at all, then only on the surface. It is part of the foundation of yoga to become conscious of the great complexity of our nature, see the different forces that move it and get over it a control of direct knowledge. We are composed of many parts each of which contributes something to the total movement of our consciousness, our thought, will, sensation, feeling, action, but we do not see the origination or the course of these impulses; we are aware only of their confused results on the surface upon which we can at best impose nothing better than a precarious shifting order".[19]

This confused or inadequate knowledge that we have of ourselves is due to the double aspect of our being, the outer and inner aspects.

The outer or external being is apparent to us, as far as it constitutes the waking-consciousness, but it also includes the individual's subconscient aspects, "an obscure mind full of obstinate impressions, associations and habitual reactions formed by our past". The ordinary man, driven by vital needs, and some intellectual and aesthetic cravings, is still as crude and undeveloped in his inner life as primitive man was in his outward life.

The outer personality is dependent on the body, but the inner personality comprises wider functions, a sort of 'psychic' existence of which the individual is normally not aware. This is called the subliminal, and though it lies beyond the range of our normal surface consciousness it is accessible to consciousness and should not be considered unconscious per se.

Behind the subliminal lies the centre of the individual existence, which Sri Aurobindo calls 'the psychic being'. Surrounding the inner and outer beings is the environmental consciousness, and above them is the superconscient.

The surface consciousness functions as an instrument of expression of the inner consciousness and the psychic; but at the same time it receives influences from the inconscient and the subconscient below, from the subliminal behind and from the superconscient above, as well as from the surrounding environment.

It is through the practice of Yoga that the seeker discovers the extraordinary complexity of his own being. For Sri Aurobindo "the individual is not composed of one but many personalities and each has its own demands and is different in nature. Our being is a roughly constituted chaos into which we have to introduce the principle of a divine order".[20]

The structure and dynamics of the psychological make-up of the being as described by Sri Aurobindo needs some more detailed elaboration in order to avoid confusion regarding this multi-layered dynamic structure.

The Outer Surface Being

In the outer being, mind, vital and physical are all mixed together and it needs an intent self-observation (regarding the mixture of thoughts, feelings and impulses) to find out the composition of one's nature and the relations and interactions of these parts with each other.

The different parts of the surface being have each a separate function and are distinct from one another, yet all of these external aspects interact with each other as constituents of one indivisible personality.

This surface being is composed of three entities;

1. The Physical being
2. The Vital being
3. The Mental being

The Physical Being

The body is just not unconscious matter, but a vehicle or expression of consciousness made up of physical energy-substance. The physical being is therefore not merely the gross body, but possesses a distinct consciousness of its own which is different from that of the mind and the vital, although interpenetrated with them. In Sri Aurobindo's words, "Each plane of our being—mental, vital, physical —has its own consciousness, separate though interconnected and interacting; but to our outer mind and sense, in our waking experience, they are all confused together. The body, for instance, has its own consciousness and acts from it, even without any mental will of our own ... and our surface mind knows very little about this body-consciousness.... It is part of the yoga to become aware of this separate consciousness of the body, to see and feel its movements and the forces that act upon it from inside or outside and to learn how to control and direct it even in its most and (to us) subconscient processes".[21]

The physical being consists of three parts;

a) The body or material physical, the most visible part of the physical being, is mostly influenced by the subconscient rather than by the mind or the vital. It is automatic and mechanical in its functioning, has its own physical instincts and is subject to illness, decay and finally death.
b) The vital physical refers to that part of the vital which is interfused with the physical consciousness. It functions as the instrument of the smaller sensations and desires of the outer

physical gross material life, and its irrational actions are completely determined by its habitual instincts and impulses.

c) The mental-physical is that aspect of the physical being which partakes of the characteristics of the mental consciousness. The mind in the physical being is fixed on physical objects and happenings. Sri Aurobindo relates the mechanical or body mind to the lower action of the mental-physical, which left to itself functions like a machine, repeating past customary thoughts and movements.

The physical being is mainly occupied with the corporeal life and the habits of life, mind and the body. This is the normal type of personality, where all other tendencies latent within the individual are subordinated to the maintenance of body and life. The physical being, clouded by obscurity and limitations, determines the greater part of our waking self.

The Vital Being

The vital consists mainly of desires, impulses, and emotions of possession and enjoyment. It is often narrow and limited and subject to dualities such as pleasure and pain. It is under the strong influence of the ego and if uncontrolled, when it is enslaved by desires and passion, it brings disorder and disaster.

Sri Aurobindo distinguishes four parts of the Vital being;

a) The central-vital consists of the stronger vital longings and reactions, e. g, ambition, pride, fear and passions of various kinds.

b) The physical or lower vital is entirely concerned with insignificant desires and feelings such as food-desire, sex-desire, anger, disliking, etc.

c) The emotional or higher vital expresses itself through various higher aspirations such as love, kindness, sympathy, altruism, etc.

d) The mental-vital gives a mental expression by thought, speech or otherwise to the emotions, desires, passions and other movements of the vital being. It expresses vital tendencies without subjecting them to the intellect. Through this mental-vital various vital passions, impulses and desires arise, which distort the thinking mind.

The vital being is mostly concerned with self-affirmation, life-enlargement, and the claims of the ego, power and excitement. The nature of the predominantly vital individual is more active, stronger, and more chaotic than that of the physical man, but it is also more creative and energetic. Though this part is obscure and full of perversions it is an indispensable mediator between the inner being and the outer life and only a vigorous vital mind can govern the kinetic vital energies. According to Sri Aurobindo, "When people speak of a vital man, they mean one under the dominition of vital force not controlled by the mind or the spirit. The vital can be a good instrument but it is a bad master. The vital has not to be killed or destroyed, but purified and transformed by the psychic and spiritual control".[22]

The Mental Being

The vital has to be clearly distinguished from the mental; on the surface they are intermingled, but in themselves they are quite separate forces. The term 'mental being' refers to that part of the human being which deals with the cognitive functions and processes, and all the mental movements that are part of the individual's intelligence.

Sri Aurobindo divides the mental being into three parts;

a) The physical mind is preoccupied with worldly pleasures and material affluence. However, the physical mental proper is less obstinate and can be more easily opened to the inner forces, because it is less dependent on the subconscious than the material and vital physical. Despite this, the physical mental being is limited in its functioning and without the influence of a widened consciousness the physical mind remains outward-oriented.
b) The vital mind, as a mediator between the vital and mental, has its utility in ordinary life and human actions, but it often limits and falsifies the mental truth according to its own desires, passions and cravings. The vital mind, though energetic and creative, does not think or reason and if it uses any thought it

does so not for the sake of reason but for the service of life-power. When it is limited by the vital movements it always imagines what can be done and acts without discipline.

c) The thinking or reasoning mind has its own defects and limitations, it knows first by analysing, only thereafter it synthesises. It can control lower nature but cannot change it. Yet the thinking mind is a higher faculty than the vital mind. It has the capacity to discriminate between good and evil, virtue and vice; but in the performance of these functions it is often influenced by the physical or vital mind and not free. Only by a strong will and severe self-discipline is the former able to rule the latter.

Human beings are complex entities. The material body, as the individual's foundation, supports a conscious life principle and a mental functioning; although it is often difficult to distinguish these from each other, they remain separate entities in a dual experience. Not only can these various parts of the being be at war with each other, but each one is also divided against itself—each different part of the being has its different movements and all these discordant movements obstruct and influence each other.

For Sri Aurobindo the outer being is only a means of expression and not one's real self. The seeker is advised not to identify with it, for then the individual can change it so as to express the true inner personality of the Light.

The Inner or Subliminal Being

The outer being is by no means complete in itself, and the individual's total existence is much larger than his apparent surface nature. This external being which we suppose to be ourselves is a confused mixture of mind-formations, life movements and physical functions. When the individual goes behind, into the hidden planes of his being, he discovers a large inner or subliminal existence.

However, there is often a struggle between the inner and outer parts, the latter remaining attached to the things of the ordinary life while the former wants the Divine.

The inner being, unlike the outer being, receives and responds to the physical and universal world directly, through the subtle senses of its more subtle inner bodies. It has the power to enter into direct contact with another consciousness or with other ojects, and is able to achieve immediate knowledge of the occult.

By entering into the subliminal or identifying oneself with it the seeker is able to observe the springs of his thoughts and feelings, the sources and motives of his actions.

Like the outer being, the inner being is also comprised of three levels.

a) The inner or subtle physical "is closest to the physical, and most like it. But yet the conditions are different. For instance, the subtle physical has a freedom, plasticity, intensity, power, colour, wide and manifold play of which, as yet, we have no possibility on earth".[23] By identifying oneself with the inner physical being the individual can observe the operative energies that build up the surface personality.
b) The inner vital, unlike the surface vital, is wide, vast and strong, without limitations. When purified it can be an instrumental force for all the divine realisations, as it is without ego and knows itself to be a projection and instrument of the Divine.
c) The inner mental is much more comprehensive than the outer mental, it exceeds the physical mind and physical organs although it is aware of them.

The subliminal is connected with the small outer personality by certain centres of consciousness. Only a little of the inner being reaches outer life, but according to Sri Aurobindo "that little is the best part of ourselves and responsible for our art, poetry, philosophy, ideals, religious aspirations, efforts at knowledge and perfection".[24] So our surface being, though largely influenced by the subconscient, is also influenced to a significant extent by the subliminal where it receives its inspirations, intuitions, etc.

The subliminal creates a larger, wider awareness and is able to open, penetrate and illuminate the submental and the subconscient, though it does not wholly enlighten those hidden areas.

The movement of going and living within brings a rush of new experiences, a larger capacity, greater vision and an enlargement richer than any delight gained in the vital and mental existence. An awakening of the inner being is characterised by the development of a state of neutral equanimity, an absence of attachments, and this quietude slowly penetrates the deeper layers of the being preparing for a first change of the outer life.

Nevertheless, the subliminal is not practically one with the soul and the universal self but it is open to it through its universal experience.

The Subliminal and the Circumconscient

The subliminal is delimited from the environing cosmic consciousness through a limitation of subtler sheaths of our being.

The environmental consciousness, also called the circumconscient, serves as a medium of transition between the individual and the universal inner consciousness. Whereas the inner physical consciousness can be thought of as "connected with" the body, and the higher consciousness as "above" the body, so the environmental consciousness "surrounds" the body, and through it the individual comes into contact with cosmic forces and with other beings.

The universal forces are not poured directly into the individual, they first enter his environmental consciousness. Sri Aurobindo explains, "The subliminal extends itself into an enveloping consciousness through which it receives the shock of currents and wave-circuits pouring upon us from the universal Mind, universal Life, universal subtler Matter-forces".[26]

Experiences rejected from the surface consciousness either sink into the subconscious or settle into the environmental consciousness, from where they try to return even after long intervals. After subconscious movements have been expelled by the conscious self, these rejected movements do not re-enter the subconscious or get abolished, but move into the individual's circumconscient where they no longer belong to the individual self. It is through this subtle circumconscient medium that waves of universal forces, such as desire, sex, etc, come in and take possession of the external being. However, according to Sri Aurobindo, "If the wall that separates this inner existence from the outer self were penetrated, we could know and deal with the sources of our present mind-energies and life-action and could control instead of undergoing their results."[27] But this can only be done when the individual has acquired a high degree of self-mastery.

The Subliminal and the Subconscient

Though the individual is usually not aware of one's inner being, it should therefore not be considered merely unconscious. The subconscient is an obscure half-consciousness below, inferior to the individual's organised waking consciousness, whereas the subliminal is a much wider, luminous consciousness behind, more in possession of itself than that of the surface consciousness. Sri Aurobindo describes the difference between the two as, "The subliminal, with the subconscious as an annexe of itself, —for the subconscious is also part of the behind-the-veil entity, —is the seer of inner things and of supraphysical experiences; the surface subconscious is only a transcriber".[25] The subliminal lies beyond the surface subconscious, and though the latter is normally unaware of these mysterious areas, the subliminal is nevertheless invariably more conscious than the surface consciousness. However veiled from the surface consciousness, this subliminal part of the being is not at all obscure and incoherent, it has the same capacities as our waking being, but is more developed and more sovereign.

The Subconscient

According to Sri Aurobindo there are different parts of the subconscient.

The so called Inconscient is not really inconscient at all, but rather a suppressed "sub-conscience" in which there is everything but in which nothing is expressed or formulated. The inconscient, as a concealed consciousness, is an inverse reproduction of the supreme superconscience but lost in itself which makes it look like Non-Existence. The first emergence from the Inconscient is Matter, and when Life and Mind emerges they turn Matter into an instrument for their manifestation. In this way the Inconscient and its primary works are penetrated by a succession of higher powers of being and its limitations are thereby diminished.

Usually, the unconscious is referred to as the absence of certain operations of mentality and sense, but for Sri Aurobindo consciousness can exist where there are no overt operations; it is intrinsic in being, self-existent and not abolished by action. Nothing is therefore truly unconscious, consciousness is there in the being even when there seems to be an absence or annulment of awareness. What modern psychology calls the unconscious is only that part which lies outside the surface consciousness and of which the mind is not conscious.

Sri Aurobindo also distinguishes the submental from the subconscient though both appear to the individual as inconscient. The submental refers to an automatical dynamic mode of consciousness which has its own separate reactions to contacts and which does not depend on the mind's response, i.e., it is below and inferior to mind, void of mentality and less in possession of itself. The subconscient proper lies below even the physical and vital consciousness, it is the Inconscient vibrating on the borders of consciousness.

The real subconscient, the lowest occult province of the being's nature, is a rather diminished consciousness close to the Inconscient. It is that area of the inner being where the Inconscient struggles in the process of becoming conscious, "the antechamber of the Inconscient through which its formations rise into our waking or our subliminal being".[28] It includes past impressions and all material which is rejected from the surface mind of which we bring ordinarily so much to the surface as our waking psycho-physical awareness needs for its purpose. However, much of the dormant rejected material is able to surge up in any absence of mental functioning; the risings are mostly automatic, uncontrolled and involuntary, causing forms of psychological abnormality and nervous disturbances or forms of disease, unbalance and morbidity. This blind and instinctive subconscient, characterised by an obscure universalism and individualism, does not allow any light. Sri Aurobindo describes the subconscient as "that quite submerged part of our being in which there is no wakingly conscious and coherent thought, will or feeling or organized reaction, but which yet receives obscurely the impressions of all things and stores them up in itself ... there is an obscure mind full of obstinate Sanskaras, impressions, associations, fixed notions, habitual reactions formed by our past, an obscure vital full of the seeds of habitual desires, sensations and nervous reactions, a most obscure material which governs much that has to do with the condition of the body".[29]

The Inmost or Psychic Being

The individual's external consciousness is rarely aware of his inner being because it is veiled from it. But once the inner being is awake, it opens inwardly to the soul and above to the Self. Within this inner being of man is revealed the central being, the transcendent and universal Atman. Sri Aurobindo distinguishes two aspects of the central being, the upper and the lower.

The upper part, the Jivatman, is that aspect of man which is outside evolution and transcends time, whereas the lower part, termed the psychic being, represents the true individuality in the process of evolution. The Jivatman transcends the individual expressions of life and mind in each individual.

The psychic being, as the centre of the individual self, is almost a deputy of the Jivatman, expressing itself in each individual life and existence and supporting it. It realises its oneness with Jivatman but does not change into it.

At its origin the psychic being is only a spark of the divine consciousness, it is not a fully individualised being and master of itself and it is only through successive lives that it builds up a conscious individuality.

Sri Aurobindo differentiates the psychic being from the vital being. The psychic entity, in its manifestation, takes two forms;

1. The surface desire-soul, a superficial psychological element which is involved in vital cravings, desires, emotions, happiness and mental intelligence. It is centred around the individual's egoistic existence and this external form therefore creates the basis for one's egoistic self.
2. The true soul, a pure power of love, light and joy, "Is the psychic personality in us that flowers as the saint, the sage, the seer; when it reaches its full strength, it turns the being towards the knowledge of Self and the Divine, towards the supreme Truth, the supreme Good, the supreme Beauty, Love and Bliss, and opens us to the touch of spiritual sympathy, universality, oneness".[30]

Only when the true soul comes forward is the individual able to gradually overcome egoistic existence and begins to grow towards a divine nature, i.e., by turning towards the Divine the soul can come truly forward and impose its power on the impure surface being.

The innermost being in its one-pointed orientation towards the Divine does not create a rigidity like the intellect, or a bigotry of impulses like the one-pointed vital forces. "Its action is like a searchlight showing up all that has to be changed in the Nature"; it sees the Divine essence everywhere. Sri Aurobindo describes the character of the psychic being thus: "In the first long stage of its growth and immature existence it has leaned on earthly love, affection, tenderness, goodwill, compassion, benevolence ... on all that can help to refine and purify the grossness and commonness of human nature; but it knows how mixed are these human movements at their best and at their worst how fallen and stamped with the mark of ego and self-deceptive sentimental falsehood.... It may still admit the human forms of movements, but on condition that they are turned towards the One alone.... It lifts the being towards a transcendent Ecstacy ... but it calls down also this transcendent Love and Beatitude to deliver and transform this world of hatred and strife and darkness. It opens to a universal Divine Love, a vast compassion, an intense and immense will for the good of all.... It is not attracted or misled by mental imitations or any vital misuse of these great deep-seated Truths of existence; it exposes them with its detecting search-ray and calls down the entire truth of divine Love to heal these malformations"....[31]

The psychic being makes it possible for the individual to open and uplift the whole lower nature to the Divine and suffuse them with a spiritual consciousness; but it can also contribute to a quieting and purification of the mental, vital and physical consciousness if they submit to the psychic influence. For if the psychic is in front it becomes easy to remain conscious of the things that have to be changed in the external nature and it is comparatively easy to change them.

The psychic personality is connected with Prakriti (Nature) and therefore not purely metaphysical but empirico-metaphysical.

In itself it carries all divine possibilities, but in its actions the psychic being is affected by the limitations of the mental, vital and physical, i.e., exteriorised in the ignorance of the outer being it assumes the imperfection of Nature. The soul is therefore not the overt guide and master of one's thoughts and actions; it has to rely on the outer instruments and its expression is not always pure since it is mixed with the activities of the outer being. It is only by the heart's aspiration to the divine that the psychic being gets free from these disabilities and can rediscover its inherent self-knowledge.

The psychic is ordinarily deep within, but as it begins to open up it is able by its influence to dominate and transform the surface movements which become fit instruments of the Divine. It is this psychic being, often the greatest help in man's spiritual life, which has to be brought from behind to the front during the practice of integral Yoga.

The Higher Being

Like an opening of the heart centre within to the psychic being there is also an opening of the mind centre above towards a higher divine spiritual consciousness. The psychic and the spiritual belong to different planes, the psychic is involved in the external manifestation and is able to create a spiritual aspiration, whereas the spiritual is concentrated in the Divine above the external manifestation. The spiritual realm is independent of the psychic but gives the latter more strength and wideness. Usually consciousness is imprisoned in the mental, emotional and sensational centres, but when the individual opens up the surface being begins to ascend in order to join itself to this higher consciousness, a vast consciousness full of freedom, peace and light. This is described by Sri Aurobindo thus: "We are not merely embodied minds; there is a spiritual being, a spiritual plane of Nature. Into that we have to heighten our force of consciousness... Our imperfect mental instrumentation is not the last word of our possibilities; for there are in us, dormant or invisibly and imperfectly active, other principles beyond mind and closer to the spiritual nature, there are more direct powers and luminous instruments, there are greater ranges of dynamic action than those that belong to our present physical, vital and mental existence".[32]

The higher consciousness is a concentrated consciousness in the Divine unity, and not running around mental ideas, vital desires or physical needs as in the ordinary human consciousness. This higher consciousness is always in touch with the Self whereas the lower consciousness is separated from it by the activities of the Ignorance. When the higher consciousness is intensely felt there is usually an opening of the limited personal being into the Cosmic Existence in which the limited personal consciousness is lost in the cosmic consciousness.

The spiritual or higher mind is distinct from the ordinary mind, the latter is not a power of knowledge; it sees as if through distorting spectacles and its knowledge is coloured by its instruments. The higher mind is open to all knowledge from above, it does not think with the brain as it has larger means of awareness than thought. It is marked by oneness and through this pure consciousness the seeker enters into the awareness of the Spirit and is able to see all things in its essential reality.

The spiritual planes above the mind is the meeting place of the ascending and descending forces; they range from what Sri Aurobindo terms the Higher mind, through the Illumined mind and the Intuitive mind to the Overmind and the Supermind.

The Higher mind as "a luminous thought mind" functions as an instrument of truth-cognition in its cognitive aspects, as it seems to be in possession of Truth. This thought is not an acquired knowledge but a self-revelation of eternal Wisdom. In its conative aspects it is marked by the effectuation of the Truth, laying a foundation of change and preparing the whole being for a superior truth of existence. By realisation of the Higher mind the seeker becomes less bound to the automatism of the lower vital nature; the latter is now mastered by a greater enlightened thought, sight and will which is in touch with the Infinite.

In the Illumined mind the seeker proceeds from the power of Truth-thought to the power of Truth-sight. In the Illumined mind thought is only a subordinate movement expressive of sight. The perceptual power of inner sight is a greater power for knowledge than the perceptual power of thought. The Illumined mind, turning the spiritual thinker into a mystic seer, illumines and transforms the thinking mind, the vital and physical being with its direct inner vision, inspiration and spiritual sight.

The Intuitive mind, as power of Truth-vision, can take up into itself the intuitive functionings of all the parts of one's nature and recast them into its own higher mode, thereby achieving a more intense integration of the being than was yet possible. Intuition can perform all the functions of reason and intelligence but by a superior process, grasping the object directly.

Sri Aurobindo distinguishes various forms of intuition; a power of revelatory truth-seeing, a power of truth-hearing, a power of truth-touch, and a power of true discrimination of the exact relation of truth to truth.

But in the present stage of evolution the action of intuition in the individual is imperfect in kind as well as intermittent in action; it is clouded and altered to the needs of the heart or intellect. Intuition being frequently interrupted by the mental movement is therefore not in a position to give the individual that integral experience which alone can reveal the ultimate truth.

The Overmind: Intuition is the culmination of mental efforts but by effort alone pure knowledge cannot be attained. Sri Aurobindo describes the Overmind as a superconscient cosmic Mind which is in direct contact with the supramental Truth-consciousness. The preceding stages are not cosmic in nature but in the Overmind the consciousness expands and widens itself to become a principle of cosmic Truth. To the vertical ascent is added a vast horizontal expansion of consciousness and in this boundless largeness the separate ego-sense entirely disappears. Egocentric movements may still continue but the centralising ego-sense is entirely subordinated and only occurs as a ripple in the cosmic wideness. The Overmind can unite the individual mind with the cosmic mind, but it cannot lead beyond itself; it cannot dynamize the Transcendent, for it is only the Supermind that has the direct power of manifestation of the Transcendence.

The Supermind is difficult to describe in our ordinary mental language, for it is a different consciousness altogether and acts in a different way. Whatever may be said of it is likely to be misunderstood and only by growing into it the seeker can know what it is. As a general description the Supermind may be characterised as a Truth-consciousness free from ignorance in which the sense of integrality is never lost.

The Supramental vision is marked by an original unity in which there is no division. It differentiates but does not divide, maintaining the many in unity always acting on the truth of the indivisible unity. The Self is in each, each is in the Self, and each is the Self; but the Self here is not the hard core of the ego in ignorance but the divine Self. All existence in all its variety and the whole cosmos is contained in the Supermind, but it also transcends the cosmos. In its transcendental vision the Supermind sees the universe in its right relation to the eternal reality of which it is one expression, and in its universal vision it sees all that is individual in the terms of the universal as well as in its own individual terms; yet it also knows each in its inmost essence, of which everything else is a resultant expression.

Man with his many personalities consists of a multi-layered dynamic structure. The gradation of the various planes as a whole appears to be a great connected complex movement, although it is often difficult to distinguish them from each other. Mind identifies itself with the movements of the various parts, but when the seeker draws back he discovers that each part has a consciousness of its own. Each different part of the being has its different movements and all sorts of discordant movements obstruct and influence each other. Nevertheless, the various parts of the being are interdependent and the development of each of them depends on the development of all the other parts. The higher, from which the lower is derived and to which it is destined to be converted, precipitate their influences on the lower, and the lower react to the higher, manifesting within themselves something that corresponds to the higher power and its action.

It must be remembered, however, that while this classification is helpful for psychological self-knowledge, discipline and practice, it should not be erected into too rigid a formula. As these things run very much into each other, a synthetical sense of these powers is as necessary as the analysis.

Man in his real nature is a spirit using the various parts of the outer being for an individual and communal experience and self-manifestation in the universe. This spirit, as an infinite existence, limits itself in apparent being for individual experience, i.e., it assumes in the universal and individual nature the complexity of the infinite in the finite. The Supermind, mind, life and the body are the four instruments which the Spirit is using for its manifestation in the workings of Nature.

The results of Sri Aurobindo's psychological interrogations may not be very concrete in its conclusions but its methods imply a broader base for understanding the various planes and parts of the being and human life; it includes the discovery of the inmost and highest self of man. Sri Aurobindo's metaphysical language is not always expressed in psychological terms but this does not mean that these assuptions have no psychological significance.

Notes:

1. Sri Aurobindo;Letters on Yoga, Sri Aurobindo Ashram Press, Pondicherry. 5th impression 1988, p. 236.
2. Sri Aurobindo;The Hour of God, Sri Aurobindo Ashram Press, Pondicherry, p. 21.
3. Sri Aurobindo; The Supramental Manifestation, Sri Aurobindo Ashram Press, Pondicherry. 2nd edition 1989, p. 328.
4. Sri Aurobindo; The Synthesis of Yoga, Sri Aurobindo Ashram Press, Pondicherry. 9th impression 1992, p. 2.
5. Ibid., p. 39.
6. Ibid., p. 66.
7. Sri Aurobindo; The Human Cycle, Sri Aurobindo Ashram Press, Pondicherry. 6th impression 1992, p. 171.
8. Sri Aurobindo; The Life Divine, Sri Aurobindo Ashram Press, Pondicherry. 10th impression 1993, p. 883–884.
9. Sri Aurobindo; The Human Cycle, Sri Aurobindo Ashram Press, Pondicherry. 6th impression 1992, p. 247.
10. Sri Aurobindo;Letters on Yoga, Sri Aurobindo Ashram Press, Pondicherry. 5th impression 1988, p. 1668.
11. Sri Aurobindo Archives and Research, December 1982, p. 197.
12. Sri Aurobindo; The Synthesis of Yoga, Sri Aurobindo Ashram Press, Pondicherry. 9th impression 1992, p. 57.
13. Sri Aurobindo;Letters on Yoga, Sri Aurobindo Ashram Press, Pondicherry. 5th impression 1988, p. 848.
14. Sri Aurobindo; The Synthesis of Yoga, Sri Aurobindo Ashram Press, Pondicherry. 9th impression 1992, p. 563.
15. Sri Aurobindo;Letters on Yoga, Sri Aurobindo Ashram Press, Pondicherry. 5th impression 1988, p. 848–849.
16. Ibid., p. 1052.
17. Ibid., p. 1630.
18. Ibid., p. 573.
19. Ibid., p. 233.
20. Sri Aurobindo; The Synthesis of Yoga, Sri Aurobindo Ashram Press, Pondicherry. 9th impression 1992, p. 69.
21. Sri Aurobindo;Letters on Yoga, Sri Aurobindo Ashram Press, Pondicherry. 5th impression 1988, p. 347.
22. Ibid., p. 346.
23. Ibid., p. 255.
24. Ibid., p. 1165.
25. Sri Aurobindo; The Life Divine, Sri Aurobindo Ashram Press, Pondicherry. 10th impression 1993, p. 426–427.
26. Ibid., p. 735.

27. Ibid., p. 736.
28. Ibid., p. 423.
29. Sri Aurobindo;Letters on Yoga, Sri Aurobindo Ashram Press, Pondicherry. 5th impression 1988, p. 353.
30. Sri Aurobindo; The Life Divine, Sri Aurobindo Ashram Press, Pondicherry. 10th impression 1993, p. 226.
31. Sri Aurobindo; The Synthesis of Yoga, Sri Aurobindo Ashram Press, Pondicherry. 9th impression 1992, p. 146–147.
32. Sri Aurobindo; The Life Divine, Sri Aurobindo Ashram Press, Pondicherry. 10th impression 1993, p. 731–732.

CHAPTER VI

SADHANA

The literal Sanskrit meaning of Sadhana "means to an end", is derived from the Sanskrit root Sadh, to exert; the essential preliminary discipline that leads to the realisation of the divine experience, i.e., the discipline that functions as an instrument which is helpful in the achievement of the spiritual life. Sadhana, as a science of spiritual discipline, is related to the gradual unfoldment of the divine consciousness present in each and every being and which ultimately leads to the Divine life. It is an attempt at bridging the gulf between the individual's surface consciousness and that which lies beyond. The aim of sadhana is to gradually unfold the latent capacities of man, through conscious effort, which leads the sadhak (the spiritual seeker on the path of sadhana) from a state of discord to a state of harmony, or from finiteness to infinitude.

Sadhana needs an inner preparedness and determined effort with a corresponding discipline and right practice to get into closer contact with the sadhak's inner and higher nature. The sadhak has to transform his normal chaotic state into a state of equanimity through a long process of preparatory psycho-spiritual practices, based on psychological and contemplative experiments rather than on verbal communication.

Sadhana as the spiritual practice or discipline of Yoga is described by M. P. Pandit as a purposeful action; "an activity done with a definite purpose, consistently, regularly ... it is not something erratic, something coming to light at one movement and receding at the next ... but converting the entire life activity into a powerful movement towards God".[1]

Sadhana is the means to an end and not an aim in itself;through sadhana the object of yoga is gained.

The all important thing in Sri Aurobindo's integral sadhana must be the growth into a new consciousness and new inner life in which the surface personality, if looked at from the true and larger consciousness, becomes an instrument for its own perfection. For Sri Aurobindo sadhana means "the purification of the nature, the consecration of the being, the opening of the psyhic and the inner mind and vital, the contact and presence of the Divine, the realisation of the Divine in all things, surrender, devotion, the widening of the consciousness into the cosmic Consciousness, the Self one in all, the psychic and the spiritual transformation of the nature".[2]

The practice of yoga brings the seeker in contact with the extraordinary complexity of his own being and the embarrassing multiplicity of his personality. The average human being who lives in the waking surface psychological existence appears fairly simple, but as soon as the seeker goes deep within himself, he discovers that his being is "a roughly constituted chaos, surrounded by a whole complex world into which we have to introduce the principle of a divine order". During sadhana the sadhak becomes aware of the different parts of being—the physical, vital and mental—each of which has a separate individuality; through sadhana they can be separated from each other and gradually developed as independent entities.

The sadhana of integral Yoga, unlike traditional yogas, does not proceed through any set of mental teaching or prescribed forms of meditation or liberation, but by aspiration, a self-concentration inwards or upwards, a self-opening to the Divine Power above and within, and a rejection of all that is foreign to these things.

The aim of Sri Aurobindo's integral sadhana is to discover the true Self or God within and thus rise out of the lower life of ignorance into the felicities of the higher realms of the Spirit. It is hardly the function of sadhana to prepare the seeker for ordinary life in the world, but its purpose is to enter into a spiritual consciousness which can only be done when the individual has entered into a complete unity with the Divine. The first reason for seeking the spiritual life therefore is to find the Divine, the Self, and to know the work the Divine demands from the seeker rather than to work for humanity; the working out of a moral, mental principle cannot be the first true object of the spiritual seeker, though it can be a means or help towards finding the Divine.

The other object of integral sadhana is the change of the nature described by Sri Aurobindo as; "Yoga is directed towards God, not towards man. If a divine supramental consciousness and power can be brought down and established in the material world, that obviously would mean an immense change for the earth including humanity and its life. But the effect on humanity would only be one result of the change; it cannot be the object of the sadhana. The object of the sadhana can only be to live in the divine consciousness and to manifest it in life".[3]

The object of sadhana is not to remove all "limitations" on the expansion of the ego or to fulfill the ideas of the human mind or the desires of the ego-centred life-force, but to create a world in which the Divine Will is able to manifest its truth without being deformed by the vital desire or ignorance. According to Sri Aurobindo, "Our yoga is not for our own sake but for the sake of the Divine. It is not our own personal manifestation that we are to seek, the manifestation of the individual ego freed from all bounds and from all bonds, but the manifestation of the Divine ... a constant forgetfulness of this simple and central truth, a conscious, half-conscious or wholly ignorant confusion about it has been at the root of most of the vital revolts that have spoiled many an individual sadhana here".[4][in the Ashram].

Sadhana conceives of a divine life upon earth and liberation of earth-nature itself as part of a total purpose of the embodiment of the spirit here. It is not an escape from the world to God, but a transformation of the seeker's integral being into the terms of God-existence, i.e., to transform one's entire being into God, "so that in a sense God Himself, the real person in us, becomes the Sadhaka of the Sadhana".

The perception of an non-ideal and unsatisfactory world marked by suffering, evil and inadequacy is in a way the starting point of sadhana. However, this imperfection is not the very essence of Nature but only a passage, and the spiritual possibility of perfection brings some hope in the darkness of the present existence. The rich human egoistic life does not offer a final satisfaction, except for those who are too trivial to seek anything else. It is often the soul within and the higher mind and vital which are dissatisfied, and if the mind and vital can feel the soul's sheer love for the Divine for

His own sake, then the sadhana gets its full power. According to Sri Aurobindo, "the Divine can come early or it can come late [in the practice of sadhana], but come it will if one is faithful to one's call.... The Divine knows best and one has to have trust in his wisdom and attune oneself with his will. Length of time is no proof of an ultimate incapacity to arrive; it is only a sign that there is something in oneself which has to be overcome, ... when a demand is there for the Divine, a sincere call, it is bound one day to have its fulfilment. It is only if there is a strong insincerity somewhere, a hankering after something else, —power, ambition, etc. —which counterbalances the inner call that the logic is no longer applicable".[5] This optimism is not a mere intellectual or philosophic view but the soul's aspiration towards light and truth. This spiritual aspiration is innate in man and a sure sign of Nature's will for a higher way to fulfilment. The mental part within the individual might recognize the individual's imperfection but there is the psychic part which rejects it. The soul's dissatisfaction with imperfection as a law of life upon earth is a kind of divine dissatisfaction and spiritual growth aims at the victory over imperfection. The growth of the soul is the growth out of darkness into light, out of falsehood into truth.

Imperfection, such as evil, error, falsehood, is relative in its nature and not absolute like Truth, Good and Beauty, the inherent aspects of the eternal self-existence. Once the imperfection has been faced and endured it has to be rejected, overcome and transformed.

The Ashram has been created as a centre and a field of practice for the attainment of divinity and perfection; as such it has nothing to do with asceticism, an escape from all conflicts or retreat from the world. Sri Aurobindo's aim is not only to rise above the limited human consciousness into the divine consciousness, but to bring the power of the divine consciousness into the surface layers of the mind, life and body, transform them, and create a divine life on earth. The Ashram is set up as a centre which serves as a practical training ground for integral Yoga, a spiritual commune to serve as a basis for a divine life on earth. The work in the Ashram is not done as a service to humanity or the sadhaks of the Ashram, but "as a service to the Divine and as a field for the inner opening to the Divine, surrender to the Divine alone, rejection of the ego and all the ordinary vital movements and the training in a psychic elevation, renunciation of all mental, vital or other self assertion of the limited personality".[6]

Life in the Ashram is not a place where the mind and the vital can hope to be satisfied or fulfilled, but a field of inner training for the discovery and purification of the seeker's egoistic mental, vital and physical nature, and for the ascension into the transcendent consciousness.

1. Foundation of Sadhana

Sadhana, as a process, turns the human soul from the egoistic state of consciousness to a higher state in which the Transcendent and Universal can pour itself into the individual being and transform it.

There are two main objects to be secured with reference to the foundation of this sadhana—the opening of the psychic being and the realisation of the self above. The triple effort of aspiration, rejection and surrender are the main supports of the integral sadhana.

Aspiration: Integral Yoga can be successfully undertaken and followed only if there is a strong aspiration to the necessity of a larger spiritual existence. Aspiration has in it the conviction that spiritual progress is not so much a personal affair but a work for the Divine and of the Divine. True aspiration is to be traced to the psychic being rather than to the hankering of the individual's vital ambitions. Aspiration which is more effective than capacities is not a form of desire but the feeling of the inner soul's need to turn towards the Divine. As such aspiration is a call to the Divine and relates to the full descent of the Truth and the victory over falsehood in the world.

Self-opening: The whole principle in integral Yoga is to open oneself to the Divine Influence and this self-opening to the Divine Power above and the Divine Presence in the heart can only come by faith, aspiration and surrender. The object of the self-opening is to allow the force of the Divine to flow in and do the work of transformation. If there is a sincerity in the aspiration and a patient will to arrive at the higher conciousness, in spite of all obstacles, the opening in one form or another is sure to come. The self-opening is of two kinds; the inward self-opening and upward self-opening. The former consists in opening oneself to the subliminal and the psychic within in which a personal relation is established with the individual Divine, the latter lies in opening oneself to the ranges of the superconscient above, in which the seeker is put in active touch with the Universal and Transcendent Divine. The self-opening specifies the directions in which the surrendered consciousness is to move for an encounter with the Divine.

Capacity: all individuals can practice some form of yoga according to their nature provided they have the capacity, will and sincerity to it. Capacity alone is not enough but must be supplemented by the will to seek after the Divine and persistance in following the path. To be sincere needs an unsparing scrutiny of self-observation and self-criticism. There are only "a few of whom it can be said that they have the capacity for this yoga",[7] [Integral Yoga], i.e. , nobody can do it by one's own capacities; personal capacity, will and sincerity needs to be aided by the Grace of the Divine·

Faith: Aspiration springs from a mystic faith in a new meaning of creation, towards new unexplored horizons in the service of the Divine. This faith in the Divine or in the truth of the sadhana is a feeling of the whole being and in accordance with reason. For Sri Aurobindo faith is a spiritual certitude of the souls's ideal, even when the immediate facts or persistent circumstances seem to deny it. Sri Aurobindo describes faith as "the soul's witness to something not yet manifested, achieved or realised, but which yet the Knower within us, even in the absence of all indications, feels to be true or supremely worth following or achieving. This thing within us can last even when there is no fixed belief in the mind, even when the vital struggles and revolts and refuses".[8] This dynamic intuitive conviction is not an ignorant but a luminous faith, not a crude mental belief but the knowledge of the soul to the guiding light within.

Doubt, as an enemy of faith has its utility only in the lower knowledge. For Sri Aurobindo blind and ignorant faith is a better possession than sceptical doubt which turns its back on the sadhak's spiritual possibilities. The fundamental faith in integral sadhana gives the seeker equanimity in times of difficulties; it accepts what happens, not definitively, but as something that has to be gone through on the way. Faith is therefore necessary as in its absence when the sadhak trusts only his critical intelligence there can be no possibility for him to live up to the greater knowledge, the higher truth. This higher truth has to be lived rather than being disputed in the mind's darkness. Those whose faith is not strong or surrender not complete can arrive at the full realisation of the true Self, but they usually have, at first, to go by small steps and face the difficulties of their nature until by perseverance they make a sufficient opening.

Rejection of the mind's preferences and opinions, of the vital's desires, passions and greed, and of the physical's obscurity and unwillingness; putting these elements out from the consciousness itself as it does not belong to the true self, should not be confused with suppression, or with a mental or moral control. Suppression with inner indulgence in subtle forms is not a cure, but expression in outer indulgence is still less a cure. In order to make a complete cure the seeker has to become conscious of the various wrong movements of the lower plane, reject them till they have been completely thrown out from his existence and replace them by the psychic and spiritual Nature.

In sadhana the control of one's thoughts, vital desires and movements of the body is indispensable. Outer discipline is necessary for their purification, otherwise they remain at the mercy of their own impulses. However, mental control by itself cannot eradicate anything entirely out of the being. The mind is often deluded by the vital and physical desires and tries to justify by its reasonings their wrong movements. Man's mental control is therefore only partially able to control, it does not liberate and is not a cure.

In sadhana the mental, moral and social control have to be gradually replaced by an inner self-control of the spirit; this can be done through the higher Nature that works within, and a greater control from above, the psychic and the spiritual. Nevertheless the sadhak is warned not to loose mental control at once, but to replace it gradually by the psychic or spiritual as many seekers loose the mental control before the spiritual is ready.

Rejection, however, is only an instrument and not an object in the practice of sadhana. It is only a stage through which the soul must pass at some period of its progress; when the soul no longer seeks objects as objects but the divine they express, no longer seeks pleasure but posseses the delight of the Divine, then the sadhak is released into the liberty of the Spirit.

Surrender: Complete surrender, as a means of fulfilment in integral sadhana, is impossible as long as the seeker is unable to give up his mental ideas, personal will, feelings and personality, and replace them by a greater Knowledge, luminous Will, divine Love, and the one Person respectively.

Mind formations, life impulses and instigations of the ego may easily betray the sadhak into a false experience. In the complete surrender the knot of the ego is cut in each part of the being, and the Divine is accepted for the Divine's sake and for no other motive and no other conditions.

For Sri Aurobindo surrender means, "to consecrate everything in oneself to the Divine, to offer all one is and has, not to insist on one's ideas, desires, habits, etc, but to allow the divine Truth to replace them by its knowledge, will and action everywhere".[9]

Sri Aurobindo distinguishes the active from the passive surrender, the latter being fraught with dangers. A state of inert passivity, until the psychic being comes to the front, is likely to bring about an uprush of the forces of Ignorance, i.e., in passive surrender everything is left entirely to the Divine and it often turns out that the seeker surrenders to the lower nature under the pretext of surrendering to the Divine. Active surrender involves a vigilant watch upon the forces of Darkness and a dynamic self-identification with the Divine Will to the complete elimination of all egoistic motivations. In active surrender the sadhak associates his will with the Divine Will and rejects all that is not related to the Divine.

However, surrender is not easy as it is restricted by a large part of the lower nature. The state of growing surrender does not come to all sadhaks at the early stage of sadhana, many have a long journey of purification and discipline to go through before the true being opens. It depends on a predisposition in the heart to open to the Light of the Divine Guidance. "One has to begin with the soul's inherent longing, then the struggle with the nature to get the temple ready, then the unveiling of the Image, the permanent Presence in the sanctuary".[10]

Often in the initial stages surrender is a doubtful kind of self-giving with a demand in it. It is only the psyhic that is able to bring about a sudden and true surrender of the whole being and until the psychic awakes personal effort is better than inertia.

Sri Aurobindo advises the sadhak in the early stages of the sadhana not to leave everything to the Divine without the need of one's own endeavour. By personal effort a preliminary change can be effected, it contributes to a greater spiritualising of the sadhak's mental motives and temperament, and a mastery of the vital and physical life. So long as there is not some measure of sustained identity with the Divine, personal effort must predominate. Only by a prolonged period of intentional effort in which the seeker has to reject the darkness and distortions of the lower nature, only then, when this has been truly done, the surrender of the lower to the higher can be effected.

However, personal effort alone may take a long time and its results are usually uncertain and fragmentary compared to the results of an opening inwards and upwards. In the later transitional stage of sadhana the personal effort should be gradually replaced by a more luminous response to the Divine Force, and in the last period there should be no effort at all; the Divine becomes the direct master of the sadhana and effects the entire spiritual conversion of the being.

The secret of integral sadhana lies in the complete replacement of individual effort by the cooperation of the upward-tending force of aspiration from below and the downward pressing force of Grace from above.

Divine Grace does not only elevate man into a higher plane of consciousness but also descends into the sadhak's being in order to take up the burden of his sadhana, and to transform the lower parts of his nature.

The miracle of Grace comes often after much difficulties and struggles and not at once. Grace is a power that is superior to any rule and its action is therefore incalculable. Aspiration and intensity of the psychic being can awaken it, yet it acts sometimes without any apparent cause. But when the power of Grace comes it makes the rest of the sadhana sure and secure, pushing the sadhak towards the goal to be attained. Faith in the Divine Grace gives the seeker all the strength to go through various trials, obstacles and dangers during the process of sadhana, as it is able to lift sadhaks beyond the present possibilities of their nature. However, for the full Grace to manifest, sadhaks must make themselves ready by a sincere surrender and self-opening to the Divine, and a rejection of falsehood, as the supreme Grace acts only in the conditions of Light and Truth. The more complete the sadhak's pure faith and surrender the more Grace will descend and protect the sadhak.

2. The Three Constituent Elements of Yoga in Sadhana: Purification, Liberation and Perfection

The passage from the human to the divine involves necessarily two stages; one of preparation as elaborated above, in which the soul and its instruments must become fit, and another of actual illumination and realisation in the prepared soul through its fit instruments. These two stages are not clearly separated, they are necessary to each other and continue simultaneously.

The object of the 3 constituent elements is to arrive at the whole truth of the seeker's self and Spirit, and the knowledge and bliss of the sadhak's complete being. To arrive at freedom, mastery and perfection, but also to arrive at his true relation with his own and with universal nature, the sadhak has to go back to the real self and soul within. The cultivation of these three elements makes the nature a fit instrument for divine works. The characteristic powers of the instruments, mind, life and body, must not only be purified of defects but also raised to a capacity for a greater action of the enlarged Divine Power and in the end they must undergo a spiritual and supramental transformation.

Purification: The first necessity for an active perfection of the being is the purification of all its members. The being itself, the spirit in man, needs no purification; it is pure in itself and is not affected by the faults of its instrumentation of mind, heart and body, the seats of impurity. This instrumentation must be rectified if the working of the spirit is not to be marred by its present concession to the pleasure of the lower nature.

Sri Aurobindo describes purification as a release, "it is a throwing away of limiting, binding, obscuring imperfections and confusions; purification from desire brings the freedom of the psychic Prana [the pure activity which gives the sadhak a psycho-physical base], purification from wrong emotions and troubling reactions the freedom of the heart, purification from the obscuring limited thought of the sense-mind the freedom of the intelligence, purification from mere intellectuality the freedom of the gnosis".[11] The object of purification is to make the lower being a clear mirror in which the divine reality can be reflected, i.e., a preparation of nature for its final transformation into the Supernature.

This purity has an integral character, the complete purification of one instrument depends on the complete purification of all the others. In the words of Sri Aurobindo, "the purification of each member of our being profits by the clarifying of every other, the progressive tranquillisation of the emotional heart helping for instance the purification of the understanding while equally a purified understanding imposes calm and light on the turbid and darkened workings of the yet impure emotions; ... yet love itself needs to be clarified by divine knowledge".[12]

This integral purification is therefore a great source of difficulties and disappointments as when the sadhak thinks that his intelligence is purified it is still subject to be clouded by the emotions of the heart and the will which, in their turn, are still affected by the impurities of the lower nature, and therefore prevent it from reflecting the pure truth. But the sadhak need not despair, as one important instrument, sufficiently purified can be used as a means for the purification of others, "one step firmly taken makes easier all the others and gets rid of a host of difficulties".

Vital craving in the form of desire is one of the main causes which prevents purification of the lower parts of the being. Desire as the root of all sorrow and affliction is always a straining of the being as it carries into its pursuit a sense of limitation, dissatisfaction and early disappointment. To get rid of desire is therefore indispensable for the purification of the lower instruments.

To turn the vital being from a troublesome power into the obedient instrument of an unattached mind is the first step in the purification of the lower being. As this deformation of the vital being is corrected, the purification of the vital and physical mind is facilitated. However, it is the psychic being which makes it possible for the seeker to open the whole lower nature to the Divine and purify the mind, vital and physical being if they submit to the psychic influence. For this penetration into the luminous soul the sadhak has to go through a difficult passage, facing all the intervening vital stuff. As useful aids during this difficult passage Sri Aurobindo advises" The method of detachment from the insistence of all mental and vital and physical claims, and calls and impulsions, a concentration in the heart, austerity, self-purification and rejection of the old mind-movements and life-movements, rejection of the ego of desire, rejection of false needs and false habits . . . and surrender of ourselves and of our parts of nature to the Divine Being".[13] All these methods are useful aids during this difficult passage.

According to Sri Aurobindo the systematic purification of the whole being can be done through the triple method of yoga—knowledge, love and works—in a growing attitude of self-surrender, a growing vision of the psychic being, and an implicit faith in the divine guidance.

It must be clear by now that for Sri Aurobindo this total purification of the complex instrumentality in all the parts of the being is not, ultimately, the narrower moral purification of the ethical nature. The inhibition of certain forms of mental and moral capacities, these things are secondary signs of the seeker's derivative being. In integral sadhana the sadhak has to gain a more deep-rooted psychological insight regarding the primary forces of one's nature, to strike at their roots rather than understanding and changing the symptoms of impurity.

Liberation: Purification as an instrumental liberation prepares the ground for a spiritual liberation which is of a larger and more essential character. Sri Aurobindo describes liberation as, "that inner change which is essential to perfection and indispensable to spiritual freedom ... it implies always two things, a rejection and an assumption, a negative and a positive side; the negative movement of freedom is a liberation from the principal bonds, the master-knots of the lower soul-nature, the positive side an opening or growth into the higher spiritual existence".[14] The instrumental knots of the mind and the heart come to the seeker in the form of ego and desire, and the liberation from ego and desire together form the central spiritual freedom.

The ego, as the fulcrum of ignorance and bondage, supports the falsehood of a separate existence rather than dwelling upon the idea of oneness and unity. An intellectual knowledge of the spiritual truth of oneness or the elimination of the active sense of the ego is not the true spiritual liberation. For Sri Aurobindo a spiritualised liberation from the ego means the replacement of the ego by a oneness in the Transcendental Divine and identification with the universal Being. This transcendent existence, a universal Spirit, is a truth which the purified intelligence can apprehend but it can only be realised and lived in the spirit.

However, liberation is not only the freedom of an unbroken contact of the individual being in all its parts with the Divine, but an integral liberation includes the acquisition of the divine nature, the complete and final release of all. The liberation of the individual soul is the primary divine necessity and the pivot on which all else turns, but there is a tendency of this single liberated soul to extend the same divine self-consciousness in other individual souls of our terrestrial humanity.

Perfection. Purification and liberation are the indispensable antecedents of perfection: when the self is purified and liberated into its self-existent being then spiritual perfection becomes possible; A human perfection aims at a more outward social action, towards our fellow-men and our environment. It is concerned with a good, happy and rich way of life, or as a more subjective ideal it endeavours to raise the intelligence and will, and to heighten a nobler ethical and finer emotional being. This human perfection must include self-mastery and a mastery of the surroundings; man's urge of self-perfection is to be self-ruler and king. But the ideal of yoga takes up this aim and places it on a wider spiritual basis opening it to the divine degrees of the Spirit, and Sri Aurobindo distinguishes therefore this human perfection from integral spiritual perfection. Perfection as used in integral Yoga refers to a growth out of a lower undivine into a higher divine nature. Sri Aurobindo describes perfection as "a divine spirit and a divine nature which will admit of a divine relation and action in the world; it will mean also in its entirety a divinising of the whole nature, a rejection of all its wrong knots of being and action, but no rejection of any part of our being or of any field of our action".[15]

Integral perfection is concerned with the sadhak's growth into the truth and power of the Spirit and using that power for the spiritual perfection in all our nature , "a living of man in the Divine and a divine living of the Spirit in humanity".

An integral liberation is a divine unity of supreme Spirit and its supreme nature, and when this liberation of the Nature becomes one with the liberation of the spirit, then there is founded, in the integral freedom, the integral perfection. In other words, an integral purity enabling a perfect reflection of the divine being in oneself and the perfect outpouring of its Truth in us, is the condition of an integral liberty which in its turn prepares the integral perfection of humanity, a perfection founded on a certian free universality of being, of love and joy, of knowledge and will in unegoistic action. It is this integrality which is aimed at in integral Yoga.

3. The Various Parts of the Being in the Course of Sadhana

According to Sri Aurobindo, "the practice of Yoga brings us face to face with the extraordinary complexity of our own being, the stimulating but also embarrassing multiplicity of our personality, the rich endless confusion of Nature".[16] Man's confusion about himself arises from the double aspect of his nature—one part external (natural) and the other inner (spiritual)—and the seeker's surface being is rarely aware of his inner being because it is veiled from it. It is the ordinary unenlightened activity of the external being that is an obstacle in spiritual development.

As explained previously, each plane of the being—mental, vital, phsyical—has its own conciousness, separate though interconnected and interacting, but in the outer surface nature they are all mixed together. Their division is the cause of most of the acute difficulties in the practice of sadhana. It is part of the sadhana to become aware of these separate parts of the being, to see and feel its movements and the forces that act upon them from inside or outside, and to control and direct them.

For Sri Aurobindo no integral Yoga is possible if the sadhak does not go back from the defects of the outer self and becomes aware of this inner being and inner nature. When the sahdak turns more inward he finds the sources of all his surface actions, sees the mixed up physical, vital and mental as separate forces in themselves and is able to analyse their surface mixtures. When living more and more in this inner being, the outer becomes an instrumental personality for the inner's self-expression in the material world.

The inner being is aware of the play of forces, personal or universal, for it is in conscious touch with the universal action. By going inside the sadhak is able to break the limitations of the ignorant external self and becomes directly aware of this universal consciousness and the universal forces that play through and around the seeker. It becomes possible for the sadhak to exercise a control, a rejection, a selection and a harmonisation of these forces, things which the surface personality only imperfectly posseses. As the sadhana progresses, the sadhak becomes aware of the two kinds of consciousness together; be in the inner and yet with his surface self fully active and awake, i.e., the inner influence behind the outer action.

Sri Aurobindo describes the awakening of this inner consciousness in the sadhak as "a calm, pure existence without any movement, but eternally tranquil, unmoved and separate from the outer nature. This comes as a result of detaching oneself from the movements and it is a very important movement of the sadhana. The first result of it is an entire quietude but afterwards that quietude begins (without the quietude ceasing) to fill with the psychic and other inner movements which create a true inner and spiritual life behind the outer life and nature. It is then easier to govern and change the latter".[17]

But there is another reason why it is absolutely necessary for the sadhak to become conscious of these regions; if they are not awake the psychic being has no proper and sufficient instrumentation for its activities.

The inmost or psychic being, as the individual soul-being, is quite distinct from the inner being. This inmost being supports all the other mental, vital and physical parts of the being in Nature, and when the psychic being can by sadhana become dominant and freely use its instruments then the transformation of the surface being and not merely its liberation becomes possible. For if the psychic is in front it becomes easy to remain conscious of the things that have to be changed in the external nature and it is comparatively easy to change them.

Sri Aurobindo describes the contribution of the psychic being in sadhana as, "love and bhakti, a love not vital, demanding and egoistic but unconditioned and without claims, self-existent; the contact or the presence of the Mother [divine consciousness] within; the unerring guidance from within; a quieting and purification of the mind, vital and physical consciousness by their subjection to the psychic influence and guidance; the opening up of all this lower consciousness to the higher spiritual consciousness above for its descent into a nature prepared to receive it with a complete receptivity and right attitude".[18]

At a certain stage, when the mind is sufficiently quieted, the vital subdued, and the physical altered then the psychic being is able to come forward and take up the lead of the sadhana. This psychic in the individual suffuses mind, life-force and physical consciousness with its inner light and changes with its purifying fineness their dark obscurities.

The subconscient below the ordinary waking consciousness, unlike the inner behind, is an automatic, incoherent half-conscious realm into which light and awareness can only come with difficulty. It is the lower basis of the Ignorance and affects mostly the lower vital and physical movements. This obscure consciousness is shut up in itself and the mind does not know its movements. Its actions are therefore irrational and mechanical, as it is not in touch with reason or the mental will. During the practice of sadhana the sahdak is bound to be confronted with these dark wells of the subconscient. These areas too have to be cleared of old movements before there can be a permanent and total change in the nature. It must be trained by a persistent insistence of the higher parts of the being. "But even before that, one [the sadhak] can minimise the trouble by putting the right will and the right habit of reaction in the subconscient parts".[19]

The higher being. During sadhana when there is a sufficient aspiration from the various mental, vital and physical planes, then the ascent into the higher ranges of consciousness or the upward movement takes place; each plane ascends above the mind where it can receive the origination of all its movements from above. But the higher descends also when there is a receptive quietude and openness in the various planes of the being to receive the higher. Mental effort in this process is only used as a temporary means until there is the natural openness towards these higher planes of consciousness.

The opening upwards does not only lead to peace and silence, but the sadhak also becomes aware of a vast Force, Light and Bliss, and when the personal consciousness is prepared sufficiently and the peace is established, this higher Force, Light and Bliss from above can descend and work in the sahdak. According to Sri Aurobindo, "The action of the higher consciousness does not usually begin by changing the outer nature—it works on the inner being, prepares that and then goes outward. Before that, whatever change is done in the outer nature has to be done by the psychic".[20]

In all it can be said that the ascent into the higher ranges of consciousness has to be followed by the descent of this higher consciousness into the different parts of the being, and aided by the psychic development it changes the external nature.

All these different actions of the inward and upward movements are intended to open up the lower nature from above, below and horizontal. The action from above opens it to the descent of forces from above the Mind and for the ascent of consciousness above the ordinary human mind. The horizontal or widening action opens it to the cosmic consciousness on all its levels, whereas the action from below helps to connect the superconscient with the subconscient.

Obstacles During the Process of Inward Movement

In the process of going inwards two complementary movements take place; the outward-coming of the inner being and the inward-going of the consciousness to become aware of the inner self and nature. The outer being is not the source of the spiritual urge; it is the inner being which seeks after union and when the inner being comes to the front all becomes possible which is impossible for the outer nature left to itself.

The movement of going inward should be done by a natural movement without haste as the sadhak has to pass through an intermediate zone before entering the field of pure Truth, Light, Power and Ananda. If the movement is done in an excessive hurry and eagerness, with an exaggerated self-confidence relying only on the sadhak's mind, then such movement is mixed with all sorts of mental and vital delusions.

A very uncertain and mixed beginning is characterised by an excessive pre-occupation with the illusions or rather incertitudes and incompleteness of the supraphysical or subtle worlds. When the sadhak gets in touch with the larger mental or vital world, which pours down with a great force, he feels himself freed from the normal limits, overwhelmed by the first rush of power of a supernormal condition. But this intermediate stage, when the screen between the individual and universal consciousness is removed and the inner being is brought forward, is not definite and final; it usually lacks the necessary knowledge and experience. Error and a mixture of Ignorance takes place freely allowing the sadhak to be tested by the world-forces, " to grow through imperfection towards perfection". This zone of transition may be crossed without being hurt, but the sadhak may also go astray in it which ends in a spiritual disaster; or the seeker may remain in this intermediate zone building up some half-truths taking them for the whole truth.

According to Sri Aurobindo, "This is a zone which many sadhaks have to cross, in which many wander for a long time and out of which a great many never emerge. Especially if their sadhana is mainly in the mental and vital, they have to meet here many difficulties and much danger; only those who follow scrupulously a strict guidance or have the psychic being prominent in their nature pass easily . . . A central sincerity, a fundamental humility also save much danger and trouble. One can then pass quickly beyond into a clearer Light where if there is still much mixture, incertitude and struggle, yet the orientation is towards the cosmic Truth and not to a half-illumined prolongation of Maya and ignorance".[21]

The best safeguard against the lures of the intermediate stage in the earlier practice of sadhana is the establishment of an inner purity and sincerity in which the sadhak is motivated only by the higher call until the psychic is in the front, and an opening of a wider higher consciousness from above rather than a larger vital consciousness.

Obstacles During the Process of Upward Movement

The repeated movement of ascent of the lower consciousness enables the mind, the vital and the physical to come into touch with the higer planes upto the supramental and get permeated with their light and power, whereas the repeated movement of descent of the higher spiritual consciousness enables the transformation of the whole being. The descent works at the same time for perfection as well as liberation; it deals with the whole nature, part by part, rejecting what has to be rejected, creating what has to be created. The upward opening puts the sadhak into direct relation with the whole Divine and is able to create within the seeker a new birth of the spirit.

However, this upward movement, like the inward movement, has its dangers for the practitioners of sadhana. The intermediate zone in the upward movement is related to a confused condition in which the sadhak is opening into the cosmic realm without having yet transcended the human mind levels. The sadhak is able to receive indirectly some divine Truth, but he is not in direct contact with the divine Truth on its own levels.

In the process of descent from above often the forces of the lower nature are stimulated and excited, and want to mix with it and turn it to their profit.

The main difficulty of the errors and stumblings of this intermediate zone are its powers to deceive and mislead the sadhak, attributing creations and formations of his own mind, vital or ego to the power of the Divine. It often happens that some undivine Powers present themselves as the supreme divine Power and demands the sadhak's service and surrender. The undivine Powers, eager to create a mental and vital formation in the earth life, use the thought and will of the sadhak making him their instrument for some apparently brilliant but ignorant formation. When this is accepted there will be disastrous consequences.

If the vaster and more powerful consciousness and its unlimited possibilities are tied to one's ego, then the sadhak becomes much more egoistic than the average man. Although there is no ego in the spiritual planes, yet by the spiritual experience the ego on the lower planes may get aggrandised through the wrong perception of the experience; a delusion of egolessness often covers an exaggerated ego. These things are always possible so long as the higher and the lower consciousness are not harmonised in the being, and the lower not transformed into the nature of the higher. A magnified ego becomes one of the most perilous obstacles to liberation and perfection.

4. The Ego in Sadhana

It must be clear by now that the ego is, from the sadhana point of view, the main obstacle and one of the greatest dangers in the process of spiritual development. However, after coming to this conclusion it is essential to place the characteristic role of the ego in evolution, understand its origin and analyse its limitations, its elimination and its transcendence.

All the sadhak does, thinks and feels has the stamp of the ego on it, and as long as his ego continues to be preoccupied with himself and remains in the forefront he cannot give himself unquestioningly to the Divine. It is only in those parts where the ego is too strong for us that the application of the divine principle becomes extremely difficult. The ego is only a result and a circumstance of our mode of world-existence and not the cause of our world existence. God does not move around the ego as the centre of existence, but the Divine is itself the centre; the experience of the individual only finds its true truth when it is known in the terms of the universal and the transcendent. The sadhak's spiritual individuality, unlike his ego, does not preclude its universality and transcendence, but at present the soul allows itself to be confused with the idea of the ego.

In order to be a possessor of one's being, the sadhak must find out his highest self, the real man within rather than one's mental, vital and physical ego.

Sri Aurobindo describes the ego as "not a lasting truth, much less our essential part; it is only a formation of Nature, a mental form of thought-centralisation in the perceiving and discriminating mind, a vital form of the centralisation of feeling and sensation in our parts of life, a form of physical conscious reception centralising substance and function of substance in our bodies. All that we internally are is not ego, but consciousness, soul or spirit. All that we externally and superficially are and do is not ego but Nature".[22]

The ego, constituted by nature is meant to aid in centralising and individualising the outer consciousness and action. It serves to separate and sharply differentiate and is indispensable to the evolution of the lower life. In the course of its development the ego did all sorts of things the individual might never have done otherwise such as ambition, vanity, power, possession, etc. It became the basis on which the individual binds together his experiences and relations in the midst of the complex contacts in which he lives.

The ego also makes the individual, through egoistic thoughts, feelings, will and desire, a tool of the universal forces. Nature puts a compulsion on the ego to grow in being until it can merge into the larger self and becomes one with the rest of existence.

In the evolution of the lower consciousness ego is a necessity; as long as the higher consciousness does not descend, ego remains essential even in aspiring and surrendering towards the Divine. It is the ego that at once initiates this surrender and self-offering through personal effort.

However, this ego is not one's real self but an instrumentation of nature by which it has developed a separate individual being, and by this instrumentation the individual acts as if he were a separate existence in the material universe. The individual soul, as the true spiritual being, appears in its complete truth when the sadhak gets rid of the ego and of his false separative sense of individuality. When the true being is discovered the utility of the ego is changed and this formation gradually disappears.

The ego, as a practical constitution of the individual's consciousness divised to centralise the activities of Nature in the individual, is a pragmatic and effective fiction, a subjective substitute for the true self. As the sadhak wants to get in touch with a higher nature the ego comes badly on the way and has to be dissolved.

Sri Aurobindo meaningfully describes the function of the ego thus; "Man the individual has to affirm, to distinguish his personality against Nature, to be powerfully himself, to evolve all his human capacities of force and knowledge and enjoyment so that he may turn them upon her and upon the world with more and more mastery and force; his self-discriminating egoism is given him as a means for this primary purpose. Until he has thus developed his individuality, his personality, his separate capacity, he cannot be fit for the greater work before him or successfully turn his faculties to higher, larger and more divine ends ... it is only when he has found himself that he can become spiritually one with all; if he tries to achieve that oneness in the mind, in the vital, in the physical and has not yet a sufficiently strong individuality, he may be overpowered by the mass-consciousness and lose his soul-fulfilment...; he has to find himself as a mental and vital ego before he can find himself as the soul or spirit."[23]

Nevertheless the ego has its limits, it is only an instrument, an image, and at every moment the slave of countless forces and influences in universal Nature. The ego principle has created separate individualities in the human beings but no divine centres of luminous self-awareness. As a false centre of unity it tries to find completeness of one's being in an identification with a changing surface personality, not with the eternal self or one's total existence. The ego in its self-enlargement may perceive its unity with others but this perception is mainly a mental idea or sentiment not based on inner experience. It is only in the spiritual self that the sadhak is able to find and possess the true unity.

The dissolution of this limited ego is therefore the necessary means for the cosmic Life to arrive at its divine fruition. In ordinary life there must be a control of the ego, but when the sadhak rises above the surface layers of one's being to a higher divine life, the elimination of the ego rather than only its control or purification becomes indispensable. By abolishing successively this practical ego-sense the sadhak comes to the realisation of the true self and is able to make this self one with the cosmic Spirit and with the inexpressible but not unknowable Transcendence. The disappearance of the ego does not bring with it the destruction of one's true individuality, one's spiritual existence, but the separate ego is replaced by the true spiritual Person and the sadhak can become a pure instrument of the Divine.

Ego transcendence includes a fusion in the wider cosmic I which comprehends all the smaller selves, and the transcendent. But Sri Aurobindo distinguishes very clearly this cosmic self from the collective existence; the former is spiritual in essence and in experience, whereas the latter is connected with the life of human society or human mankind, i.e., the sum total of individual egos.

The subordination of the ego to the progress and happiness of the human race belongs to the mental and moral world of ethics and not to a spiritual ideal. Humanitarian interests have an undeniable purifying effect but can only remove the grosser forms of the ego. According to Sri Aurobindo, "The greatest service to humanity, ... is to prepare or find the way by which the individual and the collective man can transcend the ego and live in its true self, no longer bound to ignorance, incapacity, disharmony and sorrow".[24]

In all sadhaks the ego is proven to be a stumbling-block and it is not possible to get rid of the ego movements all at once. The ego and its desires are one of the main causes of the spiritual casualties that takes place in sadhana.

Even the possibility of detachment and sublimation of the ego are not entirely free from serious dangers.

It is not very difficult to starve the ego by rejecting all its impulses of action or exalt it into a trance of peace or ecstacy, but in sadhana the more difficult problem is to arrive at a divine manhood which shall be the perfect instrument of a divine action; each difficulty has to be entirely experienced and entirely mastered.

The first stages of sadhana are with almost all sadhaks ego-centric, one's own endeavour is inevitable for most as without it there would be no sufficient push or will to bring about the first necessary changes. However, the expulsion and rejection of the ego cannot be done only by the will and its efforts.

At a certain stage of preparation, the negative attempt by a denial of the reality of the ego and its rejection must be replaced by the positive side of the sadhana, i.e., fixing one's thoughts constantly upon the One and the Infinite everywhere.

During the progress in sadhana the sadhak becomes gradually able to get rid of the ego altogether by an uncompromising rejection of all egoistic habits and insistences, along with a constant and exclusive opening to the Divine Force and an unreserved surrender in the whole being and nature to its guidance. Another means of release from the ego is the control of the psychic being within, exerting its influence directly upon the rebellious parts and forcing them to surrender. After this inner centre is discovered the progressive widening and ascent of consciousness becomes another effective means of release from the ego; the light of the higher nature penetrates into the lower mechanism and little by little the knots of the ego loosen or break. For a complete elimination of the ego-sense the sadhak has to rise into the Supermind beyond the Overmind and bring down its consciousness into the lower active nature.

5. The Three Means to the Object of Sadhana

Corresponding to the three principal faculties of the human being—will, knowledge and love, —there are three corresponding yogas; Karma yoga or the yoga of works, Jnana yoga or the yoga of knowledge and Bhakti yoga or the yoga of love and devotion.

The yoga of knowledge seeks fulfilment in the intellectual being of man, the yoga of works envisages union with the Will, and the yoga of devotion in the eternal Delight. In traditional yogas one main power of the being or one group of its powers is made the means on the path, but in Sri Aurobindo's synthetic yoga all powers are included and combined in the transforming instrumentation. An integral turning of the whole human being through action, knowledge and love, will have the unique result of an integral self-fulfilment. Sri Aurobindo's integral Yoga absorbs this cardinal principle of the Gita but he adds the ideal of higher planes and the supramental Truth-Consciousness, and the bringing down of that consciousness as a means of the complete transformation of earthly life.

In integral sadhana, it is not only the heart that has to turn to the Divine, but also the mind and the will of action. But since men differ in nature each sadhak will approach the sadhana in one's own way—one through work, one through devotion, one through meditation—and those who are capable of it through all together. Each method is a preparative help towards the proper direction of the realisation of the sadhana in the three parts of the being.

The three paths succeed only if they are done with the right spiritual aspiration, gathering up the whole life and nature and turning it towards the Divine, rather than work done for the service of humanity, a life-fleeing exclusive meditation or an emotional devotion shut up in its own ecstasy.

a. Sadhana Through Work

Karma yoga selects for its instrumentation the will as the doer of action; by purification, concentration, and some form of discipline it becomes a means for contact of the sadhak's soul with the divine Soul of the universe.

Sri Aurobindo refers to work not as an action of philanthropy which the mind of man substitutes for the deeper truth of works, but as action done for and in union with the Divine. Any work done as a sacrifice to the Divine, as a means of self-dedication through karma, is a field of inner training. Such self-dedication depends on the spirit in which all work is done and not on the nature of the work itself. Work done as a training in the spirit of Karma yoga aims, as the Gita insists, not at the work done for its own sake but at the dedication of every human activity to the supreme Will. It begins by the rejection of all egoistic aim for our works and all pursuit of action for the sake of a worldly result.

In the path of works, action is the knot to be loosened first, and the sadhak must endeavour to loosen it where it is centrally tied, in desire and in ego. The first law of action—egoistic indulgence of desire—in order to be exhausted must be put away from the sadhak with the help of the supreme Power within. There is no need to flee from action or take refuge in a blissful inertia. For Sri Aurobindo the elimination of desire does not mean the extinction of the energy that impels it, but the egoistic form it takes and which has to be dissolved; the force and energy that feeds them must not be abandoned but offered to the Divine. Desires can never be completely eliminated except through action, for it is only in an active life that they rise to the surface of the sadhak's consciousness and press for their satisfaction. However, in integral Yoga suppressed desires are not merely controlled by mental inhibitions; through the intervention of a higher spiritual force these suppressed desires are compelled to be converted into their spiritual counterparts. Once the sadhak's yoga has reached a certain culmination, works are done without any compelling ignorance, and actions are developed through the spontaneity of a supreme Force by which one's instruments are possessed.

The total surrender of all the sadhak's actions to a supreme Will, to something eternal within him, replacing the ordinary working of the ego-nature, is the way and end of Karma yoga. Desireless work carries along with it three results that are of central importance for the sadhak's spiritual ideal. 1) It leads inevitably towards the essence of an integral devotion, 2) it turns by communion with the Divine Will and Force into a way of Knowledge more integral than any human intelligence can construct or discover, 3) in renouncing egoism of the sadhak's mind, will and action, all these actions become now directed towards the Divine. In this way all works become a dynamic worship and source of the Divine. According to Sri Aurobindo, "All action must be done in a more and more Godward and finally a God-possessed consciousness; our works must be a sacrifice to the Divine and in the end a surrender of all our being, mind, will, heart, sense, life and body to the One must make God-love and God-service our only motive. This transformation of the motive-force and very character of works is indeed its master idea; it is the foundation of its unique synthesis of works, love and knowledge".[25]

Ordinary men work from the usual motives of the vital being, but in the practice of sadhana these ordinary motives have to be replaced by psychic and spiritual motives in which the sadhak does no longer work for himself but for the Divine. By constantly attributing all one's works to the Divine, the psychic being comes forward and spiritually purifies all works; works done in this spirit are quite as effective as devotion or meditation.

For Sri Aurobindo Karma yoga is therefore not only practiced as a means for liberation, but also as a very effective and indispensable means of transformation. If the sadhak follows the lead of the Divine, opening to its guidance and inspiration, he is able to heighten the powers and faculties of his nature and transform the whole instrumentation of his personality. Until work is done on the basis of the true inner self and a new consciousness, it can be only a means of sadhana and not a self-fulfilment.

In the Ashram work is of value only as a field for spiritual self-culture, as a field for the inner opening to the Divine. In the field of spiritual growth the path of works helps the sadhak to keep up the balance between the internal experience and the external development; work has its utility for the discovery and purification of the sadhak's egoistic mental, vital and physical nature. However "the work in the Ashram was not meant as a service to humanity or to a section of it called the sadhaks of the Ashram.... The work was meant as a service to the Divine and as a field for the training in a psychic elevation, selflessness, obedience, renunciation of all mental, vital or other self-assertion of the limited personality.... The merging of the little ego in union with the Divine, purification, surrender, the substitution of the Divine guidance for one's own ignorant self-guidance based on one's personal ideas and personal feelings is the aim of Karmayoga, the surrender of one's will to the Divine Will".[26]

b. Sadhana Through Knowledge and Meditation

In Sri Aurobindo's spiritual psychology knowledge does not mean mental knowledge; mental knowledge refers to the sum total of objects that the mind grasps, but it never penetrates into the essential unity of things. Besides, the mind can know only the surface of things and not their essential substance and reality. In spiritual life the ultimate aim of knowledge is not mental understanding or enlightenment, but being and becoming. Intellectual illumination may be able to lead to a right arrangement of clear and true conceptions, but is in itself ineffective because the change of the being may not at all take place. The central aim of knowledge is the recovery of the Self, the Self as a reality, and the universe as a reality of the Self and not of mere material force. This aim presupposes the admission that one's present mode of being is not one's true self-existence. This Self is not only the reality behind the movement of one's psychological being but also behind the transcendent and universal Existence.

For Sri Aurobindo the path of knowledge first leads to "God-possession, it is to possess God and be possessed by him through consciousness, through identification, through reflection of the divine Reality.... It is to possess oneness with God and through that to possess also oneness with the universal, with the cosmos and all existences; ... secondly it is to raise our being into the divine being, our consciousness into the divine consciousness, our energy into the divine energy, our delight of existence into the divine delight of being. And it is not only to lift ourselves into this higher consciousness, but to widen into it in all our being".[27] Integral Yoga does not proceed by the elimination of the lower parts of the being in order to merge into the quiescent Self, but the only thing that is to be eliminated is ignorance. The method of sadhana through knowledge must be regarded as a process of turning inward—a penetration into surface appearances of outer things, arriving at the one eternal reality within. Psychological analysis is a great and effective introduction to this turning inwards and therefore an important part of the Yoga of Knowledge, but its object is only to remove a difficulty rather than to arrive at the final and positive result of this path.

Besides, psychological self-knowledge is merely an intellectual conception or an enlightened psychological experience of the modes of the Self, but integral knowledge is based on "realisation, " the realisation of the Self in its pure being. As a first approach, psychological self-knowledge has to be followed till the wide infinite level is attained. Besides turning inwards into the core of one's being, purification and concentration are two other important means for the attainment of knowledge. Purity and concentration are two aspects of the same status of being in the path of knowledge and a necessary preparation towards the Divine Truth. Purity helps to bring about concentration, as without purification concentration would only lead to a state of eternal repose.

Traditionally concentration, as the removal of the thought from all distracting activities, implied a release from the world and an ascent into the absolute and transcendent state of Samadhi [trance].

But for Sri Aurobindo Samadhi has a more profound meaning , it is not merely a state withdrawn from all consciousness of the outward into the absorbed bliss or peace of the supracosmic Undifferentiated, but a unified state of consciousness in which the connections with the outside world are not eliminated. These experiences of trance have their utility for opening the being, but it is only when the realisation is constant in the waking state that it becomes the condition for the spiritual transformation of the inner and outer being.

Meditation: Concentration, when the consciousness is fixed in a particular state or movement, must be distinguished from meditation where the inner quiet mind remains concentrated on a single series of ideas which work out a single subject. Meditation as a method for calling down the true consciousness is a process leading towards knowledge and is one of the means in the approach to the Divine. According to Sri Aurobindo "in meditation, as the way to knowledge, there comes the opening above, the quietude or silence of the mind and the descent of peace, etc. of the higher consciousness generally till it envelops the being and fills the body and begins to take up all the movements. But this involves a passage through silence and certain emptiness of the ordinary activities".[28]

Sri Aurobindo distinguishes three forms of meditation; in the first form of concentrated meditation the discursive mind is accustomed to a settled pursuit of a single course of connected thought on a single subject, i.e., the strenuous meditation on the one subject. This process of concentrated meditation is common in the sadhak's ordinary life but it becomes more difficult when it has to be practiced by inward concentration.

The second process is related to the fixation of the whole mind on the essence of the idea only, so as to reach the very essence of the thing behind the idea rather than the psychological experience of the subject, i.e., the streneous contemplation of the one object of thought-vision. However, as already discussed in the trance state, this state into which the sadhak rises must be called down to take possession of the lower being.

The third process is related to the tranquillisation of the mind altogether which can be done in two ways; a) to stand back from the mental action altogether, watching it until it falls into an absolute quiet, b) to reject all thought-suggestions and firmly hold to the peace of the being which always exists behind the trouble of the mind. On the basis of this calm the sadhak penetrates into the deeper truth of the divine manifestation and is no longer dependent on the external phenomena of things.

The first two forms are the condition of any Yoga, but for Sri Aurobindo they are only a subsidiary helpful process. The last form of meditation is a more direct and powerful process for the integral sadhana, as by now the strenuous concentration is replaced by a free concentration on the divine Will which gives light to the lower members, remoulding these in the forms of the Divine.

A harmonised concentration of the whole being in all its parts on the Divine is the essential character of the sadhana and its character must determine its practice. Nevertheless, it must be clear that meditation is a purely mental activity, the other parts of the being are left inactive so that they may not disturb the meditation. In mastering the mind nothing is directly done for the other parts of the being and meditation therefore needs to be supplemented by the path of work and devotion.

Dreams: Ordinarily in sleep there is no longer any waking consciousness for all has been withdrawn within into the inner realm of which the sadhak is not aware in the waking state. For Sri Aurobindo, like Freud, dreams are a continuation of the process of clearing out remnants of old movements from the subconscious realm. According to Sri Aurobindo, "Sleep is a going inward in which the surface self and the outside world are put away from our sense and vision. But in ordinary sleep we do not become aware of the worlds within; the being seems submerged in a deep subconscience. On the surface of this subconscience floats an obscure layer in which dreams take place"...[29] Usually dreams seem to be incoherent, fragmentary or distorted records of experiences which are going on behind the veil of the sadhak's subconscient, but for Sri Aurobindo this lack of coherence and complete significance is due to the sadhak's limitation of understanding, and when the seeker goes within and begins to see it from within, these dreams assume a complete connected coherence.

There is maintained in sleep an obscure subconscious element which is a receptacle for one's dream experiences. But the subconscious is not only one's sole dream-builder, behind it is the depth of one's concealed inner being and consciousness which is of quite another order. When the sadhak goes deeper inward he discovers that the activity of the inner dream consciousness continues behind the veil of the subconscient surface, but this continued dream activity is revealed to the sadhak only when he becomes more inwardly conscious.

Often a large part of one's consciousness in sleep does not get sunk into its subconscious state; it passes into the subliminal planes of existence and influences the sadhak without his knowledge. But by the growth of this inner consciousness these dream experiences increase in number and coherence, and the sadhak becomes able to understand its significance for his inner life. At a certain stage, after sufficient training, when the inner sleep consciousness grows, this kind of sleep experience can replace the ordinary subconscious slumber. In the course of sadhana the subconscious ceases to predominate and is replaced by this kind of larger dreams, which are able to stamp their activities on the individual's waking memory.

According to Sri Aurobindo, " If the subliminal thus comes to the front in our dream-consciousness, there is sometimes an activity of our subliminal intelligence, —dream becomes a series of thoughts, often strangely or vividly figured, problems are solved which our waking consciousness could not solve, warnings, premonitions, indications of the future, veridical dreams replace the normal subconscious incoherence".[30]

Imagination: Another method of reaching and understanding the structure, potentialities and complexity of the inner consciousness is the usage of imagination and visions.

As one of the creative faculties of mind imagination is often used to stimulate spiritual growth as it offers the seeker not only a symbolic connection to his unconscious or subliminal layers of existence but also inevitably expands his awareness about himself and his relation with the world.

Visions are valued because they are often the first key to enter into the experience of one's inner consciousness (as distinguished from the planes of cosmic consciousness) of which most beginning practitioners are not aware. These inner visions also enable the sadhak to establish a first contact with the Divine, the hearing and seeing of the Voice and Light that guides.

Visions are a step on the way to realisations and often come in the earliest stages of sadhana, but most of the things seen at this stage are formations of the mental plane and are unlike the images seen in inner vision.

In mental imagination the images are invented by the mind and are partly true whereas in the later stages of sadhana the inner vision opens to the realm of the subtle images of inner thought and will, and always contain a truth in it. According to Sri Aurobindo, "there are visions and visions, just as there are dreams and dreams, and one has to develop discrimination and a sense of values and things and know how to understand and make use of these powers".[31]

Sri Aurobindo does give importance to dream experiences and imaginations, but they are of subsidiary help only. They are open doors to the inner planes of being which give room for a wider truth and experience, but it is not the only or most important door.

Even though these visions and inner dreams can have a considerable importance in the development of the first yogic consciousness or for an occult understanding of the universe, in the main his integral Yoga calls for self-surrender and the bringing down of the supramental consciouness for the integral transformation.

c. *Sadhana Through Love and Devotion*

Aiming at the unity of the human soul with the supreme Spirit, devotion selects the emotional powers of the soul and turns them all Godwards. Bhakti yoga, as a culture of spiritual emotions, exclusively turns the human heart towards the love of the Divine.

Traditional Bhakti yoga rejects a complete union with God as it does not want to abolish all one's individuality in the absorbed rapture of the union; this would only mean a dissolution of the individual.

Sri Aurobindo's approach to love is more comprehensive as compared to the orthodox principles and practice of Bhakti yoga. In integral Yoga it is the integral Divine who is the object of the sadhak's love and devotion. Love as the greatest power of the Divine delivers the seeker from all egoistic limitations, but this love must carry with it the expansion of knowledge and the action of the divine Will. Though love and bhakti are two aspects of the psychic feeling, Sri Aurobindo distinguishes them as follows; "The nature of Bhakti is adoration, worship, self-offering to what is greater than oneself; the nature of love is a feeling or a seeking for closeness and union. Self-giving is the character of both; both are necessary in the yoga and each gets its full force when supported by the other".[32]

In the beginning of sadhana the sadhak's love offered to the Divine is not always of the purest kind. Often the spiritual emotions when turned towards the Divine are mixed with the egoistic desires and demands of the seeker's unpurified nature. The purest and most spontaneous love comes from the psychic, which seeks for an integral divine union in the context of the terrestrial existence. Its love for God is capable of bringing down the transforming light of divine Love upon earth. When the psychic love unites with the divine Love it can draw freely upon the latter's omnipotence.

Divine love must include the more impersonal spiritual and the more personal psychic love. Spiritual love is universal in nature and based on the change of the personal into a wide, universal consciousness free from all attachments and ignorance. The spiritual element brings the individual in contact and union with the source of one's being, consciousness and bliss, i.e., the Divine.

Psychic love is a form taken by divine love in the human being. Human love can take a pure unselfish form only if it is touched by the psychic. The psychic element is the love of the inmost being for self-giving and union with the Divine Beloved. In itself psychic love is pure, but it is usually not left pure in the attraction of human beings to one another.

In sadhana emotion itself is not a bad element, it is a necessary part of human nature, but the sadhak has to be on one's guard against the so-called mission of psychic love as justification for yielding to a vital attraction or attachment. If the love and bhakti are too vital then there is likely to be a whirling around the sadhak's own ego instead of a straight flight towards the Divine.

This vital love is a passion good enough to serve a temporary purpose but in the end it doesn't last as it never gets satisfied and brings only suffering and disappointment. The vital emotions must therefore aspire for purification and once the psychic emotions come in front they become a powerful help to the sadhak and no longer a cause of suffering.

Human love is often blended by the confusion of the individual's confused consciousness stumbling in the frailty of one's inferior nature. It is made up of vital movements, emotions, passions, desires, etc, which are indispensable in human nature. But integral Yoga goes beyond this vital movement to the height and depth of Divine love. Divine love is a different consciousness with a different movement and substance, and is not merely a sublimation of human emotions. However, Sri Aurobindo does not want to eliminate human love, but from human love the sadhak proceeds to arrive at divine Love, transforming the former into the latter.

In sadhana, love based on the mental craving and vital passion is gradually replaced by psychic and spiritual love, with the mind, vital and physical as manifesting instruments of this divine love. They are a means and a part of the complete expression of divine love, provided they have the right movement of pure expression without the vital mixture of ego and desire.

This transformation of the nature of love from the character of a limited human emotion to an all-embracing divine love is not only applicable to the individual but also to universal Love. All sympathy, universal benevolence, love of mankind, are at first used as instruments of expression of human nature. But as consciousness deepens, heightens and changes, it is able to grow into a greater eternal love, transforming human love into the unifying divine love. The unity of the divine love takes hold of all living relations and turns them Godwards.

In the Gita's triple path of Yoga, neither Karma yoga—will, nor Bhakti yoga—feeling, nor Jnana yoga—thought, can be separated, each need for its fullness the incorporation and fusion of the others. In the integral view these three paths are one; works fulfil themselves in knowledge, the latter is not complete without the former, and the crown of the union of knowledge and works is love; for love is the delight of union. As the power of divine self-delight it brings richness and fullness. Fulfilled love includes knowledge and is not inconsistent with divine works.

In the practice of integral Yoga the sadhak may begin with knowledge or with devotion or with works or may combine them all in one movement; there is no single rule for it, all depends on the sadhak's personality and nature. Each must follow one's nature, and difficulties have to be accepted for some time in the pursuit of the sadhak's path of yoga.

It is possible to start with Godward emotion or with knowledge, but these subjective experiences create a tendency to live too exclusively within and it becomes difficult later on to apply to life the sadhak's gains in the higher Nature, and transforming the outer life and body. The outer action follows its old confused imperfect paths which does not correspond with the inner light.

Sri Aurobindo therefore advises the sadhak to start from works and proceed by works, although at each step works are supposed to be moved more and more by a divine love and divine knowledge. According to Sri Aurobindo: "Action is the first power of life; … therefore it is that by turning his action Godwards the life of man best and most surely begins to become divine. It is the door of first access, the starting-point of initiation. When the will in him is made one with the divine will and the whole action of the being proceeds from the Divine and is directed towards the Divine, the union in works is perfectly accomplished".[33]

The difficulty any sadhak feels about sadhana is not really a question of meditation versus bhakti versus works. It is a difficulty of the attitude or approach to be taken. They are the three means to the object of sadhana: to lift the nature wholly to the Divine. In the words of Sri Aurobindo, "work done as sadhana—done as an outflow of energy from the Divine and offered to the Divine or work done for the sake of the Divine or work done in a spirit of devotion is a powerful means of sadhana and that such work is especially necessary in this yoga. Work, bhakti and meditation are the three supports of yoga. One can do with all three or two or one. There are people who can't meditate in the set way that one calls meditation, but they progress through work or through bhakti or through the two together. By work and bhakti one can develop a consciousness in which eventually a natural meditation and realisation becomes possible".[34]

The Gita's mental perfection resulting from a mental synthesis of knowledge, love and works can resolve many discords of the human nature, but it cannot be the authentic work of the Divine in man. The practice of sadhana raises this synthesis from a spiritual-mental to a supramental perfection and aims at an ascent beyond mind into Supermind and then its descent, guided by the Light of the Supramental, into the chaos of the subconscient. An integral Yoga includes the conversion of the whole being into a higher spiritual consciousness and a larger divine existence, and on the level of the supramental existence the integration of knowledge, devotion and works becomes consummate.

6. The Process of Transformation in Sadhana

One of the meanings of integral sadhana is related to the psychic and spiritual transformation; it may be helpful to give a comprehensive explanation regarding the terms integration and transformation before arriving at Sri Aurobindo's integral transformation.

a) Integration: In passing from one level to another, climbing to higher spiritual levels, the lower faculty is compelled to take up as much as it can assimilate of the higher, enlarging itself and arriving at a more ample self-accommodation to the higher faculties.

The rudiments of the higher principles are already present in the lower grades; it would not be possible for the lower to evolve into the higher unless the potentiality of the higher were already inherent within the lower. The lower levels of development contain within themselves the essential principle of that which exceeds them.

Integration takes up what has already been evolved into each higher grade as it is reached; each ascent, a successive fixing in higher principles, does not carry with it the abandonment of the lower grades but brings out of it higher potentialities surcharging them with a deeper and finer significance. The higher is able to manifest itself in the lower gradation which brings with it a partial change of the old nature.

Integration is not only a process of heightening, an ascent to a new level and a taking up of the lower levels, but is also a process of widening the range of consciousness. The mental, vital, and physical existences are not lessened or impaired by being spiritualised, but they do become richer, more powerful and more perfect; in their divine change they break into possibilities which could not be realised in their unspiritualised condition; man becomes able to take in more of himself and the world.

For Sri Aurobindo integration is related to the transformation of the different, often conflicting parts of the being brought about by the control and the working of a higher principle into an organic whole, so that they can move in perfect union with the divine Will.

Integration implies the reconciliation of the disparate parts of the being, the conscious and the unconscious parts but also the concealed subliminal and superconscious parts of the being. A sufficient integration of one part has to be complete before an ascent to the next higher status can be entirely secure.

True integration is not a superficial association between various parts and cannot be done by the mental and vital being but only from within by the soul, as only the spirit is the centraliser of truth and can harmonize with the truth of the other parts. This integrative principle has the double function of inner purification and integrating the outer instruments.

The integral spiritual consciousness links the highest to the lowest through all the mediating terms and achieves an indivisible whole. This integral consciousness is not a thing that has to be created by the mind but must be uncovered for it is veiled in the individual's greater and deeper self.

b) Transformation: In a spiritual sense, a realisation makes the experience more real and dynamic and implies "the making real to ourselves and in ourselves of the Self, the transcendent and universal Divine". For Sri Aurobindo a spiritual realisation may bring an opening or heightening or widening of the consciousness but by itself does not necessarily transform the being as a whole. One can realise the Divine everywhere, the summit experience in spiritual life, yet remain untransformed in one's nature. It is therefore only one means towards the Divine transformation along with self-perfection and spiritual emancipation from Nature. The ideal of self-realisation figures as a means to self-manifestation.

Transformation expresses certain spiritual concepts and spiritual facts of integral Yoga. For Sri Aurobindo transformation does not mean mere purification of the nature by the influence of the Spirit, this is only part of a psycho-spiritual change, but he means by spiritual transformation a bringing down of the static and dynamic divine consciousness into every part of the being; the entire replacement of the present consciousness by the spiritual consciousness. There must be a descent of the Light and Power not merely into the mind but into all the parts of the being down to the physical and below in the subconscient before a real transformation can take place. Transformation in integral Yoga is therefore not a moral or spiritual purification but a radical and integral transformation of human nature.

In transformation when the higher consciousness from above comes down into the mind, vital or body then the imperfections of these instruments have to be faced and mended. Once they have been fundamentally purified and made capable of receiving what is beyond them then transformation can take place.

Sri Aurobindo uses transformation in a special sense, "a change of consciousness radical and complete and of a certain specific kind which is so conceived as to bring about a strong and assured step forward in the spiritual evolution of the being of a greater and higher kind and of a larger sweep and completeness than what took place when a mentalised being first appeared in a vital and material animal world".[35] In this radical change and conversion of the natural parts into their spiritual equivalents, the whole of human nature may be sublimated and transfigured into the divine Supernature. Such a transformation of human nature can only be achieved when the essence of the being is permeated in the spiritual principle in which all the movements become a harmonised process of the Spirit.

Sri Aurobindo's transformation enables the sadhak to live in the Divine not only in the absorbed ecstasy of trance but to live the Life Divine on earth at all times, in all the parts and elements of the being—physically, vitally, mentally and spiritually.

c) Triple transformation in sadhana: The transition beyond the human into the Divine, a transformation effected by sadhana, needs to be based on a total and integral change of consciousness. A descent of the whole higher consciousness into the mind may change the mind but need not change the vital nature; a higher power in the vital may enlarge the vital movements but leaves the physical consciousness unchanged; the descent of Light may change the inner being while the outer remains an imperfect instrument. According to Sri Aurobindo, "Spirituality has been up till now a power for the mental being to escape from itself or to refine and raise itself to a spiritual poise, it has availed for the release of the Spirit from mind and for the enlargement of the being in a spiritualised mind and heart, but not,—or rather not yet sufficiently,—for the self-affirmation of the Spirit in its own dynamic and sovereign mastery free from the mind's limitations and from the mental instrumentation. The development of another instrumentation has begun, but has yet to become total and effective; ... this cannot be done so long as the spiritual-mental being has not risen fully to Supermind and brought down its powers into terrestrial existence".[36]

For Sri Aurobindo transformation can be complete only when the psychic movement inward to the inner being and the opening upward to the higher existence are supported by the action of the Supramental Consciousness and Force. The descending force of the Divine which works through the Supermind transforms the mental, vital and physical status of the person; but so long as there is a hiatus between the Divine and earth existence there can be no radical change of the surface existence. This hiatus between mind and Supermind can be bridged through the process of triple transformation. As Sri Aurobindo says, "the gulf between Mind and Supermind has to be bridged.... This can be done only by the triple transformation; there must be the psychic change, the conversion of our whole present nature into a soul-instrumentation; along with that there must be the spiritual change, the descent of a higher Light, Knowledge, Power, Force, Bliss, Purity into the whole being; last there must supervene the supramental transmutation—there must take place as a crowning movement the ascent into the Supermind and the transforming descent of the supramental Consciousness into our entire being and nature".[37]

Psychic Transformation

Each time there is a purification of the outer nature it becomes more possible for the inner being to reveal itself and once the psychic being is in front the sadhana becomes natural.

Psychicisation, the first step in the process of the triple transformation, brings a psychic entity to the front of the being. It leads to a psychic change of the lower nature bringing right vision into the mind, right feeling into the vital and right movement into the physical.

Sri Aurobindo describes psychic transformation as, "a modification of the substance of the consciousness especially in the vital-emotional part, and as such a modification prolonged or repeated till it became permanent would mean a great step in what I call the psychic transformation of the being. It is just these modifications in the inner substance that make transformation possible".[38]

Sri Aurobindo distinguishes three main elements in the psychic transformation; "(i) the opening of the occult inner mind, inner vital, inner physical, so that one becomes aware of all that lies behind the surface mind, life and body—(2) the opening of the psychic being or soul by which it comes forward and governs the mind, life and body turning all to the Divine—(3) the opening of the whole lower being to the spiritual truth—this last may be called the psycho-spiritual part of the change".[39]

The psychic being with its spontaneous self-giving at once lights up the thoughts, emotional movements, vital and physical habits. It substitutes right movements for wrong ones and makes them pure instruments of the innermost psychic within.

The psychic's characteristic power is "to turn everything towards the Divine, to bring a fire of purification, aspiration, devotion, true light of discernment, feeling, will, an action which transforms by degrees the whole nature. Quietude, peace and silence in the heart and therefore in the vital part of the being are necessary to reach the psychic".[40] It is the psychic personality which is able to awake the spiritual force which must stamp itself upon heart, mind and life, and give them their upward orientation, purify and uplift their motions and suffuse them with a higher consciousness.

However, the intervention of the psychic dynamic principle may take long to succeed due to resistances in the lower parts of the being. To overcome this difficulty Sri Aurobindo advises the sadhak to open up one's inner being (the subliminal) and its centres of action. Once the inner mental, vital and physical consciousness is liberated into action, bringing to bear their powers on the whole range of the being, then the difficult task which the surface being could not achieve becomes more possible.

Only when the sadhak has got rid of the mixture of vital forces during his sadhana, is the psychic being able to fully open. Purity, sincerity, aspiration and an unegoistic self-offering are the conditions of an entire opening of the psychic being; psychicisation means to live and do sadhana for the sake of the Divine and not for one's own sake. When all the parts of the being become purified, a guidance from within repels all that is opposed to the divine realisation and enables the sadhak to have a free inflow of all kinds of spiritual experiences. The guidance of the soul brings into all the sadhak's experiences the tendency of integration and harmony.

In spite of all these inner changes the psychic transformation has certain limitations. In its action the psychic being gets mixed with the surface disabilities which it has to use to express itself and therefore it does not remain distinct in its purity. The inferior instrumentation reflects a modified manifestation of things as the psychic intimations get jumbled with mental ideas, vital desires and habitual physical tendencies. In these conditions the true psychic light gets diminished in the mind into a mere idea, the psychic feeling in the heart into a mere sentiment and the psychic will to action into a blind vital enthusiasm.

For a spiritual change the psychic or more widely speaking the psycho-spiritual transformation is essential but not sufficient. The old yogas have been mainly confined to the psycho-spiritual occult range of experiences, a kind of static liberation without any dynamic descent. In integral Yoga when the lower field has been prepared by a certain amount of psycho-spiritual experiences the sadhak's consciousness is drawn upward to ranges belonging to the spiritual consciousness, not merely to receive from there but to live there and bring it down to change the lower consciousness altogether. Without the inner psycho-spiritual experience nothing lasting can be done, but there must be also a realisation of the Divine in the outer consciousness and life. If the sadhak does not go beyond the psychic transformation then there is only an inner change whereas the outer nature continues to be moved by the mechanical effects of past energies and may become a field of apparent incoherence.

Also, by itself the psychic being at a certain stage might be content to create a formation of truth, good and beauty and become purely passive, remote from mastery and action in the world.

Spiritual Transformation

The psychic development has to be attained before a perfect spiritual descent can take place. It prepares the lower nature to receive the higher spiritual consciousness with a complete receptivity and right attitude. To explore spiritual experiences before purification often creates a dangerous situation; an ambition or any other vital motive mixed up with the spiritual seeking may easily lead to the growth of an exaggerated egoism. Sri Aurobindo advises the sadhak not to plunge into spiritual experiences in sadhana without a fairly long period of preparation and purification. When the soul is in front the sadhak gets the right guidance from within which makes the descent of the higher consciousness safe and easy.

While psychicisation, as a change from within, unifies the depth of the being with the surface, spiritualisation, as a change that descends from above, unites the manifested existence with what is above by the descent of a higher Light, Knowledge, Power, Bliss and Purity into the whole being.

These two movements indicate the two necessities in sadhana and are complementary to each other; if the spiritual ascent and descent are not made, the spiritual transformation of the nature cannot happen, if the full psychic opening is not made the transformation cannot be complete.

For a complete spiritual transformation a permanent ascension to the higher ranges of consciousness is needed because only such a permanent ascent can guarantee complete freedom from the distortions of the lower medium. According to Sri Aurobindo, "It is the aim of the sadhana that the consciousness should rise out of the body and take its station above.... Thus liberated one opens to all that is above this station, above the ordinary mind, receives there all that descends from the heights, observes from there all that is below. Thus it is possible to witness in all freedom and to control all that is below and to be a recipient or a channel for all that comes down and presses into the body, which it will prepare to be an instrument of a higher manifestation, remoulded into a higher consciousness and nature".[41]

When the being opens, the mental, vital and physical consciousness begin to ascend in order to join themselves to a higher spiritual or divine consciousness. This upward opening necessarily results in a vision of a vast static and silent Self, the foundation of a spiritual tranquility.

When the higher consciousness descends there is usually an opening of the limited personal being into the Cosmic Existence and an awakening to the existence of higher supernormal levels. This new consciousness brings to the sadhak spiritual awareness of the Infinite which is able to remove barriers and break down the limitations of the lower nature. The descent of the higher Force, descending from centre to centre till it has occupied the whole being, often comes down in an extremely intense way and its influence is often resisted by the lower instruments. But according to Sri Aurobindo, "What is needed is the establishment of the calm and wide consciousness at the base of the whole Nature, so that when the lower nature appears it will not be as an attack or struggle but as if a Master of forces were there seeing the defects of the present machinery and doing step by step what is necessary to remedy and change it".[42]

Spiritual transformation, like psychic transformation, has its limitations. The spiritual consciousness, like the inner consciousness is diminished in its working by having to depend on the human instrumentation of mind, vital and physical; in this way it is difficult to work out the full power of the higher principle. The light and the power of the higher comes down but gets diminished and modified, and its truth gets mixed with mental and vital error.

Again, the spiritual mind can unite the individual mind with the cosmic mind on its highest plane and give to the nature an action of universality but it cannot transform the whole human nature (the Inconscient) into the Supernature. In the words of Sri Aurobindo, " The Power has to come at intervals and work meanwhile behind the veil or hold itself back through long periods of obscure assimilation or preparation of recalcitrant parts of Nature; the Light has to work in darkness or semi-darkness on the regions in us that are still in the Night".[43]

The psychic transformation after rising into the spiritual change has to be completed, integralised and uplifted by a supramental transformation.

The Supramental or Integral Transformation

The psychic opening puts the sadhak primarily into connection with the individual Divine, whereas the upward opening puts the seeker into direct relation with the Divine All. The psychic change takes place within the limits of the natural instrumentation and effectuates only a modified manifestation of the heavenly riches such as peace and bliss. The spiritual change gives a vision of a heightened truth and brings down into the terrestrial embodied existence the dynamic self-luminous instrumentation of the transcendent Self.

But all these powers of consciousness suffer a diminution of their dynamic capacities when they descend and work in the obscurity of the lower regions; they are therefore not able to bring about the integral transformation, the complete divine dynamisation of nature, the total and radical transmutation of even the darkest and most inconscient parts of the mind, life and body.

However, these instruments of the Spirit are not condemned to function forever on the irretrievable basis of division and darkness but are meant to recover their essential unity and be converted into the divine counterparts of light and purity; a union of the sadhak's instrumental being no less than of his soul and spirit must change his imperfect nature into the very likeness of Divine Nature. It is only the dynamic descent of the supramental Truth-Force with its perfect unity of Truth-knowledge and Truth-will which can establish in the outer and inner existence the harmony of the Spirit.

The supramental transformation must carry with it an uplifting of the lower nature into a greater way of being, not through the abolishment and suppression of the powers of this lower nature but the perfection and fulfilment of them by the self-exeeding supramental Force.

However, an isolated individual transformation is not enough, "the individual change will have a permanent and cosmic significance only if the individual becomes a centre and a sign for the establishment of the supramental Consciousness-Force as an overtly operative power in the terrestrial workings of Nature".[44] This emergent Force must be active within the terrestrial whole so as to make the manifestation of the Divine in the earth-consciousness possible. The difficult result of an integral transformation can become possible only "if there is an immense conversion, a total reversal of our consciousness, a supernormal entire transfiguration of the nature. There must be an ascension of the whole being, an ascension of spirit chained here and trammelled by its instruments and its environment to sheer Spirit free above, an ascension of soul towards some blissful Super-soul, an ascension of mind towards some luminous Supermind, an ascension of life towards some vast Super-life, an ascension of our very physicality to join its origin in some pure and plastic spirit-substance.... At the same time there must be a descent too to affirm below what we have gained above: on each height we conquer we have to turn to bring down its power and its illumination into the lower mortal movement".[45]

The integral transformation of human nature and life will be the ultimate perfection of man. The labour of this transformation must be inevitably a long battle with oneself and one's environment, for the old ignorant nature will contend repeatedly with the transforming influence and is supported in its strong resistance by most of the established forces of environing universal Nature. However, after a prolonged, often painful period of preparation and purification, two inner changes take place within the sadhak which help to convert what now seems impossible into a thing possible. There takes place a coming into the front of the inmost soul within by which an inner Yogic conciousness gradually replaces the sadhak's ordinary views of things, natural movements and motives of life, and there will come about, as a result, a growth of the Divine Presence into all the conscious and subconscious ranges of the sadhak's nature.

The three steps of transformation as described above should not be considered as strictly successive; the spiritual transformation may begin before the psychic transformation has reached its culmination or the integral transformation may intervene in the midst of the psychic or spiritual transformation in order to speed up its pace and shorten the long way.

Sri Aurobindo does not ask everybody to become supramental; in the first step of transformation he asks the sadhaks to make their love psychic and use the vital not for its own sake, but as an expression of the soul's realisation. The difficult supramental change must be regarded as the end of a far-off perspective, it must not be turned into a first aim or an immediate objective.

Transformation is not the central object of the traditional yogas, but for Sri Aurobindo a full descent of a new consciousness into the whole nature of man is essential to transform life, rather than a spiritual escape from life or a departure into some kind of celestial transcendence. Sri Aurobindo has formulated the idea behind the philosophy of transformation thus: "An integral transformation is the integral aim of the Being in Nature ... the process of Nature is not confined to a heightening of herself into a new principle . . it brings with it a widening and establishes a larger field of life in which the power of the new principle may have sufficient play and room for its emergence ... it includes a taking up of that which is lower into the higher ... Our mental, physical, vital existence need not be destroyed by our self-exceeding, nor are they lessened and impaired by being spiritualised; they can and do become much richer, greater, more powerful and more perfect: in their divine change they break into possibilities which in their unspiritualised condition could not be practicable or imaginable".[46]

7. Conclusion

Sadhana is not an easy and smooth practice, long periods of despondency and crises of despair seem incurable by their continuity and persistence; therefore "a strong mind and body and life-force are needed in the sadhana". In Sri Aurobindo's Yoga the spiritual seeker must already be a balanced individual with a developed emotional stability, intellectual knowledge, physical health and a definite spiritual orientation. Not everyone is suited for the practice of integral Yoga, as it is a difficult and trying yoga to follow, "a way for heroes not for weaklings". Capacity of the outer nature is not enough; there must be also the call and will to seek after the Divine, and courage and persistence in the practice. According to Sri Aurobindo, "There can be for the seeker of the integral Yoga no clinging to resting—places on the road or to half-way houses; he cannot be satisfied till he has laid down all the great enduring bases of his perfection and broken out into its large and free infinities".[47]

It is necessary from the beginning of the practice to understand and accept the arduous difficulties the sadhak has to face. Faith in the sadhana and faith as a support from above prevent these attacks. If the sadhana fails in its immediate aim it is because the Divine has intended the failure, and if difficulties still come the sadhak has to go through them as soon as possible and get back into the sun.

It is essential for the seeker to go inside oneself with a complete dedication to the spiritual life, without clinging to mental preferences or insistence on vital craving and attachments. "If the little external personality is to persist in retaining its obscure and limited, its petty and ignoble, its selfish and false and stupid human consciousness, this amounts to a flat negation of the sadhana".[48]

Sadhana includes a discipline far more difficult than mere ethical and physical austerities and the seeker must enter this path only if he is sure of the psychic call. Nevertheless, not all can approach at once the Divine in the pure psychic way and need to be supported in the beginning of the practice by the mental and vital approaches.

Difficulties in the sadhana such as failures, struggle, lapses or states of darkness are hurtful to spiritual progress. The rule in sadhana is not to let any of these difficulties depress the sadhak, but to stand back from them, observe its cause and remove the cause, for the cause is always the sadhak himself. These superficial difficulties are not created by the practice of yoga, in yoga the seeker becomes conscious of their movements and their causes. During sadhana the struggle is transferred to the psychological plane where it will be much easier to sort the disturbing matter out, and gradually the sadhak comes out of the struggle; these superficial disturbances may afterwards still touch but cannot destroy the seeker.

But besides the difficulties in the movements of the outer parts of the being which are attached to the realm of the lower nature, there are also the difficulties to be faced in the transformation of the human nature. If the higher part is dominant, then the lower is kept under control and does not cause much trouble. The real difficulty lies in the change of the lower nature because of the obstinate resistance from the sadhak's ignorant nature. Even when the inner being gets free the outer still follows its fixed nature, clinging to its old mechanical habits and manners. However, in the later stages of sadhana after the laborious preparation of the whole lower nature by the divine working to receive the higher Nature, an eventual transformation becomes possible.

It is known that the movements of the lower human and higher spiritual nature pull different ways and that the lower is at first much stronger. But it must be clear by now that sadhana does not leave the lower and higher nature separate so that the sadhak can live a double life, one spiritual above, the other material in earthly living. The lower realm is remoulded in the light and joy of the higher and the two realms can be united in the oneness of the Divine.

The object of sadhana is to change the sadhak's human nature into the divine nature, but as discussed before, this divine nature is not a mental or moral but a spiritual condition which is difficult to achieve. It needs a long stage of preparation in order to arrive at the proper inner psychological condition in which the seeker is ready to receive the new consciousness without being disturbed by the impure layers of the surface being.

In spite of all these difficulties Sri Aurobindo is also clear that those who are sincere and faithful in heart and those who rely on the Divine will arrive at the kingdom in spite of all difficulties. If the call of the soul is there, although not yet full, there can be no irretrievable failure. After each stumble the soul brings back the light and the sadhak forges ahead on the path. An acute struggle does not mean that the sadhak is unfit for the sadhana, as described by Sri Aurobindo; "To all sadhaks, even to the best and strongest there come interruptions in the flow of the sadhana; that is not a cause for thinking one-self unfit and wanting to go away with the idea that there is no hope. A little quietude would bring back the flow.... These difficulties always come and have to be overcome. Once overcome by the working of the Force, the sadhana goes on as before.... No sadhak ought ever to indulge thoughts of unfitness and hopelessness —they are quite irrelevant because it is not one's personal fitness and worthiness that makes one succeed, but the Mother's grace and power and the consent of the soul to her grace and the workings of her Force".[49]

All these difficulties can also be cured by the sunlit path in which the sadhak goes forward in absolute reliance of the divine Force, fearing nothing, and in which the old persistent habit of raising up and stressing the difficulties are rejected. Sri Aurobindo describes the sunlit path thus: "do not be always thinking of your defects and wrong movements. Concentrate more upon what you are to be, on the ideal, with the faith that, since it is the goal before you, it must and will come.... Turn your eyes more to the coming light and less to any immediate darkness".[50]

The sunlit path can be followed by those who are able to practice surrender, trusting the inner guidance or, in the absence of these two, the habitual practice of turning one's face to the sun. This does not mean that the sunlit man has no difficulties but with confidence in the ultimate victory, the sadhak regards them cheerfully as "all in the day's work", which makes the progress much swifter.

Notes:

1. M. P. Pandit; "What is Spirituality and what is Sadhana", p. 12.
2. Sri Aurobindo; Letters on Yoga, Sri Aurobindo Ashram Press, Pondicherry. 5th impression 1988, p. 1271.
3. Ibid., p. 149.
4. Ibid., p. 1313–1314.
5. Ibid., p. 792–793.
6. Ibid., p. 850.
7. Ibid., p. 551.
8. Ibid., p. 573.
9. Ibid., p. 603.
10. Ibid., p. 789.
11. Sri Aurobindo; The Synthesis of Yoga, Sri Aurobindo Ashram Press, Pondicherry. 9th impression 1992, p. 647.
12. Ibid., p. 295.
13. Sri Aurobindo; The Life Divine, Sri Aurobindo Ashram Press, Pondicherry. 10th impression 1993, p. 907.
14. Sri Aurobindo; The Synthesis of Yoga, Sri Aurobindo Ashram Press, Pondicherry. 9th impression 1992, p. 647.
15. Ibid., p. 664.
16. Ibid., p. 68.
17. Sri Aurobindo; Letters on Yoga, Sri Aurobindo Ashram Press, Pondicherry. 5th impression 1988, p. 1003.
18. Ibid., p. 298–299.
19. Ibid., p. 360.

20. Ibid., p. 1211.
21. Ibid., p. 1043.
22. Sri Aurobindo; The Synthesis of Yoga, Sri Aurobindo Ashram Press, Pondicherry. 9th impression 1992, p. 203.
23. Sri Aurobindo; The Life Divine, Sri Aurobindo Ashram Press, Pondicherry. 10th impression 1993, p. 692–694.
24. Sri Aurobindo; The Synthesis of Yoga, Sri Aurobindo Ashram Press, Pondicherry. 9th impression 1992, p. 344.
25. Ibid., p. 97.
26. Sri Aurobindo; Letters on Yoga, Sri Aurobindo Ashram Press, Pondicherry. 5th impression 1988, p. 850.
27. Sri Aurobindo; The Synthesis of Yoga, Sri Aurobindo Ashram Press, Pondicherry. 9th impression 1992, p. 490.
28. Sri Aurobindo; Letters on Yoga, Sri Aurobindo Ashram Press, Pondicherry. 5th impression 1988, p. 534.
29. Ibid., p. 1023.
30. Sri Aurobindo; The Life Divine, Sri Aurobindo Ashram Press, Pondicherry. 10th impression 1993, p. 424.
31. Sri Aurobindo; Letters on Yoga, Sri Aurobindo Ashram Press, Pondicherry. 5th impression 1988, p. 933.
32. Ibid., p. 776.
33. Synthesis of Yoga;p. 521.
34. Letters on Yoga;536.
35. Ibid. p. 98.
36. Sri Aurobindo; The Life Divine, Sri Aurobindo Ashram Press, Pondicherry. 10th impression 1993, p. 890.
37. Ibid. p. 891.
38. Sri Aurobindo; Letters on Yoga, Sri Aurobindo Ashram Press, Pondicherry. 5th impression 1988, p. 1113.
39. Ibid. p. 1092.
40. Ibid. p. 1197.
41. Ibid. p. 1128.
42. Ibid. p. 1677.
43. Sri Aurobindo; The Life Divine, Sri Aurobindo Ashram Press, Pondicherry. 10th impression 1993, p. 915.
44. Ibid. p. 962.
45. Sri Aurobindo; The Synthesis of Yoga, Sri Aurobindo Ashram Press, Pondicherry. 9th impression 1992, p. 123.
46. Sri Aurobindo; The Life Divine, Sri Aurobindo Ashram Press, Pondicherry. 10th impression 1993, p. 727–728.
47. Sri Aurobindo; The Synthesis of Yoga, Sri Aurobindo Ashram Press, Pondicherry. 9th impression 1992, p. 748.

48. Sri Aurobindo; Letters on Yoga, Sri Aurobindo Ashram Press, Pondicherry. 5th impression 1988, p. 1306.
49. Ibid. p. 1704.
50. Ibid. p. 1687.

CHAPTER VII

SRI AUROBINDO'S SADHANA COMPARED WITH THE TRANSPERSONAL APPROACH

1. Psychotherapy and Integral Yoga Psychology

As mentioned previously, the common element in each psychotherapy is based on a greater awareness and integrity of the various aspects of the being. Many systems of psychotherapy agree that individuals are able to change by increasing their self-consciousness, though such changes are only related to the client's psychological disturbances. Systems of psychotherapy and Sri Aurobindo's sadhana include the development of insight and the deepening of awareness pertaining to aspects of behaviour of which the seeker is more or less unaware. A genuine insight into the unconscious dynamics of the individual's psychological disturbance has in itself a strong therapeutic effect. But awareness gained through psychotherapy does not in itself bring about the psychological state of total well-being. For Sri Aurobindo consciousness is also power or will-force and to attain psychological health is therefore not only to be fully aware of one's being but also to possess the full force of consciousness.

While integral Yoga psychology and psychotherapy both try to delve into the hidden nature of the suffering being through illuminating insight, in the capacity and degree of illuminating power they differ widely.

The therapeutical reductionist theory in which the individual has to recognize himself in his subconscient energies reduces the higher to the lower. It attempts to explain spiritual experiences in terms of familiar psychological processes, which often fails to provide insight into the inner nature of the experience. Psychotherapy, in its therapeutical remedies, tends to externalise the individual's subtle spiritual nature and remains therefore a treatment of technical manipulations of the sensitiveness of the soul.

For Sri Aurobindo, the individual, in the process of self-discovery, should know the highest first by transcending his psycho-physical nature before entering and understanding the lowest, i.e., the higher cannot be explained by the lower as the lower represents only a part of reality. It is only in the light of the Infinite that the truth of the finite can be properly understood. Sri Aurobindo's Yoga therefore tries to find the solution of the problem in man's higher nature through combining psycho-spiritual processes with contemplative awareness.

Nevertheless integral Yoga psychology incorporates the basic elements of psychotherapy by insisting on the need for inward self-opening, the joining of the surface consciousness with the depth of the being. It confirms the modern psychological theory in which the subconscious is seen as a storehouse of repressed material which powerfully influences the behaviour of the individual. It is full of irrational habits and "is largely responsible for chronic illness". In psychotherapy the individual is able to become aware of his unconscious repressed vital and mental capacities, and in order to consciously control them psychotherapy can be beneficial as a preliminary treatment. Through a conscious control of one's vital and mental capacities, that is to say a mature prepared mind, the individual is able to transcend one's ego attachment and obtain the strength of the Spirit.

In psychotherapy the vital and mental movements are accepted as a natural allowable part of the human nature and only so far as society discourages such movements people try to control them. In sadhana complete mastery is essential and the sadhak has even to become conscious of suppressed impulses and eliminate them. In this process the impulses are raised up in the consciousness, so as to be cleared out of the being, but they are not raised up into action. Sri Aurobindo advises the sadhak to become conscious and recognize one's weaknesses, lay oneself before the light, draw back from them and finally change. A mental control can certainly effect a change, but usually it takes a long time and the success at the beginning may be only partial and is often accompanied by many failures. The sadhak in sadhana does not solely rely on his effort alone, but also places reliance on the Grace and the power of the Divine.

Actually, the object of sadhana is not to make unlimited room for the fulfilment of the ideas of the human mind or the desires of the ego-centred life-force, but to create a world in which the Divine Will can manifest its truth rather than a world in which the sadhak is able to do what he likes. As such sadhana is a living thing and not a set method of mental principles. Each sadhak has to be dealt with according to his nature, capacities, real needs and according to what is best for one's spiritual welfare.

Again, the goal in most Western systems of psychotherapy is to make the individual aware of his hidden motivations and thus to enable him to adjust better to ordinary life. Its object is to strengthen the ego rather than to dissolve it. The various psychotherapeutic approaches utilize the positive aspects of the ego for overcoming psychological disturbances.

For Sri Aurobindo, on the other hand, all psychological disturbances are different forms of an exacerbated egoistic state, true well-being can only come from the true Self. To enter integral Yoga demands the abolition of the ego and its demands, an infinite trust, patience and self-discipline. Psychotherapy aims at psycho-physical health and psychological maturity, but it does not reach into the depths beyond the surface psyche. Integral Yoga psychology is essentially an art of spiritual life and is not much concerned with healing psychopathological symptoms. As such it cannot be seen as a form of therapy, but as a methodical process of surrendering the ego-self to the larger spiritual self. Sri Aurobindo's sadhana assumes a level of personality organisation in which an integrated sense of the ego is already complete.

However, difficulties arise when this assumption of mature selfhood is not understood, and psychotherapy can be very useful in stabilizing this fragile and vulnerable sense of self before the seeker enters into the slippery process of transcending the ego-sense, i.e., "to become somebody before one can be nobody".

Finally, according to Sri Aurobindo psychological difficulties do not disappear by the mind brooding on them. These difficulties, no doubt, have to be observed but if the mind stresses psychological difficulties then they tend to stick without a solution and may even increase. Sri Aurobindo wants the seeker to put his whole stress on faith and aspiration, a change in the poise and attitude of the mind, as it is from something above and outside the difficulties that the solution must come. This does not mean that the mind has no role to play in solving psychological difficulties, but the mind's task of concentrating on details and putting them right should be a subordinate process. In a tardy and slow progress the mind tries to construct out of the details some general result, however, progress is much more rapid when the seeker makes an opening to a larger consciousness the main method. In the process of opening, the higher ranges of the mind tend to bring about an essential change and it is this change that will be the most helpful process.

With these views in the background some of Sri Aurobindo's commentaries regarding the various traditional Western psychotherapeutic approaches will be more easily understood.

Behaviourism bases the study of mind upon the study of the body and leaves out any hidden profundities of one's subjective existence. The behaviour psychologist attempts to explain the complex behaviour of the human organism in terms of the same physiological and biological principles applicable to behaviour of the animal organism.

But, as explained in the chapter on the various parts of the being, life and mind are not merely looked upon as phenomena in Matter, but as energies other than the material with their own peculiar qualities, powers and workings. Only a limited range of the phenomena of life and mind can be satisfied by a purely bio-physical or psycho-physical explanation.

The behaviour therapist studies others from outside rather than seeing his true field of knowledge and laboratory of experiment in himself. For Sri Aurobindo the seeker must proceed from one's self-knowledge to the knowledge of others.

The knowledge of one's superficial mentality and the laws of one's bodily life do not bring the seeker to the hidden and mysterious depth behind the surface consciousness as, "psychological enquiry in Europe (and without enquiry there can be no sound knowledge) is only beginning and has not gone very far, and what has reigned in men's minds up to now is a superficial statement of the superficial appearances of our consciousness as they look to us at first view and nothing more. But knowledge only begins when we get away from the surface phenomenona and look behind them for their true operations and causes".[1]

In integral Yoga behaviourism as a scientific psychology, with a materialistic basis which assumes human mind as only a subtle development from the life and the body, cannot be of much help. This superficial psychology has its value in the mental and vital realms, but in the spiritual realm it has to be turned into a higher end, where the lower realms are transmuted and then become capable of linking the sadhak's consciousness with the Divine. In the words of Sri Aurobindo: "In yoga we have to travel beyond the physical nature and the superficial man and to discover the workings of the whole nature of the real man. In other words, we must arrive at and use a psycho-physical knowledge with a spiritual foundation".[2]

Humanistic psychology like Sri Aurobindo's psychology emphasises the inherent principle of personal growth and the unity of consciousness rather than the sum total of separate instincts and perceptions. Each individual is responsible for his own actions and for his own choices among the possibilities for growth. The root cause of the problem lies within oneself and only through a deeper understanding of oneself will the seeker become able to cope with the problems of life. For Sri Aurobindo as well as the humanist psychologist man is a never-finished product of evolution with endless potentialities for inner growth and this inner reality need not depend on the exclusive sphere of religion. However, the humanist's unifying process is based on mechanical principles rather than spiritual ones. The humanist considers men primarily as biological organisms and in their vitalistic biological approach they give insufficient significance to the spiritual dimension of human development, in contrast with Sri Aurobindo who assumes the divine essence of man. According to Sri Aurobindo, "The mundane ideal regards man always as a mental, vital and physical being and it aims at a human perfection well within these limits.... It is a wide and full aim, but yet not sufficiently full and wide, because it ignores that other greater element of our being which the mind vaguely conceives as the spiritual element and leaves it either undeveloped or insufficiently satisfied.... Its aim besides is limited to a terrestrial perfection of the normal human life".[3]

Existentialism offers the seeker a heightened awareness of existential limits and suffering, and to accept them with authenticity and courage.

Sri Aurobindo would not pay so much attention to the importance given by the existential psychologists to despair and anguish as central to human existence. In its lack of spiritual depth of man it has little to offer in helping humanity to evolve towards higher levels of being, to move towards a more optimistic view of human destiny. For Sri Aurobindo this existential attitude is a preliminary rather than a final wisdom. In the deeper integral wisdom suffering can be transcended through transforming all those parts which seem to suffer.

Gestalt therapy: Sri Aurobindo agrees with the Gestalt therapist that the individual should know the whole first before entering into the various parts; this wholeness is the soul of the individual's self-actualising tendency.

The Gestalt therapist, like Sri Aurobindo, aims at an emotional transformation through cultivation of positive emotions, equanimity, and reduction of destructive emotions, not through suppression or repression but through a clear awareness of them and consciously relinquishing them where necessary.

But Sri Aurobindo may question the Gestalt therapists regarding the importance of one's limited ego in relation to outer realms (the environment). They do not give any value of the annihilation of the ego; a transcended ego need not defend itself and brings together the inner and outer realm.

Sri Aurobindo does not integrate Gestalt's concept of holism in his integralism.

The New Encyclopeadia Britannica defines holism as "a philosophical theory based on the presuppositions of emergent evolution, that entirely new things—'wholes' are produced by a creative force within the universe; they are consequently more than mere rearrangements of particles that already existed".

In Gestalt holism refers to a theory according to which a whole cannot be analysed without residue into the sum of its parts, it emphasises the organic or functional relation between parts and wholes rather than an atomistic approach. Even though holism includes the spiritual realm of Being into its unitive principles it appears that this holistic integrative principle is more or less based on the external superficial association between various parts.

For Sri Aurobindo the interrelations between the various parts of the being are very complex and many-sided and cannot be expressed in a single formula like holism. The organic unity of the various parts is a characteristic only of the external being, but their true synthesis can be discovered only in a deeper unitary principle of the power of the Spirit within the individual, i.e., the psychic or spiritual being. Diverse principles do not unite on their original level but are first transformed and then enter into a greater synthesis. Only this self-realising power of the Spirit, which is not the structure of an artificial or natural organism, is able to effectively unite the chaotic parts of the being.

Psychoanalysis: Sri Aurobindo agrees with Freud's basic views regarding the contents of the unconscious; "It is the sub-mental base of the being and is made up of impressions, instincts, habitual movements that are stored there; it contains the potentiality of all primitive reactions of life ... it retains the impressions of all our past experiences of life and they can come up from there in dream forms ... but also all that is consciously experienced sinks down into the subconscient as obscure yet obstinate impressions of experiences.... All too that is suppressed without being wholly got rid of sinks down there and remains as seed ready to surge up or sprout up at any moment.... The action of the subconscient is irrational, mechanical, repetitive, ... it is a thing of habits and memories and repeats persistently or whenever it can old suppressed reactions, reflexes, mental, vital or physical responses ... the subconscient is the main cause why all things repeat themselves and nothing gets changed except in appearance".[4]

However, this part of the subconscient must not be confused with the subliminal part of the being which is not at all incoherent but well organised. It is in full possession of a mind, a life-force and a clear subtle-physical sense of things; it has the same capacities as one's waking being only more developed, more sovereign. Freud's lower vital subconscious is only a very inferior portion of the subliminal whole. According to Sri Aurobindo, "When we go back into ourselves very deep away from the surface appearance, we find that the mind, heart and sensational being of man are moved by forces not under his own control and that he can become an instrument in the hands of Energies of a cosmic character without knowing the origin of his actions.... He can realise that he is not a conscious creature inexplicably produced in an unconscious world out of a seed of inconscient Matter and moving about in an obscure self-ignorance, but an embodied soul through whose action cosmic Nature is seeking to fulfil itself".[5]

For Freud the meaning of likeness between "oceanic feeling" and psychopathology is unambiguous, these feelings usually involve something in disguise and are often related to a regression of the individual's earliest encounters of his past rather than the positive unfolding aspects of a creative experience. Much of religion and spiritual behaviour is a projection of unconscious wishes and the transcendent state of consciousness has no validity on its own; it is only an infantile aberration to turn the adult away from reality. But it seems Freud mixes up the copresence of different orders of experience, explaining one in terms of the other.

According to Sri Aurobindo, "They [the Freudians] look from down up and explain the higher lights by the lower obscurities; but the foundation of these things is above and not below".[6]

Freud described the oceanic feeling as a sense of unbounded oneness with the universe that seeks "the resurrection of infantile helplessness". But for Sri Aurobindo annihilation of the ego is not a return to the feelings of infancy but a return of the true spiritual person in which the seeker is no longer bound to ignorance and disharmony.

Sri Aurobindo is aware that many psychological problems can be traced to the chaotic action of the subconscient elements of the being. For an integral transformation the subconscient must be made conscious and completely conquered.

However, for Sri Aurobindo, psychoanalysis using mental analysis in its method for gaining insight into unconscious processes remains relatively fragmentary. Mind according to Sri Aurobindo, as an instrument of analysis and synthesis has its inherent limitations and is therefore incapable of knowing the whole in its essential nature as described by him; "Mind in its essence is a consciousness which measures, limits, cuts out forms of things from the indivisible whole and contains them as if each were a separate integer ... this essential characteristic of Mind conditions the workings of all its operative powers, whether conception, perception, sensation or the dealings of creative thought.... All its action and enjoyment deal thus with wholes that form part of a greater whole, and these subordinate wholes again are broken up into parts which are also treated as wholes for the particular purposes they serve".[7] This limited mind views every phenomenon as a thing-in-itself, separating part from a whole without arriving at the sense of true unity. Psychoanalysis describes the whole of a vast complexity in terms of a small part, but for Sri Aurobindo the mind must know the whole first before it can know the part.

As the seeker has no knowledge and therefore no control of the obscure part of the subconscient, Sri Aurobindo advises the sadhak not to descend into this part of the subconscient. A mental insight can give the seeker only some indirect insight of these hidden activities and often the sadhak plunges into incoherence or is likely to fall into many confusions. On the other hand, it is only by drawing back into the subliminal or by ascending into the superconscient and from there looking down into these obscure depths that the seeker can become directly aware of and gain control over the dark areas of one's subconscient nature.

No doubt, in sadhana the seeker can minimize the trouble by putting the right will and right habit of reaction in the subconscient parts, but this will not yield to a deep-rooted change; only when the higher consciousness and Truth-light are brought to the subconscient it is able to change.

Sri Aurobindo would differ with the Freudian method of raising up and stressing psychological difficulties, accepting and approving their presence as the only way to get rid them. In sadhana it is a mistake to dwell too much on the lower nature and its obstacles. They are not to be evaded but preoccupation with them is not very helpful. It is well to see what the dark side of the apparent aspect of the instrumental being is, and how it acts, but to dwell solely on the dark parts of the subconscient and its aspects of imperfection creates depression and should therefore be avoided. Certainly, the more the lower nature is purified the easier is the descent of the higher Nature, but for Sri Aurobindo it is more true that the more the higher Nature descends, the more the lower is purified. In the course of sadhana purification of the lower and descent of the higher do not come all at once but go on progressing side by side.

Sri Aurobindo's views regarding Freud's psychoanalysis is best expressed in his own words: "The psycho-analysis of Freud is the last thing that one should associate with yoga. It takes up a certain part, the darkest, the most perilous, the unhealthiest part of the nature, the lower vital subconscious layer, isolates some of its most morbid phenomena and attributes to it and them an action out of all proportion to its true role in nature.... Moreover, the exaggeration of the importance of suppressed sexual complexes is a dangerous falsehood and it can have a nasty influence and tend to make the mind and vital more and not less fundamentally impure than before. . . But the lower vital subconscious which is all that this psycho-analysis of Freud seems to know, —and even of that it knows only a few ill-lit corners, —is no more than a restricted and very inferior portion of the subliminal whole.... If one wishes to purify and transform the nature, it is the power of these higher ranges to which one must open and raise to them and change by them both the subliminal and the surface being.... But to begin by opening up the lower subconscious, risking to raise up all that is foul or obscure in it, is to go out of one's way to invite trouble. First, one should make the higher mind and vital strong and firm and full of light and peace from above; afterwards one can open up or even dive into the subconscious with more safety and some chance of a rapid and successful change".[8]

As mentioned previously, Sri Aurobindo agrees with Freud that many of the obstinate psychopathological disturbances can be traced to the subconscient elements of the being, and while recognising the influence of the past he nevertheless suggests the seeker to be cautious about re-energizing painful processes from the past. The unconscious might be relatively cleared, but it can easily accumulate a new large amount of conflictual material if the sadhak's mental habits and attitudes towards himself and life are not changed. For Sri Aurobindo the more the seeker is exclusively fixed on the darker areas the more he becomes subject to them; the innumerable rediscovered ego-desires only obscures the urge for spiritual realisation and turns the seeker away from the highest levels. "The superconscient, not the subconscient, is the true foundation of things.... That is the promise of the greater psychology awaiting its hour before which these poor gropings will disappear and come to nothing".[9]

2. Psycho-Spiritual Concepts in Transpersonal Psychology and Sri Aurobindo's Writings

There is an increased interest in psycho-spiritual concepts and their influences on psychotherapeutical processes. Various transpersonal psychologists differentiate the soul and Spirit in the widespread confusion between psychotherapy and spiritual disciplines.

Maslow relates the real self to Being, the inner core of the individual in relation to reality including the Cosmic consciousness. Maslow consciously choose not to get into metaphysical statements on the nature of reality as distinct from experience. His "enlarged self" is a fusion of the highest individual self with non-self in a metapsychological sense. It is higher than the individual self, but Maslow in his natural mysticism remains vague about the transpersonal self, it is a phenomenological state within the limits of extraordinary humanness.

Assagioli's personal self is a reflection of the spiritual or transpersonal Self. The spiritual Self is the centre around which superconscious processes take place, but it is also the cause of these processes and the source of the energy which makes these processes possible. It is the eternal, unchangeable reality in which individuality merges and unites with universality. Assagioli's concept of the spiritual Self closely approaches the concept of "Atman" in Indian psychology.

Wilber differentiates the soul from psyche and spirit. In the soul realm, the soul communes with God but there still remains an irreducible boundary between them, whereas in the realm of Spirit, the soul becomes Being. Beyond the transpersonal realm lies the Absolute Spirit, Spirit as the ground of the process of human evolution. For Wilber, like Sri Aurobindo, evolution is related to the process of self-actualisation of the Spirit, where the Self is united with its infinite and eternal Wholeness.

The term psyche, often replaced by the term soul, refers mostly to the psychological self-awareness at any level of the spectrum, (like Jung's totality of all psychological principles and functions in man) whereas the soul refers to the subtle self-sense in the various realms of existence, (like Jung's inner personality.)

Vaughan distinguishes the transpersonal Self from the soul, she considers them not identical. "The term soul in relation to psychotherapy has religious connotations and as simple subject of awareness may be identified with any level of consciousness [Wilber's Spectrum of Consciousness] whereas the transpersonal Self has transcended former identifications".[10]

Vaughan's transpersonal self, though it is beyond the personal, does not deny the validity or importance of individual uniqueness and it is therefore not yet Absolute Spirit. She distinguishes the transpersonal from the transcendent in that the former refers to the transcendental as manifested in and through the person. "The transpersonal Self that transcends personal boundaries, remains as an experiencer, distinct from what is experienced".[11] The transpersonal Self includes awareness of the soul but is not exclusively identified with it; it is an integrated principle operating at every level of development.

Washburn takes the Dynamic Ground as Spirit, the ultimate and greater Self against the subordinate ego as a lesser self. The small self is an actually existing self but in itself incomplete, beneath it there exists the big Self, the ultimate Ground. In Washburn's dynamic dialectical model psychological development ultimately leads to the unification of the higher Self of Spirit and the lower self of the ego-subject. The power of the Spirit is a fundamental reality of the soul and not merely an explanatory construction. "As psychic energy, it amplifies experience across all dimensions and, as spirit, it effects dramatic transformations of the ego and of subjective life generally".[12]

Hillman in his "Re-visioning Psychology" equates the soul with psyche, "By having its own realm psyche has its has its own logic-psychology—which is neither a science of physical things nor a metaphysics of spiritual things".[13] However, the soul has become identified with spirit but the world of spirit is different indeed. It moves and operates in a field of transcendence among ultimates and absolutes, whereas soul sticks to the realm of experiences and to reflections within experiences.

For Sri Aurobindo psyche and spirit are two different things and should not be confused together.

The Spirit is an essential entity which does not need to think or perceive, because whatever knowledge it has is direct or essential knowledge.

The psyche is related to psychological principles whereas the Spirit is identified with metaphysical principles. Each realm has its own rules and perspectives.

For Sri Aurobindo, the Spirit is the Atman, Brahman, which is always in oneness with the Divine, "In its supreme status the Spirit is the supreme Conscious Being and the Consciousness-Force in his supreme Nature, ...; in the supreme spiritual status it becomes the Being of Bliss and pure Existence".[14]

Sri Aurobindo's self is the highest centre of pure consciousness also called Atman which is free, eternal and transcendent. This Self is more than universal or individual mind, life and body, they are only its forms and not the true Self. By detaching oneself from all identifications with these forms the individual can get back to the consciousness of the true Individual, the eternal Being and pure Existence. The Self is immanent in all things, embracing the individual in the universal as well as transcending the universe. It is something self-existent, pure and eternal.

Sri Aurobindo makes no distinction between the Self and Spirit, the Self is the divine element within the individual that is not affected by the evolution. The Spirit is always one with the Divine and in its nature is either transcendent or universal. When it individualises it is called the Jivatman which remains aware of its oneness with the universal and transcendent, but at the same time feels its central identity/individuality as a portion of the Divine.

Sri Aurobindo regards the Self an entity in itself, and as the ultimate source of consciousness with its illuminative and transformative capabilities: it is considered as a portion of the Divine, involving itself in Matter and transforming it through several mutations into the Divine.

In the embodied individual the Spirit appears as the *psychic Entity*, a pure power of light, love and refined essence of being, "the inner voice of the mystic".

The word psychic is ordinarily used as anything phenomenal in psychology (such as the ego), but Sri Aurobindo uses the word psychic for the soul differentiating it from the mental-vital consciousness. According to Sri Aurobindo, "the word psychic is used in English to indicate anything that is other or deeper than the external mind, life and body or it indicates sometimes anything occult or supraphysical; but that is a use which brings confusion and error and we have almost entirely to discard it".[15]

All movements of the soul are related to the psychic, and where the mind and vital predominate the movements are called psychological, i.e., the Western psychologist dealing with mental movements. Sri Aurobindo uses the term psychic as "a spark come from the Divine which is there in all things and as the individual evolves it grows in him and manifests as the psychic being, the soul, seeking always for the Divine and the Truth".[16]

The soul, as a representative of the Jivatman is not a compound but a thing in itself, it is a power of the Divine Consciousness which does not disintegrate and is always turned towards Truth, Good and Beauty.

This psychic part within the individual has in its origin divine possibilities and it supports the lower triple manifestation of mind, life and body.

The divine element within each individual is not at first developed but hidden behind the ordinary consciousness; once it grows by the accumulation of deeper and higher movements it develops into a psychic individuality, *the psychic being,* which is often the secret cause of man's turning to the spiritual life.

The psychic being, as a psychic individuality, stands behind the mental, vital and physical nature, transforming them until all is ready for the union with the Divine.

The psychic entity, the soul in its essence, and *the psychic being,* the soul in its individual form are therefore not the same. The soul as the eternal essence is the divine spark that dwells at the centre of each being, whereas the psychic being is shaped progressively around the soul during terrestrial evolution. According to Sri Aurobindo, "It is the psychic personality in us that flowers as the saint, the sage, the seer; when it reaches its full strength, it turns the being towards the Knowledge of Self and the Divine, towards the supreme Truth, the supreme Good, the supreme Beauty, Love and Bliss, the divine heights and largeness, and opens us to the touch of spiritual sympathy, universality, oneness".[17]

The psychic being can be located in the transpersonal realm as it forms the depth-dimension of the inner reality and opens the individual towards universality and is in constant relation with it.

3. Transpersonal Psychology and Integral Yoga Psychology

Transpersonal psychology considers the human psyche as an open and transcendental system of consciousness. Its purpose is to widen the concept of human nature and bring about a synthesis between the modern scientific approach and traditional Eastern and Western insights into human psychology. It provides a basis for cross-cultural psychology emphasising the study of transcendental and religious experiences and man's higher functions, so as to become able to grasp the unifying and universal elements which are characteristic of all cultures.

Transpersonal psychology as well as integral Yoga psychology take consciousness as the true subject matter of psychology. Both are concerned with the utmost development of the latent possibilities of human nature and both aim at a higher state of consciousness through the transcendence of the ego.

Transpersonal psychology endeavours to carry life to perfection through the realisation of the various higher values of humanity and emphasises the need for a spiritual reorientation of life. According to R. Walsh and F. Vaughan in the introduction of Paths Beyond Ego; "There exist within us, however, latent but unexplored creative capacities, depths of psyche, states of consciousness, and stages of development undreamed of by most people. Transpersonal disciplines have emerged to explore these possibilities, they emerged first in psychology".[18]

In the last 25 years Transpersonal psychology has moved beyond its psychological investigation and now includes areas such as transpersonal sociology, anthropology and psychiatry. Its studies are no longer used only by transpersonal psychologists but also by social scientists, mental health practitioners and clinicians.

Sri Aurobindo explains in a similar way man's potential for spiritual growth as he writes; "if the common human mind has begun to admit the ideas proper to the higher order that is in the end to be, and the heart of man has begun to be stirred by aspirations born of these ideas, then there is a hope of some advance in the not distant future. And here the first essential sign must be the idea of the soul, the inner being, its powers, its possibilities, its growth, its expression and the creation of a true, beautiful and helpful environment for it as the one thing of first and last importance".[19] However, these favourable ideas are not enough, more is needed. The general aspiration of mankind toward the idea of the kingdom of God on earth to be effective must be supported by a dynamic recreation of individual manhood in the spiritual type.

The transpersonal psychologist focuses on the psychological interpretation of the seeker's spiritual concerns and in its aim towards spiritual humanitarianism he admits the possibility of a cosmic consciousness in humanity but the transpersonal psychologist remains simultaneously exclusively occupied with humanity. For Sri Aurobindo the feeling of oneness with all beings does not mean humanity only, but includes all earth-life. Man is here to affirm himself in the universe, but also to evolve and finally to exceed himself.

In integral Yoga psychology the values of humanity have been subordinated to those of the Spirit as it is the soul which is the source of all values. The supreme end of life is the realisation of higher spiritual values, but without neglecting the values of life and humanity. Integral Yoga psychology aims at the integration of the values of humanity with the realisation of spiritual self-perfection. But for Sri Aurobindo, unlike transpersonal psychology, human nature cannot have its complete fulfilment without a dynamic realisation of the unity and identity of the self in the Spirit, "the outflowering of the Divine in man". He is convinced of the higher grades of self-manifestation of the Divine in the life of evolving humanity.

Both psychologies are optimistic regarding the possibility of the development of higher spiritual actualities unknown so far, but for Sri Aurobindo not only higher principles will be at work in the near future, he also claims the growth of new principles which cannot be understood by any of the principles which are recognised today by our present state of knowledge.

The emergence of new principles is not based on the inactivity or disappearance of the older principles. In order to give rise to the new, it changes the nature of the older so that they may become fit instruments for the new and will continue in a transformed condition. The acceptance of this new illuminative spiritual principle is not merely based on an intellectual seeking of something higher beyond, (mental will and interest) but has to be seized by the heart's aspiration, i, e., has to be lived.

Consequently, this spiritual ideal is of no avail for humanity until it is lived, lived inwardly while outward life flows out of this inward living.

Wilber "does not think that the world is entering anything resembling a 'new age' or 'transpersonal transformation' but he believes that transpersonal studies always will be that one beacon to men and women who see Spirit in the world and the world in Spirit".[20] Sri Aurobindo, on the contrary, maintains that "the dynamic side of the spiritual urge has not been absent, —the aspiration to a spiritual mastery and mutation of Nature, to a spiritual perfection of the being, a divinisation of the mind, the heart and the very body; there has even been the dream or a psychic prevision of a fulfilment exceeding the individual transformation, a new earth and heaven, a city of God, a divine descent upon earth, a kingdom of God not only within us but outside, in a collective human life. However obscure may have been some of the forms taken by this aspiration, the indication they contain of the urge of the occult spiritual being within to emergence in earth-nature is unmistakable".[21]

Integral Yoga psychology and Transpersonal psychology view man as an evolutionary being, the existential status of man is not denied but needs to be actualised, and both are concerned with the earnest enquiry into the deeper significance of life.

Transpersonal psychologists in their transpersonal orientation confine themselves to the evocation of the highest potential in human beings, the full realisation of human possibilities thereby restricting themselves to the mental realm.

For Sri Aurobindo mind can never be a perfect instrument for the Spirit, it can exceed its own sphere into a higher range of existence peculiar to the superior hemisphere, but it cannot bring down its greater spiritual nature into the lower triple nature. A spiritualised mind is essential for the fullness of one's total inner growth, as without it this inner growth may be erratic and mixed with unspiritual elements.

However, for Sri Aurobindo, unlike the transpersonal psychologist, this spiritualised mind may create certain inner changes but until it disengages itself from the preliminary mental approaches and opens the door to inner realisations by a transmutation of the consciousness, it cannot create in mental man the spiritual being; it can exercise an influence on earth-life but not bring about a transformation of that life. "The mental being can develop a spiritual interest or preoccupation and may evolve perhaps in consequence a spiritual as well as intellectual mentality; ... but there can be no such thing as a spiritual being taking up and transforming the mental into the spiritual nature. There is no evolution of the spiritual man; there is only an evolution of a new and possibly a finer and rarer element in a mental being".[22]

Sri Aurobindo therefore distinguishes the mental from the spiritual realisation. In transpersonal terms this could be translated as the distinction of the transpersonal realisation (the realised mental being) from the integral realisation (the realised spiritual being), characterising the latter as superior and divine and the former as inferior and human.

To the divine belongs infinite Being, Consciousness and Bliss; to the human belong the three human principles, the physical, vital and mental beings seeking the Divine. Even when the mental being realises the Divine, it sees it as a superior plane of being, as a supreme state of existence, and the gulf between the Divine being and the human being remains unbridged. Only when the mentalised being is spiritualised, and thereby changed into the image of the Divine, does a unification of the human with the Divine become possible.

When man becomes mentally aware of the Spirit as something superior to his normal mind it has some effects on his inner nature but the transpersonal psychologist, in his partial formulations of the spiritualised mind, is not able to establish a complete change within the spiritual seeker or to establish a new principle, a permanent new order of being in the field of terrestrial nature; it is the emergence of the Spirit as a new power that must finally excel the mental part and replace it as the leader of life and nature.

Spirituality for Sri Aurobindo is not a high intellectuality, moral purity, or mental belief or faith, these things are of considerable value to mind and life, preparatory movements to the spiritual evolution but in themselves they belong to the mental evolution. The spiritual being can only emerge when the Spirit is free from its present limitations of the psycho-physical instrumentation.

Nevertheless, Transpersonal psychology and integral Yoga psychology are not contradictory to each other; they are rather complementary, representing different levels of health and growth, simply dealing with different ranges of human development.

The achievement of psychological insight enhances the possibility of spiritual potentialities. In its quest for total integration Transpersonal psychology draws upon a wide range of therapies for an effective means of facilitating holistic health. It does not remain content with the investigation of the lower planes of being, but includes consideration of the vast resources of the spiritual realm, lifting the personality to higher planes of being, beyond self-actualisation.

Transpersonal psychology is therefore very useful in the preparation of the individual to become stable and strong, providing the spiritual seeker with a first illuminating insight before he enters the difficult path of Sri Aurobindo's integral Yoga.

Sri Aurobindo's psycho-spiritual perception of the integral structure of the Being includes the transpersonal views, the integration of the psychological and spiritual realms, but he also envisages an all-encompassing spiritual world-view and provides a sound working conception of an integral spiritual psychology. For Sri Aurobindo "Yoga is nothing but practical psychology".

When Transpersonal psychology and integral Yoga psychology are well combined in their true balance than their views, each with its own reality, are correlative. According to M. Reddy: "From their meeting (Yoga and psychotherapy) there may well result an enlargement and intensification of consciousness which will inaugurate a new and more hopeful era for mankind. The East by itself has not achieved it, and the West by itself has so far ignominously failed to do so. The wisdom and genius of the two combined might accomplish what neither can do alone".[23] All the experiences of the transpersonal psychologist receive their true value and are accepted by integral Yoga psychology, but ultimately they are filled with the light of a greater Spirit.

4. Transpersonal Psychotherapy and Integral Sadhana

Transpersonal psychology envisages the possibility of developing higher areas of awareness through transpersonally-oriented therapeutical activities. But as previously mentioned it seems that a medical approach to "healing" within a transpersonal perspective sounds paradoxical, as the transpersonal field has no finite limits. It could be better classified as a guidance towards a universal yearning for the transcendence of apparent human limitations or an understanding and unfoldment of a transpersonal way of life rather than as a therapy.

In man's innate spiritual aspiration there is a tendency towards inner self-discovery, a groping after the inner self and the drive towards the establishment of the spiritual consciousness in the being. For Sri Aurobindo this foundation of the spiritual consciousness is the sole preoccupation of the spiritual seeker.

Though the transpersonal psychotherapist uses transpersonal experiences as an integral part of the therapeutic process and though he aims beyond the traditional ego-goals, he nevertheless stresses the importance of establishing the ego-identity before it can be relinquished. Ego development is viewed as a stage along the way. Surrendering to something greater than oneself requires a degree of self-autonomy and self-determination.

The surrender of egocentricity is related to altruism or selfless service in the world by which the individual ego becomes less-all-important. After all, the principal focus of transpersonal effort remains centred on growth towards a fuller human functioning.

Sri Aurobindo too maintains the necessity for the development of the ego as essential for the lower life, but for the higher life the elimination of the ego becomes indispensable.

In Sri Aurobindo's views the ego needs to be replaced by the true spiritual being, individual yet universal, universal yet self-transcendent, unlike the transpersonal therapist who replaces the individual ego by a collective ego.

The transpersonal collective existence must not be confused with Sri Aurobindo's cosmic self which is spiritual in essence. The transpersonal subordination of the ego to the progress of the human race is a mental ideal and not like Sri Aurobindo's spiritual ideal; the spiritual aim is founded on a sense of the Divine in all rather than serving the sum total of individual egos.

Spirituality belongs to a world beyond the one manifested to us by our mind and senses, it can be experienced but it is difficult to explain spiritual experiences within the scope of human intellect and language. As in scientific enquiry which passes beyond the physical senses but which remains limited by the rational enquiry, so the search for the vast field of spiritual phenomena passes beyond the scientific enquiry, and ordinary reason is therefore unable to test the data of spiritual experiences and the validity of their existence. Nevertheless spiritual experiences lead the seeker to the direct essence of the Spirit and to the facts of the spiritual world, which lie beyond the phenomenal world.

Sri Aurobindo as well as the transpersonal psychotherapist look at the spiritual or mystical experience as something different from the normal waking consciousness. Both wish to give the spiritual experience a place in the natural area of experience within the human personality.

All causes and conditions for a spiritual experience are already within the individual's psyche and only need to be germinated to arrive at maturity.

They may occur in the context of virtually any activity or any situation where perfection can be attained. The spiritual experience as such refers to an expansion of human consciousness which gives the individual insight into his own inner potentials.

H. Chaudhuri maintains that although the authentic transpersonal experience—a human experience on a deeper level of consciousness—does play a vital role in our total self-development, yet no transpersonal experience can possibly be complete and final. He rightly asks: "If the transpersonal self be in the final analysis a mode of being of the person's pure consciousness wherein does the difference lie between humanistic and transpersonal psychology?".[24]

For Sri Aurobindo the transpersonal experience cannot be the highest possible experience, these experiences though transcending the ego are not necessarily integral and spiritual (pertaining to or concerning the Spirit).

The individual in the transcendent experience transcends the psychodynamic level and enters into the transpersonal realm—unifying spiritual and psychological perspectives—but for the transpersonal psychotherapist these transpersonal experiences remain a specific mode of human experience.

Though the transpersonal therapist deals with the experience of an extension of identity beyond the usual limits of the ego and personality, beyond time and space, and enquires into the essential nature of Being, these explorations remain confined to the highest reaches of human nature and it seems that the transpersonal psychotherapist is more concerned with the concept of "human" instead of the "divine".

For Sri Aurobindo the individual being cannot be nature's ultimate aim, the universal and transcendental being are closely related to it and only by an experiential understanding of these determinants is the individual able to transcend his own limited ego-aspects.

The transpersonal experience, in transcending the ego, creates the universalisation of being, an expansion of consciousness to the dimensions of the entire universe. But this universalisation of being is for Sri Aurobindo not an objective extension of the empirical consciousness. Impulses towards social consciousness are in the ultimate analysis mental impulses and therefore limited in application and not free from egoism.

In Sri Aurobindo's spiritual self-realisation the individual realises the Divine in humanity; the self-surrender towards the Divine indicates the beginning of a new life of activity, the true universalisation of being which removes the barriers between individual and collective human existence. The realisation of the Spirit in the depth of one's being expresses itself in a selfless service of humanity and therein lies the ideal reconstruction of human existence. It is the collective ideal of the Divine that carries with it the solution and remedy of the disharmonies of human existence.

For the transpersonal psychotherapist the principal focus of transpersonal effort remains centred on growth towards a fuller human functioning. But to move the present psychological situation towards a renewal, the transpersonal therapist has to abandon his most tenacious convictions regarding the functioning of man and find the comprehending essence of man, i.e., to move to the divine to meet the needs of the soul.

The transpersonal experiences are active creations of the psyche and therefore not objective contemplations about or reflections of a separate existing reality. For Sri Aurobindo, the various ways to inner freedom are accompanied by a complete personal surrender to the higher Power, the Divine, and not the surrender of the psyche to the individual potentials, whatever these potentials may be.

Transpersonal psychotherapy in its scientific approach does not recognize any transpersonal self-substance, the evolving soul of man, as an independent psychic structure beyond the limits of human consciousness.

In Transpersonal psychology the soul is only a hypothesis but in integral sadhana the realisation of the soul is pursued as a matter of experience. This reality behind the surface ego can be known by going deep within oneself, "when we have seen both ourself and our nature as a whole". The soul-entity in the transcendental realm is not identical with the chemical components of the body, although without them it would have no means of material expression. The individual can realize and conceptualise the psychic being for himself but can never localise it on the experimental table, i.e., one cannot dissect the soul under a microscope.

Transpersonal conclusions may be empirically true but this is no reason why these psychological truths must remain confined within the limits of phenomenal validity only; an attempt should be made to make these truths valid from the highest, the ultimate standpoint which transcends the empirical.

For Sri Aurobindo a constant psychic consciousness enables the seeker to feel each impure movement of his nature, not as the mental impurity of the conscient, but as the wrong play of energy casting a veil upon the divine attitude of the psychic.

Sadhana often generates an intense effect and has its potential risks of phases of chaos. However, in the course of practice the psychic transformation enables the sadhak to tackle his problems in a more orderly but also more transcendent manner, and the disintegrated mental structure gets united into a synthetic entity. For Sri Aurobindo the divine Guide of the sadhana is the psychic being, a mental rule or mental consciousness cannot be its leader. It is always the psychic being that is the real cause of man's turning to the spiritual life and his greatest help in it. It is the psychic being which opens the whole lower nature to the Divine and prepares it for the descent of the higher consciousness into this instrumental being.

Transpersonal psychology envisages the possibility of developing higher areas of awareness through transpersonally-oriented therapeutical activities. These therapeutical activities play an important role in stimulating the individual's effort in the process of psycho-spiritual growth, but are not meant to stimulate behaviour modification.

However, transpersonal psycho-spiritual methods such as meditation, dream-analysis, imagination, bodywork, etc, have a much deeper meaning for Sri Aurobindo. In integral sadhana these methods are founded on a system of psycho-spiritual thought and are seen in a wider spiritual context including the path of Karma and Bhakti.

The results of the transpersonal investigations can be questioned on the ground that spiritual issues cannot be investigated in isolation but need to be contextualised, viewing them in the light of classical ancestry; such a task can be undertaken only by those skilled investigators who are directly involved in, or a least familiar with the specific spiritual discipline and its actual practices.

The transpersonal therapist in his attempt to explore the spiritual realm, using therapeutical and scientific methods should therefore not omit the context in which spiritual disciplines are developed, and he should also describe its intending purpose as well as its conditions for a rightful application. In its application of transpersonal-therapeutical methods, the transpersonal psychotherapist might abolish all the individual's ego-limitations, but this does not automatically lead to the experience of unity with the Divine. As long as the individual lacks a proper spiritual attitude, aspiration for as well as an opening and surrender to the Divine, then all psychological methods may be very valuable for the integration of the personality but need not bring the individual into direct contact with his spiritual development.

Integral Yoga is not primarily concerned with the attainment of a particular psychological state, and though psychological health is a necessary preliminary step towards perfection and integration, it is in the elaboration of the goals of the spiritual liberated individual that Sri Aurobindo sharply diverges from any form of Western psychotherapy. If the seeking of transcendence is the highest goal for the transpersonal psychotherapist, beyond self-actualisation, then it seems inappropriate to equate the transpersonal realm with therapy.

5. Psychological Problems Inherent in the Process of Spiritual Development

Transpersonal psychotherapy as well as integral Yoga psychology aim at the inner growth of the individual, the transpersonal development beyond the ego state in which the ego does not disappear but is transcended. This process of spiritual development has its challenges and difficulties, and might be accompanied by a psycho-spiritual crisis as a spontaneous effort of the organism to heal itself.

According to S. Grof, "for some individuals the transformational journey of spiritual development becomes a 'spiritual emergency', a crisis in which the changes within are so rapid that, temporarily, these people may find it difficult to operate fully in everyday reality".[25] When taken care of, these states of mind can offer potential benefits for inner growth and the development of new levels of awareness.

For any therapist, as well as for Sri Aurobindo, a certain minimal ego-strength is necessary prior to undertaking therapy or sadhana respectively. Though transpersonal psychotherapy aims beyond the traditional ego goals, it nevertheless stresses the importance of establishing the ego-identity before it can be relinquished. The positive aspects of the ego are utilised for improving psychological growth, a fully developed ego seems to be a pre-requisite for spiritual growth and its development is viewed as a necessary stage along the way.

For Sri Aurobindo too the development of the ego is seen as necessary to the evolution of the individuality in the early stages, and is not to be regarded as evil. He considers the development of individuality as an essential precondition for spiritual growth: "Man has to find himself as a mental and vital ego before he can find himself as the soul or spirit. Untill he has thus developed his individuality, his personality, he can not be fit for the greater work before him or successfully turn his faculties to higher, larger and more divine ends".[26] However, a fortified individuality is not the essence of the being; it is not a lasting truth, although it is necessary for effective action in normal human life. Once the individual has sufficiently developed his ego, his whole existence stands in need of an explanation other than an egoistic self-affirmation. When the individual delivers himself from divisive egoistic motives, when his ego is replaced by the true spiritual person, he commands a wider life, a larger existence, and higher consciousness.

As mentioned previously, ego development is essential for the lower life, but for the higher life the reverse movement of elimination of the ego becomes indispensable. So long as the higher consciousness does not descend, the ego remains a necessity even in aspiring towards the Divine. Only in the higher consciousness can the ego be dissolved, either by ascending there or by a descent of the higher consciousness into the consciousness below.

However, he warns the sadhak against the potential danger of a pathological condition that may occur in the process of Sadhana due to the false identification of the subjective ego consciousness with the spiritual Self. This dangerous ego enlargement vanishes only through the seekers' surrender to the Divine, a subordination to the all-encompassing spiritual principle.

Contrary to this process of ego-inflation is the danger of the insufficiently developed ego in the process of ego-transcendence. In Eastern traditions the ideal of ego-transcendence in the spiritual attainment through detachment can be easily seen as an unconscious fear of human responsibilities or an escape into "Oceanic mysticism", a flight into an unknown cosmic paradise before the seeker is fully conscious of the existence of his own ego, i.e., the transcendence of an underdeveloped ego.

Spiritual techniques without a prior clear-cut understanding of the ultimate goal of dynamic self-integration with the sacred realm might provide an escape from the hardship of life into a naive paradise. Without deeper knowledge the sadhak's spiritual practice deteriorates gradually toward rigidity and the whole process becomes mechanical.

There might be a tendency of an exaggerated interpretation of emotional problems as spiritual developments, and psychopathological symptoms can be easily mistaken for transpersonal processes. In such cases Transpersonal therapy is only used to compensate major pathological conditions.

Confusion might also arise in the incompetence of the sadhak's psychological condition, when he does not *comprehend* the increasing spiritual forces operating within him due to the re-release of old patterns which are coming to the surface or some other immature ego conflicts. Spiritual experiences as altered states of consciousness can be of great value and a stepping stone on the path towards losing the limited ego, but the same experience can have a frightening effect when the sadhak is overwhelmed by the inrush of spiritual energy which might temporarily disrupt the ego rather than transcending it.

Other problems may arise during the practice of sadhana when the individual is unable to *assimilate* the inflow of spiritual forces due to an unbalanced mental-emotional excitement or inadequate ego development. In such situations the seeker is not likely to be liberated from his unconscious deep-rooted fears, habitual resistances and repressed unconscious processes or any other psychopathological obstacles in general through sadhana alone, on the contrary, such psychological obstructions are a hindrance for growth. Obstructions of serious nature are impedimental for spiritual growth and therefore remain demanding the seeker's psychological attention. Even though these problems are only temporary reactions, they do not always disappear by themselves.

These difficulties are not fully elaborated by Sri Aurobindo, his integral Yoga does not explore the formative maturation process from ego-childhood to ego-adulthood. Sri Aurobindo's mystical views as an end-product of his psycho-spiritual experiment are not always destined for the unstable beginning practitioner of integral sadhana.

For the practice of sadhana he takes the developed integral personality for granted, but by doing so he overlooks those sadhaks with psychological conflicts in their ego-maturity. Some seekers have to go through a process of painful reorganisation of unresolved ego conflicts before they can rebuild and transcend them.

It is for this reason that the transpersonal psychotherapist, working within a spiritually oriented therapy, would advise the forthcoming spiritual practitioner to work through personal psychodynamic issues first, in order to clarify underlying psychological problems before the emergence of spiritual awakening takes place. Only a strong psychological grounding, a mature level of ego organisation allows the practitioner to enter into those spiritual practices which aim at a manifestation of mature psycho-spiritual development, i.e., ego transcendence and development of awareness to cope with the powerful spiritual energies and processes. Unresolved egoic issues may unnecessarily complicate spiritual growth in the transpersonal realm.

For transpersonal psychotherapists many psychological maladies first require strengthening of ego rather than liberation from the constraints of the ego. It is their credit to deal adequately with such psychological disorders which lie at the root of a disturbed growth process, and it may add a useful component to Sri Aurobindo's integral approach.

Besides these difficulties there is the problem which is related to the unconscious defence mechanisms. Almost all the various psychotherapeutic approaches elaborate extensively on the concept of defence mechanisms. When the client is seeking guidance for the release of psychological problems he often tends to be terrified by a dual set of forces; the desire to change and simultaneously to resist change.

Many seekers change profoundly during the process of spiritual practices and many of the problems, which otherwise might have taken them to the psychotherapist, disappear without any systematic attempt to change. Others, however, become more alienated from their own hidden aspects and use spiritual knowledge to the service of their defences.

As elaborated previously resistance, as a defence mechanism, can be broadly defined as a force within the individual that opposes change of behaviour patterns, personal interactions or a general life style. Unacceptable primitive drives or physical/vital satisfactions are invariably concealed by various mental manoevers.

For Freud, every piece of behaviour is a concealment, and the interpretation of the analyst always aims at uncovering such concealments. In Freud's psychoanalysis defence mechanisms are examples of unconscious mental processes or instrumental behaviours directed towards preserving the present self-structure. They protect the individual against external threats or against internal anxiety-arousing impulses by distorting reality in some way. The individual excludes ideas or emotions from his consciousness which are unacceptable for him.

All schools of psychotherapy agree that the internal and external reality have to be integrated and that lack of insight is caused through the defences, and all are therefore concerned with identifying these mechanisms.

Subtle resistances obscure the nature of the intrapsychic conflict and consume an inappropriate amount of psychic energy; they are not easy to observe and require a great deal of struggle with the client as well as the therapist. The goal of psychotherapy is not to remove defences but replace immature and distorting defences for more mature and realistic ones.

For the transpersonal psychotherapist the question arises regarding the consequences of those initial non-identified aspects of the self which are not made conscious in the process of transcendence of the ego.

The opening and widening of the normal consciousness to the higher consciousness, through aspiration, surrender, and ego-transcendence, while letting the creative force of the Spirit act, should not be confused with the promptings which are in reality determined by unconscious forces, wishes and desires.

For the transpersonal therapist, to hand over repressed emotions to the Divine can be easily misused as a denial to reflect upon various deep-rooted dark areas of the unconscious, in the hope that one's higher self will do the work. In other cases, during the practice of intense sadhana, (which leads to spiritual insight, and expansion of consciousness) the sadhak's defence mechanism may not always be able to withstand the onslought of confrontational experiences; the sadhak may avoid and bypass deep repressed psychological issues or some unresolved psychic conflicts. The transpersonal therapist maintains that these subtle issues should be dealt with at the personal level first. The sadhak must first encounter and master the contents of repressed unacceptable elements of the personal unconscious.

Untying the knot of the various repressions can have dramatic effects during the practice of spiritual discipline and together with other unresolved flaws might be a repeated obstacle in the process of spiritual growth. It is for this reason that the transpersonal psychotherapist uses traditional psychodynamic therapy in order to deal with such problems. They can be helpful in the beginning stage of the spiritual practice, but in itself will be inadequate for further spiritual development.

A similar view is suggested by A. Deikman in his article, "Mindfulness, spiritual seeking, and psychotherapy". For Deikman, the controlled person who is looking inside is "also determined to protect the person [him or herself] by not getting into any areas that are dangerous. Much of the training of a therapist in Western psychotherapy has to do with learning to detect those places of restricted functioning and begin to open them up, so the underlying problems they conceal can be dealt with.... Some kind of outside assistance is needed, directed specifically to the areas that the client's mind does not want to look at".[27]

It is the therapist who is able to break these unconscious defences and resolve these subtle conflicting areas. However, Deikman does admit that "these issues might be improved in the course of spiritual development but only as a secondary by-product of something that has a really different focus. " Spiritual development needs a certain degree of health and he sees "psychotherapy as providing a very important foundation from which someone might gain access to larger dimensions of reality".[28]

For Sri Aurobindo resistance, as a habitual movement of the lower part of nature, necessitates a negative element in sadhana. One of the essential objects in integral Yoga to be attained by the seeker is a certain change of consciousness, the spiritual change, and it is this change of the mind, heart and will which is obstinately resisted by the sadhak's ignorant nature. Each part of the nature wants to go on with its old movements and refuses to admit a change, because this change would subject it to something higher than itself and deprive it of its sovereignty in its own field. An overactivity of the intellectual mind prevents the doors to the inner light and a refusal to go inside, the desires of the heart block the self-giving process of the heart to the Divine, whereas the inertia of the sadhak's physical consciousness comes badly in the way of the needed change.

These obstructions have to be removed or cleared out before the unimpeded working of the Divine can have its impact on the surface nature. According to Sri Aurobindo, "There is a resistance that has to be fought out or worked out—fought out if the nature is unsteady or insists violently, worked out if the will is steady and the nature moderate in its reactions. On the other hand if there has been a long preparation and the resistances of the nature have been already largely dealt with by the psychic or by the enlightened mental will, then there are no primary or later aggravations but a steady and quiet pushing through of the change."[29]

Sri Aurobindo wants the sadhak to look quietly at the resistance, detect its cause, acknowledge it, see its workings, reject it and call down the Power and Light from above for its removal.

Sri Aurobindo is more or less aware of the problems described by the transpersonal psychologists regarding the various defence mechanisms. He writes: "for the mind and vital will always find tricks and excuses for prolonging their own reign, imposing their likes and dislikes".[30] To get out of these 'imaginary obstacles', he continues: "It is why we (in integral Yoga) always express depreciation of mental constructions and vital formulations—because they are the defence-works mind and vital throw up against their capture by the Divine.... The secret is to be firm in knocking it all down and making a tabula rasa, a foundation of calm, peace, happy openness for the true building".[31]

Sri Aurobindo is aware of the frequent re-emergence of unconscious material into the conscious mind, but the goal of sadhana is to facilitate the development of the transcendence of the ego, and the eruption of unconscious material is only a secondary by-product of the practice.

Sri Aurobindo prefers the mysterious workings of the Grace of the Divine in the individual, an action from above or from within, independent of mental causes, which decides its own movement. In the end, by constant will and aspiration for change, the divine Power is brought down into the body where it can penetrate the subconscient also and convert its resistance. But such a divine intervention seems psychologically vague, as the divine Power is often working from behind, and until the clouds vanish making place for sunshine, the seeker is advised to insist quietly for the Light and waiting in faith for it to come. "It comes (Grace) of itself intervening suddenly or with an increasing force when all is ready".[32] It needs a deep-rooted faith and aspiration pervading the whole being, and the individual cannot demand Grace; Grace is something spontaneous, the Sadhak looks for it, "but he must be ready to wait in perfect reliance—even if need be, all his life—knowing that it will come, never varying in his love and surrender because it does not come now or soon".[33]

In such cases instead of waiting all one's life for the incalculable Grace which comes often as a response to a long and persistent course of sadhana *rightly* done, Transpersonal psychology can be an expedient to avoid the danger of a preoccupation with an artficially created, enlarged ego-experience or a blind euphoric enthusiasm of a self-appealed state of trance which counterbalances the inner call. It is able to establish a sufficiently stable foundation for the development of a yogic consciousness in which the Divine Grace is allowed to work in the deeper roots of the individual's inner nature by removing obstructing unconscious resistances.

Sri Aurobindo does not elaborate extensively on the concept of psychological health. He is not directly concerned with psychological health, but associates the latter with spiritual growth. However, psychological health and spiritual growth are two different concepts, spiritual development requires a certain degree of psychological health. For the resolution of psychodynamic conflicts Transpersonal psychotherapy may be considered as a useful preparation for spiritual discipline as it provides an important foundation from which the individual might gain access to larger dimensions of reality.

It seems inappropriate to this author to equate Sri Aurobindo's integral Yoga practice with the treatment of psychiatric disturbances as maintained by M. Reddy. M. Reddy assumes that in solving a greater range of mental problems, integral Yoga at a lesser or more mundane level is able to find a solution to the problems akin "as in the achievement of the aims pursued in clinical psychology, ranging from the treatment of psychiatric disturbances to psychological well-being".[34]

Deikman rightly questions the achievement of spiritual discipline and psychotherapy. Spiritual practice as a general rule is not able to remove the obscurations that causes neuroses and "there is no evidence that spiritual training will substitute for psychotherapy"[35]. The focus of attention of the two approaches is different, the sadhak in his spiritual goals requires a challenge of a different order, whereas the psychiatric client has more basic problems which needs to be addressed immediately.

Sadhana in integral Yoga as practiced for spiritual growth, requires the abolition of the ego and its demands, an infinite trust, patience and self-discipline, and therefore cannot be seen as a form of therapy. It is a methodical process of surrendering the ego-self to the larger spiritual Self and as such it is incompetent to cure any psychiatic distrubances.

Notes:

1. Sri Aurobindo; Letters on Yoga, Sri Aurobindo Ashram Press, Pondicherry. 5th impression 1988, p. 321.
2. Sri Aurobindo; The Synthesis of Yoga, Sri Aurobindo Ashram Press, Pondicherry. 9th impression 1992, p. 598.
3. Ibid., p. 593.
4. Sri Aurobindo; Letters on Yoga, Sri Aurobindo Ashram Press, Pondicherry. 5th impression 1988, p. 354–363.
5. Sri Aurobindo; The Life Divine, Sri Aurobindo Ashram Press, Pondicherry. 10th impression 1993, p. 604.
6. Sri Aurobindo; Letters on Yoga, Sri Aurobindo Ashram Press, Pondicherry. 5th impression 1988, p. 1608.
7. Sri Aurobindo; The Life Divine, Sri Aurobindo Ashram Press, Pondicherry. 10th impression 1993, p. 162.
8. Sri Aurobindo; Letters on Yoga, Sri Aurobindo Ashram Press, Pondicherry. 5th impression 1988, p. 1606.
9. Ibid., p. 1609.
10. Vaughan F; The Inward Arc; Healing and Wholeness in Psychotherapy and Spirituality, Shambhala Publ, Boston 1985, p. 46.
11. Ibid., p. 39.
12. Washburn, M; the Ego and the Dynamic Ground; A Transpersonal Theory of Human Development, State University of New York Press, Albany 1988, p. 119.
13. Hillman, James; Re-visioning Psychology, Harper Perennial, New-York 1992, p. 68.
14. Sri Aurobindo; The Life Divine, Sri Aurobindo Ashram Press, Pondicherry. 10th impression 1993, p. 350–351.

15. Sri Aurobindo; Letters on Yoga, Sri Aurobindo Ashram Press, Pondicherry. 5th impression 1988, p. 292.
16. Ibid., p. 278.
17. Sri Aurobindo; The Life Divine, Sri Aurobindo Ashram Press, Pondicherry. 10th impression 1993, p. 226.
18. Walsh, R, and F. Vaughan, Edt; Paths Beyond Ego, Jeremy Tharcher, Los Angeles 1993, p. 1.
19. Sri Aurobindo; The Human Cycle, Sri Aurobindo Ashram Press, Pondicherry. 6th impression 1992, p. 232.
20. Walsh, R, and F. Vaughan, Edt; Paths Beyond Ego, Jeremy Tharcher, Los Angeles 1993, p. 266.
21. Sri Aurobindo; The Life Divine, Sri Aurobindo Ashram Press, Pondicherry. 10th impression 1993, p. 846.
22. Ibid., p. 852.
23. Reddy, Madhusudan. V; Integral Yoga Psychology, Institute of Human Study, Hyderabad 1990, p. V.
24. H. Chaudhuri: Journal of Humanistic Psychology Vol. 15 No:1 San-Fransisco, p. 7.
25. Grof. C and S. Grof; The Stormy Search for the Self, Jeremy Tarcher Books, New-York 1992, p. 1.
26. Sri Aurobindo; The Life Divine, Sri Aurobindo Ashram Press, Pondicherry. 10th impression 1993, p. 694.
27. A. Deikman; "Mindfulness, spiritual seeking and Psychotherapy", Journal of Transpersonal Psychology, 1992, p. 30–31.
28. Ibid., p. 39.
29. Sri Aurobindo; Letters on Yoga, Sri Aurobindo Ashram Press, Pondicherry. 5th impression 1988, p. 1641.
30. Ibid., p. 612.
31. Ibid., p. 613.
32. Ibid., p. 1659.
33. Ibid., p. 790–791.
34. Reddy, Madhusudan. V; Integral Yoga Psychology, Institute of Human Study, Hyderabad 1990, p. 92.
35. A Deikman; Journal of Transpersonal Psychology 1992, p. 43.

CHAPTER VIII

FINAL CONCLUSION

1. A. Maslow and Sri Aurobindo

For Maslow and Sri Aurobindo man is a never-finished product of evolution with endless potentialities for inner growth, and has the capacity to cultivate the psyche's higher aspirations for a spiritual reality beyond the grasp of the pragmatic human intellect. The human being is impelled from within to exceed his actual state in order to actualise the latent potentials.

Both thinkers brought the depths of inner reality out of the exclusive sphere of religion and stressed the need for investigation of this inner reality.

Maslow and Sri Aurobindo share a clear-cut optimistic view of human destiny, man must learn to move towards future realisations and all that is good and helpful in the past must be integrated into the desired form for the future.

In spite of these similar views the two thinkers differ regarding some of their major concepts, such as self-actualisation/self-realisation, peak-experience/spiritual experience and the integration of personality.

a. Maslow's Self-Actualisation and Sri Aurobindo's Self-Realisation

Maslow describes self-actualisation as the drive towards the establishment of a fully evolved and authentic self, the fulfilment and actualisation of the individual's highest nature by the full use of all their talents, capacities and potentialities.

Self-actualisation implies the development of one's whole personality, and an intrinsic trend towards the development of capacities already existing in the organism as latent potentialities. However lofty Maslow's vision of self-actualisation, it is still based on the assumption of an independent existing empirical ego.

For Sri Aurobindo, self-realisation means the purification and perfection of the physical, vital and mental parts of the individual so that they can become fit instruments for the manifestation of a higher dimension of consciousness. Through expanding consciousness the individual is able to realize the Self.

In Sri Aurobindo's view, self-actualisation applies only to the mental man on the mind-plane of the pure thought and intelligence, i.e., the man of ideas, the philosopher, scientist, the poet, etc; these are mental beings at man's presently highest attained summit.

In his later years Maslow maintained that beyond self-actualisation lies the need for self-transcendence, i.e., the transpersonal. The transpersonal is centred in the cosmos rather than in human needs and interests, and goes beyond humanness. This transcendent realm is characterised by the experience of pure awareness, transcending space, form and time, and could be considered to correspond to Sri Aurobindo's dynamic Self-realisation where the personal "I" awareness merges into the awareness of the cosmic Self.

For Maslow the self-actualising process comprises many factors and embraces within its scope spiritual, psychological, social, as well as biological characteristics. He does refer to the spiritual excellence of man and his transcendence over the whole material universe, but he does not go beyond the human structure itself to postulate the existence of pure spirit or Purusha. Yet the human structure in its unity cannot be explained by the sum total of its parts, hence this harmony of the parts must be grounded in something beyond the structure itself.

For Sri Aurobindo self-realisation is not so much a biological necessity or an impulse towards the ontologically-oriented farther reaches of human nature but the metaphysical aim of human existence which expresses itself in the natural outcome of a true relationship between the human individual and his divine essence. This actualisation implies not merely the realisation of human potentials but also the actualisation of deeper psychic potentialities, and the realisation of the universal and transcendental dimensions of the Self.

b. Maslow's Peak-Experience and Sri Aurobindo's Spiritual Experience

What Maslow calls "Peak-experiences" are moments of intense ecstasy, wonder, awe and delight, with an expansion of human consciousness. They are self-validating moments which carry their own intrinsic values with it. During the peak-experience the individual feels more at peace with himself, more integrated and unified. But when Maslow attempts to investigate the peak-experiences by empirical methods he becomes less precise, admitting that this higher consciousness is not a human truth but a metaphysical truth.

Actually, Maslow's natural mystical experiences as moments of intense ecstasy, "experiences of the greatest joy or the happiest moments of life" could be easily classified as experiences of euphoria and they need not imply any spiritual upliftment.

In Sri Aurobindo's spiritual experience there is a voluntary suspension of ego-gratification, there is an experience of ego-loss in the quest for divine fulfilment. However, this divine fulfilment is not merely a replacement for human fulfilment but a transformation of the latter through the former.

According to Sri Aurobindo, the spiritual experience is able to bring about a limited transformation of our whole being into a more and more pure, powerful and luminous nature.

Maslow's peak-experience can be roughly equated with Sri Aurobindo's "rare visitations" or flashes of understanding (intuitive experiences) in the ordinary mental operations, in which the mind is flooded with light.

c. Maslow's and Sri Aurobindo's Integration of Personality

Maslow's view of the integration of personality is based on basic-need gratification. He considered the integral person as the healthy personality, and a healthy growth, a healthy process of becoming clears the way for the experience of integral moments of Being, which in turn stimulates a further progress of becoming. In Maslow's final formulation of his concept of the hierarchy of needs, he examines the search for transcendence as the highest aim of human life; the summit of integration is reached when the metaneeds are fully developed and expressed. The concept of gratification itself is transcended at the level of metamotivation, and true integration therefore takes place only in the Being-realm.

At the very heart of integral Yoga psychology lies the concept of the psychic being, the integrating principle of the total personality.

If Sri Aurobindo's ideas were to be expressed in Maslow's terminology, it may be said that the Deficiency-realm (directed towards satisfying basic needs) needs to be transformed by the psychic, they need not necessarily be gratified before they can be transcended. Sri Aurobindo would deal with the Deficiency realm in terms of control and purification rather than of gratification. Purification of the lower movements and of personal desire is a preliminary training in integral Yoga psychology.

Integration of the personality cannot be achieved by any outward arrangements but only from within by the action of the integrative principle, the unifying psychic being. All the different aspects of the personality must find their true position and role around this psychic centre which has the double work of inner purification and integration of the outer instruments. It prepares and opens each plane of the being, physical, vital and mental, so as to make them ready for union with the Divine.

In Maslow's mental integration a certain mastery or control over the lower levels can be achieved; but mastery is not the same as transformation. The changes which can be brought about are not sufficient to integrate the whole being. Only when all the different parts of the being are under the control of the central psychic individuality does a full integration of all the parts of the being become possible.

Both the thinkers in exploring man's inner being, his potentials and future growth, agree that the ordinary life is something one must pass beyond—not to any remote Heaven but in this earthly life itself, however, they differ in the methods they recommend for achieving this.

According to Sri Aurobindo man's main drive is towards the transcendence of his humanity; for Maslow it is for human fulfilment. Sri Aurobindo's motivation is a motive of the soul towards the Divine. He replaces Maslow's metamotivation for authenticity, truth, goodness, love, beauty or other higher human potentials by a psychic or spiritual motivation. What Maslow conceives of as the farther reaches of human nature is mainly founded on humanistic empirical science, whereas the basis of Sri Aurobindo's integral Yoga is essentially spiritual.

Although both these thinkers are concerned with the development of man's basic nature and share the same conviction of the individual's essential goodness, they differ radically in their descriptions of what this basic nature is.

Maslow considers man primarily as a biological organism, whereas Sri Aurobindo assumes a divine essence in man. His conception of an evolving psychic being, essentially divine, is too occult a notion for Maslow to accept, or to receive any verification from his experimental-empirical psychology.

In his secular humanism, Maslow does not ignore the spiritual dimension of man, but he remains chained to man's biological nature and is therefore unable to perceive a way to divinise humanity. Sri Aurobindo urges man to transcend his humanity, since the Divine is not to be reached by a glorification of human attributes and movements. Sri Aurobindo's aim of self-fulfilment is an integral unfolding of the divine possibilities within man, a complete evolution of the hidden divinity in the individual soul and collective life. Each man contains in himself the whole divine potentiality, and is in need of perfection of his other elements for a divine manhood. This divine potentiality in human existence seeks to realise itself in a certain harmony and unification of the individual and universal life. To follow an inferior potentiality may seem comfortable but it ends "down the abyss or in a stagnant morass", rather than in a victory.

Integral Yoga brings out these highest potentialities which lie dormant in each individual. However, Sri Aurobindo does not ignore or minimize the undivine parts of the being, they have their functions and values but they are only contrary to the Divine and not contradictory. An effective elimination of undivine forces can be achieved only when the dynamic principles of the Spirit are brought into operation in the evolving earth-consciousness.

Maslow in his attempt to restore man's dignity tends to leave out this darker side of human nature. In transcending conflicts through ecstatic-godlikeness experiences he does not mention anything about the worth of the individual undergoing them, for they can happen in the criminal or psychotic too.

Maslow's godlike experiences are not able to overcome the unbridgeable gulf of the Judaic—Christian tradition in which God and man are separated.

For Sri Aurobindo man and the universe are veiled aspects of God; in the spiritual experience the experiencer is one with God and this oneness is the characteristic of Spirit. In integral Yoga God is not a mere extra-cosmic being or only a static transcendent absolute entity , dominating man and the world as something foreign to His nature. God relates to the supra-cosmic, He embraces and includes the universe, the Cosmic Self that upholds all beings, but He is too the Self of each individual. God, if representing some Being totally different from man or life, completely outside the universe only with an external relationship, then this God can never be an actuality and in this way man can never be transformed into the Divine man. For Sri Aurobindo God out of pure self-delight reproduces Himself in the universe, and by the Grace of God man can rise from his present condition to a higher one. Integral Yoga prepares the seeker for the reception of this Divine Grace.

2. K. Wilber and Sri Aurobindo

K. Wilber in his "Spectrum of Consciousness" views the human being as a multi-levelled expression of a single consciousness, each level having its own characteristic sense of identity ranging from the all-embracing infinite identity of cosmic consciousness to the exclusive narrow identity of the ego consciousness. His innermost consciousness is identical to the ultimate reality of the universe which is infinite, eternal and outside of which nothing exists.

This viewpoint resembles Sri Aurobindo's outlook on consciousness which is described by him as, "the fundamental thing in existence, not only the macrocosm but the microcosm is nothing but consciousness arranging itself-it is not composed of parts, it is fundamental to being and itself formulates any parts it chooses to manifest".[1] However for Sri Aurobindo consciousness is not only related to the nature of awareness but also to conscious power or force which is the energy, the motion or movement that creates the universe and all that is in it. Awareness of the self is the first thing neccessary for creating a change but by itself it is not enough; it is the force that makes the consciousness effective.

In Wilber's Spectrum of Consciousness, each level of the spectrum is marked by a different sense of individual identity. Psychological development proceeds through a triple process; from identification to disidentification and on to integration. As evolution proceeds, and new higher orders emerge, the self disidentifies from the lower structure and shifts its identification to a higher structure. Because the self is differentiated from the lower structure, it transcends that structure and becomes capable of acting on that lower structure from the higher level. Sri Aurobindo, in a similar way, describes identification in the process of evolution as, "psychological experience is capable in man of a double action, mixed or dependent, pure or sovereign. Its mixed action takes place usually when the mind seeks to become aware of the external world, the object; the pure action when it seeks to become aware of itself, the subject.... In reality, all experience is in its secret nature knowledge by identity; but its true character is hidden from us because we have separated ourselves from the rest of the world by exclusion, by the distinction of ourself as subject and everything else as object, and we are compelled to develop processes by which we may again enter into communion with all that we have excluded."[2]

As previously mentioned, Wilber uses Sri Aurobindo's structural model of the hierachy of minds in his structural developmental model of consciousness. In the basic structure of the developmental stages of consciousness, Wilber distinguishes ten such stages in the individual's life as a whole.

Sri Aurobindo's model according to Wilber:	*Wilber's model*
1. Sensorimotor	– realm of sensation and perception
2. Vital-emotional	– sexual level
3. Will-mind	– representational mind
4. Sense-mind	– rule/role mind
5. Reasoning mind	– formal/reflexive mind
6. Higher mind	– vision—logic
7. Illumined mind	– psychic; the beginning of transcendence
8. Intuitive mind	– subtle; the transcendent insight
9. Overmind	– causal: universal self
10. Supermind	– ultimate: the ground of a levels

The first six stages are similar to the stages investigated by conventional psychology, whereas the higher stages, from the Illumined mind onwards, are described in contemplative or Transpersonal psychology.

But it seems that Wilber omits some essential aspects of Sri Aurobindo's model of consciousness.

Sri Aurobindo's model of consciousness consists of three systems;

a. The surface system, which is made up of the various levels of the outer being—the outer physical, vital and mental, corresponding to level 1–5 in Wilber's rendering of Sri Aurobindo's model.
b. The depth or concentric system, including the inner physical, inner vital, inner mental and behind these three, at the centre of the being, the psychic being .
c. The vertical or ascending and descending system, consisting of various levels below the mind such as the subconscient and the inconscient, as well as various levels above the ordinary mind such as the higher mind, illumined mind, intuitive mind, overmind and supermind.

In Sri Aurobindo's model the 'Transpersonal' would relate to the depth and the vertical systems, whereas Wilber's conventional stages of growth (level 1 till 5) pertain to the surface system of the outer being. However, Sri Aurobindo nowhere uses the terms sensorimotor and Will-mind; the former Wilber borrowed from Jean Piaget and relates to Sri Aurobindo's brain-mind, whereas the latter refers to the thought-mind which works upon the forms presented by the sense-mind.

In his basic structure of consciousness Wilber omits Sri Aurobindo's depth system, and he also leaves out the subconscient and inconscient of the vertical system.

Wilber equates Sri Aurobindo's levels of consciousness with his own stages of contemplative development; these two models, however, are used in a different context. There may be some similarities between Wilber's stages of contemplative development and Sri Aurobindo's vertical system, but Sri Aurobindo's levels of higher consciousness need not necessarily succeed one another in a single life cycle.

When Wilber extends the various levels of the Spectrum of Consciousness to the various different schools of psychotherapy, he seems to mix up concepts such as pathology and treatment of the medical model with the spiritual or transpersonal model, but clinical concepts and spiritual growth are two different orders. Integral Yoga is a way of life for spiritual development, whereas Wilber's Spectrum of Consciousness is based on clinical concepts and therefore not fully applicable to Sri Aurobindo's sadhana.

Besides these shortcomings in Wilber's comparative model more serious questions arise in relation to his concepts of integration, transformation and transcendence.

Wilber's Integration

Wilber conceives the psyche as a hierarchy of structural levels; each level of the psychic hierarchy is distinguished by basic and transition or replacement structures.

Transition structures, as particular social manifestations of the basic structures, are not included in the basic structures but tend to be dissolved, negated or replaced by subsequent phases of development. For Wilber the transition structures serve basically as stages. Once the higher structure is developed the transitional structure becomes inactive and returns to its prior state of "selfless function".

Basic structures, as innate underlying patterns of life are stages of development that are never outgrown, they are not abandoned but incorporated in the lower levels. Once the basic structures emerge they tend to remain in existence as relatively autonomous units. In the course of development the lower basic structures not only fulfil their own functioning but also contribute to senior structures, as they are the foundation of the higher ones. The higher structures, on the other hand, subsume, reorganise and control the lower structures.

Negotiating these structural developments is the self, which in the process of growth negates its exclusive identification with its present basic structure in order to identify with the next higher developmental structure. Wilber categorizes this self therefore as a transition structure.

For Wilber at each stage of development a higher-order structure emerges through a differentiation of the preceding lower-order level, and the self identifies its being with that particular structure. When the next higher-order structure emerges the self disidentifies with the lower structure and shifts its identity to the higher structure. When the lower structure is transcended then consciousness becomes capable of operating on that lower structure from the higher-order level. In this way all preceding levels are integrated in consciousness. Wilber is aware that the higher levels when exerting control over the lower levels can overdominate and repress lower levels leading to pathological difficulties.

For optimal spiritual growth each lower level must be enfolded into higher levels but is ultimately transcended. When the lower levels are transcended they are not abandoned but no longer constitute the essential focus of the individual's life. For Wilber each higher level contains all the capabilities of the lower ones but not vice versa.

For Sri Aurobindo all the higher gradations of consciousness are initially embedded or involved in the lower orders, and by an evolutionary development the higher realms can be attained, i.e., the higher is potentially inherent in the lower.

The question arises here whether Wilber's inclusion of the lower in the higher means the same as Sri Aurobindo's integration of the lower and the higher. In Sri Aurobindo's integration the achievements of the lower are harmonised and uplifted by the influence of the higher, the perfection of the lower level is related to perfections on other levels and all are made into a coherent whole.

Wilber's lower structure, though included in the higher, remains unchanged and his integration appears to be partial.

Conceptual emphasis on a "higher" level need not imply the completion of the lower level's task. If the lower is not transformed and is simply dominated by the higher, then the lower is not granted its proper autonomy, which may result in a distortion of the lower self.

Wilber's Transformation

Related to Wilber's concept of integration is his concept of transformation; "At each stage or level of evolution each emergent level is not so much a total negation of the previous level but rather is a transformation and transcendence of it";[3] in the ascent the lower level is now transformed and transcended and not negated or inactive.

For Wilber the evolution of consciousness is marked by a series of significant transformations upward, each of which indicates the emergence of a new and higher level. In distinguishing the terms 'basic' and 'transition' structures in the process of integration, he similarly distinguishes transformation from translation, the former belonging to the movement of the deep structure of consciousness, (embodying all the potentials and limitations of that level) whereas the latter belongs to the movement of the surface structure of consciousness (a particular manifestation of the deep structure). According to Wilber, "transformations are the movements from one level to another while translations represent a movement of the elements of any given level".[4] The mechanism of translation is based on the process of identification, then assimilation, thereafter dissolution and finally adopting a higher translation.

In Wilber's transformation the "higher" structure transcends the systematic problems of the lower structure, integrates its achievements and manifests a new and emergent structure, but for Sri Aurobindo this means a transcendence without full integration. There are three processes in the dynamics of Sri Aurobindo's transformation; heightening, widening and integration. "Heightening" refers to an ascent from a lower grade of existence to a higher grade, "widening" to the full development within one level as a result of that ascent, and "integration" to the taking up of the lower into the higher and transforming it under the influence of the higher.

For Sri Aurobindo transformation is something more than Wilber's change on the various levels; it is an alteration of the very structure of the whole being, the end product of the integration process. In the process of transformation the lower parts are purified and modified to become fit instruments for the expression of the higher consciousness, and this is completed by an integration of the higher with the lower. For this integral transformation it is neccessary that the lower totally surrenders and the higher intervenes and descends. This includes the growing awareness of one's inner laws of being, becoming master of one's lower nature and realising one's kinship with the higher law operating in Nature.

Actually Wilber seems to confuse transformation and transcendence, which are completely different matters. To transcend means to go beyond, whereas to transform implies a radical restructuring or change.

Wilber's developmental transformation represents a series of transcending movements from lower to higher levels. "The transformation into higher levels implies the death of its present level, differentiate from that level and thus transcend it to the next higher state".[5]

Sri Aurobindo distinguishes between transcendence as ascent, and transformation as ascent followed by a descent bringing about an alteration of the very structure of the being.

To sum up: Wilber's integrated full-spectrum model of human development is a laborious attempt to integrate the discoveries of both Western conventional psychology and Eastern psycho-spiritual disciplines; but unfortunately his structural model remains incomplete when he compares it with Sri Aurobindo's model. He omits various parts of Sri Aurobindo's model and he differs in opinion regarding some major concepts of integral Yoga.

Wilber's human evolution, in spite of its vaunted spirituality, lacks Sri Aurobindo's metaphysical vision; a truly spiritual view transcends Cosmic Evolution.

As we can enter into the cosmic consciousness, so we can enter into the world-transcending consciousness, superior to the cosmic existence. It embraces the universe, as the universe embraces the individual, and this Supracosmic Silence is one of the most powerful experiences which the human mind is able to achieve.

For Sri Aurobindo, universal consciousness conducts evolution along two lines, one of ascent to the discovery of the Self and Spirit, the other of descent to bring down spiritual consciousness into mind, life and body. The object of integral Yoga is to bring the Higher Consciousness down into the earth-consciousness and establish it there as a constant realised force, so as to create a new race where the principle of this Higher Consciousness governs the inner and outer individual and collective life.

Sri Aurobindo's spiritual evolution is an evolution of the present type of humanity into a spiritualised humanity which does not stop until the whole world is completely Divinised.

3. S. Grof and Sri Aurobindo

Integral Yoga begins with the will and aspiration towards a complete surrender and at the same time the seeker rejects the domination by or impulses from the lower nature; he aspires to transform the lower instrumentation by calling on the Divine Shakti (Power) to open the vital nature and bring down peace and light into all the centres. Without these preparations the sadhak runs the danger of making an unreal surrender and therefore no progress.

However, rejection does not include all those activities that can be made instruments of the sadhana, though these activities such as art, poetry, music, etc, have to find a spiritual base.

Sri Aurobindo, like Grof, aims at the quietness of mind by getting rid of the habit of the invasion of troubling thoughts, wrong feelings, and confusion of ideas. The vital is indispensable for the divine action and is not a thing to be rejected in its very nature; the lower vital has its place and is not to be killed, "it is a good instrument but a bad master", and therefore it has to be changed. The outer vital mixture, full of the lower passions, desires and ego, needs to be mastered and purified before it is able to cooperate with the spiritual action. According to Sri Aurobindo, "By what actual steps, in what order, through what processes this mastery of the lower vital shall come depends on the nature, the stress of development, the actual movement of the Yoga."[6] Sri Aurobindo therefore, unlike Grof, lays emphasis on the mastery of the vital, its subordination to the spiritual and the psychic rather than its unlimited expression. Emotions have their place in sadhana but these must be pressed inwards, opening to the psychic instead of always throwing them outwards. It is through the emotional being that the psychic most easily expresses itself, but it wants these emotions to be pure.

Sri Aurobindo, like Grof, does not support the attitude of a forceful suppression in the spiritual path, but this does not mean that the vital can go its own way and do according to its fancy. For Sri Aurobindo the lower vital should be enlightened and transformed by the higher consciousness. To do so a decreasing importance has to be attached to the gratification of the lower vital together with a certain mastery and control. But, as discussed before, mental control by itself cannot eradicate anything entirely out of the being. In due course of time sadhana replaces the seeker's mental control by a spiritual mastery.

Sri Aurobindo, like Grof, maintains that purposeful exhaustion, is valid in some cases, "especially when some natural tendency has too strong a hold or too strong a drive in it to be got rid of by the process of rejection.... But this method of purposive indulgence is always dangerous.... It succeeds only when there is a very strong will in the being towards realisation; for then indulgence brings a strong dissatisfaction and reaction".[7] Rather than Grof's free indulgement of the vital movements, Sri Aurobindo advises the seeker to draw back from them, and by detaching himself from them it becomes more possible for the sadhak to discover and get in touch with his psychic being which is not troubled by these movements.

It appears inadequate to attempt an alliance between the lower vital and the spiritual, this is only a stumbling solution of the fallible human mind groping for a transaction between the spiritual higher summits and the various lower forms of outer hedonism. Grof's "transcendental hedonism" stands in contrast with Sri Aurobindo's psycho-spiritual growth process which is a disciplined methodical effort towards integral realisation of unity between the individual, universal and transcendental Self.

For Sri Aurobindo the guiding law of spiritual growth can only come by an opening of the human consciousness to the Divine Consciousness.

Grof's human views give no lead to the psychic element within the seeker, the soul's aspiration towards light and truth, towards a victory over imperfection and evil. It is possible when the seeker lives inwardly, in the depths, to arrive at a state of inner equality which is untouched by the reactions of the outer nature.

4. R. Assagioli and Sri Aurobindo

Integration for Assagioli as well as Sri Aurobindo implies not only realisation of the transcendent dimension of the self, but it also requires actualisation of the individual's spiritual potentials as a creative unit of the evolutionary process.

Self-integration is a process of the total harmonisation of one's being. The fully integrated individual actively participates in the world affairs and through an integrated self-development encourages his own potential to realise Being as the unity of spirit and nature.

Psychosynthesis seeks to make the individual aware of the various conflicting parts of his subpersonalities bringing them under the subordination of the Self, and enabling the seeker to harmonise these multiple parts.

Sri Aurobindo in a similar way explains the different parts of the being; integral Yoga aims at becoming conscious of this great complexity of one's nature, and to experience the different forces that move it. Like Assagioli, Sri Aurobindo maintains that clarity about these various parts can only come from the light of the Divine Consciousness above. The higher planes precipitate their influences on the lower, whereas the lower, reacting to the higher, develops something that corresponds to the superior power and its action.

But such a plastic movement cannot be reduced to a rigorous logical formula. For Sri Aurobindo the relation between the different parts of the being and their interactions are more complicated and subtle than described by Assagioli. Each plane, in spite of its connections with others above and below it, is yet a world in itself with its own movements and forces. The complexity of interrelations between the various parts cannot be expressed in a single formula like holism, whose organic unity is a characteristic of the external being only. In integral Yoga only the psychic being is able to unite the chaotic parts of the being, rather than the structure of the natural organism.

Assagioli's experience of self-realisation like Sri Aurobindo's self-realisation is not a mere psychological self-analysis related to the experience of the modes of the Self, but the realisation of the Self in its pure being.

Assagioli describes self-realisation as the experience and consciousness of the united spiritual centre, the realisation of the psychic growth of the Self through the development of latent possibilities. Sri Aurobindo in a similar way describes self-realisation as the reception in the consciousness and the establishment there of the fundamental truth of the Higher Nature of the world-consciousness and of one's own real inner nature. But Sri Aurobindo divides self-realisation into the twofold aspects of the Self (the static and dynamic self) on the mental-spiritual plane and the unification of the two on the supramental plane.

The static self-realisation is the fundamental realisation of the Divine in its essential Self in which the narrow instrumental ego merges into the greater, permanent spiritual 'I'. This realisation is liberative but not unitive as the lower parts of the being remain untouched amid the play of cosmic forces.

In the dynamic self-realisation the seeker becomes one with all the outpouring of consciousness and all its creative force in Time and Space. It is characterised by the establishment of the true relation between the eternal Self and the mutable world. If the static realisation is liberating, the dynamic realisation is unitive and effective, for here the essential Self is not only one with the Eternal but also, in its active nature, an instrument of its Consciousness-Force. This cosmic-realisation may cause a change in the inner being but the outer remains an imperfect instrument. Only in the integral self-realisation, by calling down the Supramental into the outer instrument, is the latter transformed into an image of the Divine.

However, for Sri Aurobindo, unlike Assagioli, self-realisation is not the final goal, but only a means towards the Divine transformation. Self-realisation may bring an opening or heightening or widening of consciousness, but by itself does not necessarily transform the being as a whole.

Sri Aurobindo's integral psychology aims not at a mere realisation of the Divine, but at His manifestation; such a full integral realisation indicates a radical change in all the parts of the being and a new centre of consciousness which is capable of manifesting progressively the truth of the Divine on earth.

5. Metaphysics and Transpersonal Psychology

Man has a deep craving for some kind of metaphysical belief. Traditional Western metaphysics claims to give statements partly on the immanent nature and structure of existence or reality, and partly on the essence of the supreme or transcendent Reality, God, soul and the world.

The Oxford dictionary defines Metaphysics as, "That branch of speculative inquiry which treats of the first principles of things including such concepts as substance, essence, time, space, cause, identity, etc; as the branch of theoretical philosophy it deals with the ultimate science of Being and knowing and includes ontology, that which is beyond the physical or the experiential, and cosmology, that which deals with the character of the universe as a cosmos."

However, Ontological statements only clarify what the metaphysician *understands* by existence or reality within the framework of the prevailing experience of a certain culture and a certain age, but the same statements are not concerned about the reality as it exists in itself.

A metaphysical vision of reality recognizes a divine Reality substantial to the world of things, lives, and minds. In psychological language, the soul, which is identical with that divine Reality, moves beyond the limitations of the rational mind, the senses, space and time, and explores regions beyond human potentials towards inner and higher realms, i.e., the spiritual realm.

Metaphysics fully acknowledges human power and divinity, the wholeness of body, mind and spirit. Life is part of a spiritual journey, and urges the individual to reclaim his own responsibility.

A metaphysical worldview assumes that the individual creates his own reality rather than being determined by God, chance or luck. Each circumstance is a self-created opportunity to grow and recover one's responsibility and wholeness.

Presently traditional metaphysics is involved in a competitive struggle with empirical sciences. The former claims to be a superior science as it aims to offer the most fundamental explanations on the basis of absolute fundamentals, but notions such as "being in general" or "being as a whole" are not possible subjects for empirical observation. Empirical science accuses metaphysics therefore as a senseless pseudo-science.

However, empirical science observes only the periphery of existence and leaves the motivating power outside its scope. It is not concerned with the ultimate questions of life, and man's surface-consciousness serves the individual only with the interactions of external life. Even though it is clear to the common man that modern empirical science does not have all the answers to the fundamental questions of existence, yet for a large number of scientists the exploration of such questons does not lead to any finality, in fact these questions have no answer at all. It is for this reason that science declared metaphysics as an aberration of the ideative faculty, a false extension of logic, and denied one's right to recognize any metaphysical existence or anything at all which cannot be judged by or inferred from the result of the test tube, the scalpel, the microscope and the telescope.

Though science and metaphysics as different orders of reality have each their own province and method of inquiry, yet they have a common truth underlying them; truth of the physical universe can throw some light on the nature of the Force that is active in the universe. Nevertheless, science cannot dictate its conclusions to metaphysics any more than metaphysics can impose its conclusions on science.

Though the metaphysician aspires for a deliverance from the physical or material framework and the consequent "common sense" attitude, he interpretes and identifies the beyond within the prevailing framework of known entities, i.e., the immanent tendency in the traditional metaphysics. This "beyond" is only a product of reason, a mental abstraction of something that is in its own nature other than mental; it is a metaphysical speculation about and the intellectual effort is not confirmed by the metaphysicians' vision or experimental realisation of novelty and depth.

The history of Eastern metaphysics has been the history of endlessly diverse *experiments* with spiritual truth; an explorative attempt towards the unravelling of the different aspects of the Ultimate Reality. According to Sri Aurobindo, "In the East, especially in India, the metaphysical thinkers have tried, as in the West, to determine the nature of the highest Truth by the intellect. But they (Eastern thinkers) have not given mental thinking the supreme rank as an instrument in the discovery of Truth, but only a secondary status. The first rank has always been given to spiritual intuition and illumination and spiritual experience".[8] Mental intuitions of the metaphysician for the most part fall far short of a concrete spiritual experience; they are shadowy reflections, not "rays from the centre of Light".

For Sri Aurobindo metaphysics does not aim at mere rational analysis/speculation or aesthetic originality but moves on to the practical achievements of the spiritual goal, i.e., spiritual realisation.

It is not by becoming irrational that one enters supernature beyond ordinary nature, it should be done by passing through reason to "superreason".

Reason has its place in the formation of metaphysical generalisations, but it cannot claim a decisive authority in spiritual matters. Logical reasoning is indispensable in its own field; it gives the mind a certain clearness and subtlety of its own ideas and removes confusions of the obscured average human intelligence. Logical reasoning, as a partially enlightened guide, is therefore part of the preparation in the method of metaphysical dialectics.

Again, it is reason itself which supports the spiritual realisation and insight. Man's intellect needs to know the nature of the spiritual Reality, and its relation to oneself and the universe. In this way it helps to create a mental formulation of the spiritual Truth which can be applied later on in the more direct seeking. However, reason as an efficient guardian against error is not a discoverer of truth; by itself it cannot arrive at the metaphysical realisation or the full knowledge of Nature or God. One cannot judge what is beyond ordinary consciousness while remaining oneself in the ordinary consciousness.

Western metaphysical thought does not in its methods and results go beyond the intellect and remains therefore lost in speculative and mind-constructed formulae, pointing vaguely to a fragmentary representation of the supreme Truth. This speculation about truth has its utility in helping the mind to seek the idea of something beyond towards which it must turn. But intellectual speculation about the beyond does not carry the seeker far and needs to be supplemented by a practical way of entering into the supreme state of consciousness.

According to Sri Aurobindo it is only by going beyond ordinary intellect into the wider realm of consciousness that the individual can know and enter into the ultimate Reality. The beyond, the transcendence involves a change of consciousness which surpasses our established world of experience, as described by Sri Aurobindo; "the concepts of metaphysical knowledge do not in themselves fully satisfy the demand of our integral being ... until it becomes an experience. But the truths which are now in question, are of an order not subject to our normal experience.... Therefore, some other faculty of experience is necessary by which the demand of our nature can be fulfilled and this can only come, since we are dealing with the supraphysical, by an extension of psychological experience".[9]

Only in the spiritual intuition beyond the ego lies the possibility to come into conscious contact with our real Self, and this intended dimension reaches farther than any thought process will ever arrive at. Mental intelligence remains mainly a means of expression of this supreme Truth. It is not a conceptual taking possession of, but a becoming inwardly one with or a merging in Truth.

Transpersonal psychology, as a higher form of psychology, does satisfy the deeper spiritual needs of the individual. However, when it is dealing with mind, conciousness and its actual workings, it does not ascertain its ultimate nature. The transpersonal psychologist does not pursue any preconceived spiritual goal or any clear objective though its methods may yield spiritual experiences. As such it comes to an inconclusive end because without this goal it remains a searching for the sake of searching, which leaves the seeker sooner or later dissatisfied. Without essential pillars in spiritual discipline, the fascination with spiritual experiences may easily result in overindulgement or spiritual greediness. This acquisitive impuls often serves a purpose that stands in sharp contrast with the original spiritual teachings of control and detachment. To be receptive to spiritual needs the seeker must be inwardly prepared to change the very basis of his common life.

For Sri Aurobindo spiritual needs ought not to be a pursuit of truth for its own sake, but a discovery of the basic truths of all-existence which ought then to become the guiding principle of one's own existence. To gain integral importance the ultimate truth once discovered must be accomplished in one's inner being and one's outer activities.

The transpersonal approach paying tribute to the methods of science but also to the principles pertaining to the higher planes of the individual and existence, lacks a sound metaphysics which violates the true meaning of Transpersonal psychology, as it can lead only to new fragmentary views. It does not go to the metaphysical root of the problem and does not explore the why of their fundamental concepts.

As a science without a metaphysical worldview it studies isolated facts, and is therefore correct only within the special frame of its psychological presumptions. It might lead to psychological health but not to spiritual perfection or wholeness. For all transpersonal psychologists as scientific explorers of the human psyche the true nature of being remains unaccessible.

By confining themselves only to verifiable psychological facts they withhold the transcendent metaphysical reality, and the fundamental truth of man remains therefore partially hidden for them.

Transpersonal psychology's commitment toward science and hence its uncompromising devotion to empiricism forces it to explain the transcendental spiritual experiences, and what is a metaphysical reality beyond space, time and causality, in physical terms. Transpersonal psychology, insisting on scientific values but simulteneously exploring the superconscious is dragged from its empirical stronghold into the field of metaphysics which is rather controversal. As previously mentioned, the higher planes of consciousness, the unrealised human potentialities beyond the surface consciousness, cannot be satisfactorily described in terms of the conscious or unconscious.

Transpersonal psychology does not reject a metaphysical reality, but it does not explore this reality in depth and it remains therefore only a possibility. It is not concerned with the question of the truth of spirituality and its enquiry relates only to the *effects* of spirituality upon the life of the individual and humanity.

By restricting itself to the observation of spiritual phenomena, Transpersonal psychology refrains from any application of metaphysical considerations. In its therapeutical approach it does not elaborate metaphysical events that often permeate spiritual healing systems. The therapist does not presume to delineate spiritual goals. It awards God a psychological validity but avoids the ontological status of God, the identity of God and man. When Transpersonal psychology uses God as a sort of therapeutical means against the vagueness of the unsatisfying human life on earth, then this pseudo-God gets degraded to a mere projected human wish-fulfilment, unlike God as the ground of all life and all existence.

In Sri Aurobindo's metapsychological insights, the transcendental self-realisation is given an ontological status as he envisages the integration of the existential as well as the transcendental dimension of the individual.

For Sri Aurobindo spirituality is able to bring out the best in man by revealing the divinity that is already within the individual. Each soul is potentially divine and the goal of life is to manifest this divinity within. In integral Yoga psychology man's being is a microcosm of the macrocosm and the psychological nature of man is therefore intimately related to the metaphysical nature of the universe.

6. A Final Confrontation

Transpersonal psychology, in changing the contents of psychology, continues to smuggle the spiritual realm into the reductionistic-mechanical psychological realm, using the processes of the post modernistic worldview to prove its valid existence. All transpersonal psychologists struggle with the issues of mechanistic science in order to avoid rejection by the so called mainstream of Western civilization.

In exploring issues such as introspection, intuition, subjectivity and spirituality, the transpersonal psychologists move beyond the mechanistic model of the soientist, but they nevertheless hold on to and use methods and assumptions of modern science in order to prove the validity of these phenomena which cannot be studied by empirical methodology alone.

Science for Sri Aurobindo is nothing else than a support for the mind, and extremely practical and useful in dealing with physical energies in the material world. But while these practical aspects of science are valid in their own field, they do not represent the whole truth of things. The scientist, finding out more and more about the processes of the physical field, may now be able to go forward to a more open repossession of mental and psychic knowledge.

Before arriving at supraphysical certitudes the seeker still has to adhere to the rigorous methods of science, though not to its purely physical instrumentation. This supraphysical has another method of verification than that of the physical; its inner method of verification by its very nature cannot be referred to the physical.

Science in its attempt to explain the supraphysical by the physical is limited by the usual vice of the scientist's intellect. Only when the intellect surrenders itself to the Divine can it be a means of reception of the Light and an aid to the supraphysical experience.

The supraphysical is as real as the physical, in the latter the scientist is able to trace the processes of matter, whereas in the former the seeker is able to discover all that is behind the material surface, the Self, but also the spiritual way of knowledge and action. An integral solution requires the knowledge of both realms.

The preoccupation with physical existence is at the beginning necessary but it is only a preliminary step in the growth of his whole being. After the first necessary foundation in life and matter the seeker has to expand, deepen and widen his consciousness in order to penetrate into the essential nature of the individual and the universe, i.e., the Divine Reality. According to Sri Aurobindo, "The Yogin's aim in the practical sciences, whether mental and physical or occult and psychic, should be to enter into the ways of the Divine and his processes".[10] Spirituality does not cut at the root of science but lifts it out of its limitations and compels it to perceive the divine intelligence and will in the material universe. Such a science which turns its face towards the Divine must be a new science which deals directly with the forces of the life-world and the mind, so as to arrive at what is beyond Mind.

K. Wilber in his quest for a new comprehensive paradigm meaningfully tries to expose empirical science, philosophy, psychology and transcendental religion, fit them together to form a unified worldview which is in accordance with empirical science, and unravel some of the major obstacles to the emergence of such a paradigm.

He wants to integrate the empirical (physical), rational (mental), and the spiritual (transcendental) realms in his new paradigm. "We honour all spheres best by their respective tasks understanding their respective spheres".[11] Each level is valid and useful in its own field or realm and each on its own has its respective role but cannot form a complete worldview, i.e., each part cannot play the whole.

For Sri Aurobindo the real truth lies in the laws of the Spirit and only the Spiritual realm is of primary importance, all other realms are not equally valid; they are only means for the expression of the Spirit. In his spiritual insights he classifies science, religion, philosophy, psychology, etc, as secondary processes making them subservient to spirituality. But according to Wilber such an opinion may lean towards absolutistic views and metaphysical rigidity. Spiritual insights in Wilber's paradigm have meaning only in so far as they are related to the Spiritual realm, the latter does not prove the existence of the physical or mental realm. In a similar way the empirical phenomenal evidences are not able to prove the Spiritual realm, unless their instruments of investigation or methodology are changed into contemplative and spiritual disciplines.

Actually the higher realm commits a fallacy when it attempts, by itself, to fully grasp the lower realm and vice versa. In the transcendental realm, the methodology of empirical-analytical science cannot be applied, like Sri Aurobindo's 'reason' which is powerless in understanding spiritual Truth. The higher (transcendental) science is based on noumena of the transpersonal area, on nonverbal insights revealed by the superconscious and therefore related to contemplative proofs rather than empirical or rational proof.

For Wilber, Transpersonal psychology transcends the physical and mental level. However, in its investigations it uses both levels and as such it is not a science but "a state-specific enterprise".

But unfortunately Wilber when admitting sensory, intellectual and spiritual experiences in the physical, mental and spiritual realms respectively, advises Transpersonal psychologists to restrict the term empirical to its original meaning,—"knowledge grounded in sensory experience"—to avoid ambiguities with strict empirical scientists, who otherwise would reject their results. In bringing on par Transpersonal psychology with the modern scientific methodical approach Wilber seems to mix up the contemplative realm with the empirical realm in order that the former be accepted by the latter, forcing an artificial reconciliation of the eternal transpersonal realm with the temporal scientific (sensory) realm. But later on he admits that, "mysticism itself is too profound to be hitched to phases of empirical scientific theorizing. Let them appreciate each other, but premature marriages usually end in divorce".[12]

Transpersonal psychology, in rejuvenating the spiritual traditions of the West through a synthesis of Eastern and Western traditions and in maintaining true integration, should not merely accept the fundamental reality of the Spiritual realm, but in its investigations it should also establish a more solid spiritual foundation exploring the ultimate divine nature of man.

In exploring the ultimate divine nature of man Sri Aurobindo maintains that humanity is not the highest godhead, God is more than humanity, but in humanity too we have to find Him, i.e., to serve God's ways upon earth and fulfil the Godhead in man. According to Sri Aurobindo "The individual as spirit or being is not confined within his humanity; he has been less than human, he can become more than human. The universe finds itself through him even as he finds himself in the universe, but he is capable of becoming more than the universe, since he can surpass it and enter into something in himself and beyond it that is absolute".[13]

Humanity is not satisfied with the analysis of the externalities of Nature and man's unconquerable impulse directs him towards God. Man as a finite-seeming infinity is seeking after the Infinite and gradually becomes aware of God within him. The highest aim possible to man on earth is the discovery of the manifestation of the Divine within and without. God dwells in all, and only by becoming conscious of God within from within can humanity be saved; it is by helping others to awake to the veiled Divine within them that the sadhak goes the straight way to the creation of his Kingdom on earth.

For Sri Aurobindo modern society, whatever may be the splendour of its achievements, acknowledges only two gods; life and practical reason. The life-power in its manifestation appears to be concerned only with the physical good and vitalistic well-being of the individual and the community. Its primary impulse is individualistic and it makes social and national life a means for the greater satisfaction of the individual's needs, interests, aggrandisement and well-being.

Science as a manifestation of practical reason aims at a cure of conflicts by carrying artificial remedies to their acme, by a more scientific organisation of life, which means that the logical reason attempts to substitute itself for complex Nature as if humanity can be saved by machinery. In the words of Sri Aurobindo, "A rational and scientific formula of the vitalistic and materialistic human being and his life, a search for a perfected economic society and the democratic cultus of the average man are all that the modern mind presents us in this crisis as a light for its solution. Whatever the truth supporting these ideas, this is clearly not enough to meet the need of a humanity which is missioned to evolve beyond itself or, at any rate, if it is to live, must evolve far beyond anything that it at present is".[14]

The changes taking place in the present world are mostly intellectual, the spiritual revolution throws up its waves here and there, but until it comes, all interpretations of others and the prediction of man's future cannot be understood.

Humanitarianism which confines itself to "man above everything else" is supposed to be the highest form of self-sacrifice man is capable of, but for Sri Aurobindo to appreciate the full dignity of man the sadhak has not to deify himself to the rank of God, but to see man as a vehicle of manifestation of the Divine. For Sri Aurobindo the highest good of humanity is conditional upon the fulfilment of the Divine Will in the world. However, Sri Aurobindo accepts human nature as the sadhaks who enter the practice of integral Yoga are after all human. The human approach at the beginning and long after is full of excellent material, but this material should be utilised with the right spiritual attitude. Divinisation of humanity does not mean the destruction of human elements, but raising them, by purification and perfection, to their full power and that means the elevation of the whole of earthly life to its full power.

The transpersonal psychologist insists on the Divine becoming human rather than attempting to make the human Divine. Sri Aurobindo's integral Yoga is not for the sake of humanity but for the sake of the Divine which includes the individual, the cosmic and the supracosmic.

Man's highest ideal of human life is to establish the control of a strong mind, a rational will, to master the emotions and fulfil any human capacity which is useful in life. The object of the divine life, on the contrary, is to fulfil man's divine capacities and fulfil them in life as a true instrument of the Divine Power. In their apparent nature the two are opposed but it is man's aim in life to solve the difficulty of harmonising the divine life with human living. The Divine is already there immanent within the seeker and it is this reality that the sadhak has to manifest; it is that which constitutes the urge towards the divine living even in this material existence.

A divine life in a material world implies a necessary union of the spiritual summit and the material base. It is possible to change the human nature into the divine or to make it an instrument of the divine when there is a union with the supreme Being, and a unity with its universal Self in all things and beings i.e., a change in the total life of humanity or a perfect collective life in the earth nature. The human journey to the divine life is characterised by the abolition of the ego but it need not exclude earthly existence; "it will take up human being and human life, transform what can be transformed, spiritualise whatever can be spiritualised, cast its influence on the rest and effectuate either a radical or an uplifting change, bring about a deeper communion between the universal and the individual, invade the ideal with the spiritual truth of which it is a luminous shadow and help to uplift into or towards a greater and higher existence".[15]

Sri Aurobindo maintains that the ideal of a divine humanity cannot be brought to function by religious or moral sentiments but by transcending the furthest outskirts of the mental realm. It is almost impossible to achieve a harmonious adjustment of all conflicting claims by any mental principle, formula or sentiment.

An ethical solution is therefore insufficient to solve the problem of the universe and human suffering, as it has no power to transform nature. Altruism or humanitarianism are not the first true objects of spiritual seeking, they can only be a means towards finding the Divine, but in themselves they can only be temporary or local palliatives. To serve humanity is undoubtly a lofty ideal, a divine possibility which can be made a first means of the sadhak's growth into a spiritual unity of being with being, but until the seeker realises the Divine he serves humanity as humanity, i.e., to serve one's ego expanded to embrance the entire human species.

At best its method is to put a wall of a relative safety around the seeker, well expressed by H. Jacobs: "Self discovery has never been an easy task ... man is inclined to run away from himself; he seems more interested in his fellow-men whose lives he seeks to remedy in every way. Feeling indecisive, vague and lonely, he does not try to solve the problem ... he projects himself into the outer world".[16]

The ethical approach has its relevance in ordinary life and in the beginning of sadhana, but later on it can only be the mark of transition, a deeper solution must be found in a surer supra-ethical dynamic principle. It is only through integral self-surrender to the Divine Will that unity and harmony can be achieved and established in the world.

For Sri Aurobindo a perfected human world cannot be created by men who are themselves imperfect; "man in himself is little more than an ambitious nothing. He is a littleness that reaches to a wideness and a grandeur that are beyond him, a dwarf enamoured of the heights. His Mind is a dark ray in the splendours of the universal Mind. His life is a striving, exulting, suffering, an eager passion ... a blindly and dumbly longing petty moment of the universal Life. His body is a labouring perishable speck in the material Life. This cannot be the end of the mysterious upward surge of Nature, there is something beyond, something that mankind shall be ... man's greatness is not in what he is but in what he makes possible".[17]

Philosophy, religion and science insist on a knowledge of which they are incapable—the essential nature of man and the world. "Science has only one cry, society and again society and always society. But the nature of man knows that society is only a means not an end, and that society is not the whole of life".[18] For Sri Aurobindo, man should serve society for the sake of the Self and not for the sake of society.

To characterize common civilisation, culture, education, science, religion, social laws, etc, as ineffective means to change human life, because they have no power to transform human psychology and the human race, is certainly not accepted by Transpersonal psychologists.

Sri Aurobindo is aware of those critics who oppose such a rigid standard. Those who feel only the human and not divine values may argue that his truth is likely to destroy the very foundation of morality. But Sri Aurobindo maintains that at the human level the standard of conduct may be temporary yet necessary for its time, until it can be replaced by a better standard. It is in God alone, by the possession of the Divine only that all the divisions of life can be restored and the only effective way of helping mankind is the growing of man towards the Divine. For Sri Aurobindo human tendencies and human values, however noble and good, need a metaphysical justification.

But for the transpersonalist's "wordly" or "human" form of spirituality such a view deprives man of all his significance. Qualities like sympathy, righteousness, solidarity, true love and compassion are necessary constituents in reaching the wealth of a complete life; they are not qualities "about" something and need not be sustained by social, moral or religious values. On the higher planes of man's spirituality the most profound truths about these illuminative qualities resides in the depth of these qualities themselves. Descriptions of, or reflections on these unique qualities do not capture the deeper essence of them, and because many have never achieved these emotions in their deepest essence they confuse them with religious values, moral standards or social activities.

Interpreting the longings of these pure and natural human characteristics as inferior (a means only) to the ways of the Divine, subordinating the former to the supra-ethical dynamic principles, fails to imply the underlying identity between them.

In the exploration of the unknown both illuminate the essential nature of the individual's soul and one's world with a fresh vision. The transpersonal approach considers these universal, benevolent qualities and contemplative spiritual tendencies as equally real and therefore equally important; by uncovering and integrating the impact of both realms in an ever-evolving process human beings reflect the divine reality itself.

The transpersonal psychologist grants these human excellences in the higher stages of contemplative development a legitimate life of their own; they are not merely temporary palliatives but often man's only route to Godhead and can therefore never be dismissed as a mark of transition, or written off as ineffectual.

For Sri Aurobindo, these transpersonal views regarding the triumph of human's aspirations in a full and new life are certainly meaningful, but they leave out the divine origin of these human potentials, and he moves beyond the transpersonal experiences to the source of them, i.e., to God.

Man is not a self-sufficient being but supported from within and above by the divine spiritual principle. These human qualities have ultimate value only in this wider spiritual context and cannot be seperated from God.

Transpersonal psychology, in its relation with natural science, acknowledges mystical/spiritual experiences as symbols which indeed points to God, though the transpersonal psychologist remains searching for the absolute ground of everything exclusively in man rather than in the Divine.

The transpersonal exploration of the mystical dimensions of life and its preoccupation with man's spiritual aspirations for a "human spirituality" seems therefore a highly valuable self-preparation towards Sri Aurobindo's aim and destiny of human life, i.e., the evolution of a divine humanity through the mysterious "outflowering" of the Divine in man.

The seeker sees the Divine not only within himself but also equally in all others. A growing inner and perfect unity with others is a necessary condition of a perfect life. Collectively they form a new perfected life in the earth-nature superior to the present individual and common existence.

However, this dynamic cosmic identity should not be mixed up with a certain form of pantheistic thought; the Divine is here not only within the individual, nor merely as cosmic Spirit or universal Power, (it depends on the cosmic Existence but is not limited by it) but the Divine is also Beyond as an eternal Transcendence. This superconscient Transcendent, as Power as well as Existence, is not something seperated from our present existence. It is this Transcendent Divine which reveals to the seeker his supreme Existence and the perfect Source of all that he is.

Despite these differences between the two views, both in their search for the higher and deeper meaning of the inner dimensions of human existence maintain that man is a never—finished product of evolution with endless potentialities for inner growth, and has the capacity to cultivate the psyche's higher aspirations for a spiritual reality beyond the grasp of the pragmatic human intellect.

Notes:

1. Sri Aurobindo; Letters on Yoga, Sri Aurobindo Ashram Press, Pondicherry. 5th impression 1988, p. 236–237.

2. Sri Aurobindo; The Life Divine, Sri Aurobindo Ashram Press, Pondicherry. 10th impression 1993, p. 62.
3. Wilber, Ken; The Atman Project, Quest Book, Illinois 1980, p. 37.
4. Ibid., p. 45.
5. Wilber, Ken; No Boundary: Eastern and Western Approaches to Personal Growth, Shambhala, Boston 1985, p. 320.
6. Sri Aurobindo; Letters on Yoga, Sri Aurobindo Ashram Press, Pondicherry. 5th impression 1988, p. 860.
7. Ibid., p. 1607.
8. Ibid., p. . 159.
9. Sri Aurobindo; The Life Divine, Sri Aurobindo Ashram Press, Pondicherry. 10th impression 1993, p. 61.
10. Sri Aurobindo; The Synthesis of Yoga, Sri Aurobindo Ashram Press, Pondicherry. 9th impression 1992, p. 133.
11. Wilber, Ken; Spectrum of Consciousness, Theosophical Publishing House, Illinois 1982, p. 247.
12. Ibid., p. 153.
13. Sri Aurobindo; The Life Divine, Sri Aurobindo Asharam Press Pondicherry. 10th impression 1993, p. 1049.
14. Ibid., p. 1056.
15. Sri Aurobindo; The Supramental Manifestation, Sri Aurobindo Ashram Press, Pondicherry. 2nd edition 1989, p. 47.
16. Jacobs, Hans; Western Psychotherapy and Hindu Sadhana, George Allen and Urwin Ltd, London 1961, p. 92–93.
17. Sri Aurobindo; The Hour of God, Sri Aurobindo Ashram Press, Pondicherry, p. 8.
18. Ibid., p. 183.

SELECT BIBLIOGRAPHY

1. Ajaya, Swami; Psychotherapy East and West; A Unifying Paradigm, The Himalayan International Inst, Honesdale 1985.
2. Assagioli, R; Psychosynthesis, The Viking Press Inc, New-york 1971.
3. Assagioli, R; Transpersonal Development: The Dimension Beyond Psychosynthesis, Aquarian/Thorsons, London 1993.
4. Sri Aurobindo; The Synthesis of Yoga, Sri Aurobindo Ashram Press, Pondicherry. 9th impression 1992.
5. Sri Aurobindo; The Life Divine, Sri Aurobindo Ashram Press, Pondicherry. 10th impression 1993.
6. Sri Aurobindo; Letters on Yoga, I, II, III, Sri Aurobindo Ashram Press, Pondicherry. 5th impression 1988.
7. Sri Aurobindo; The Supramental Manifestation, Sri Aurobindo Ashram Press, Pondicherry. 2nd edition 1989.
8. Sri Aurobnindo; The Hour of God, Sri Aurobindo Ashram Press, Pondicherry.
9. Sri Aurobindo; The Human Cycle, Sri Aurobindo Ashram Press, Pondicherry. 6th impression 1992
10. Bannister, D. Edt; Issues and Approaches in the Psychological Therapies, John Willey and Sons, New-York 1975.
11. Bettelheim, Bruno; Freud and Man's Soul, Alfred A. Knopf, New-York 1983.
12. Boorstein, S. Edt; Transpersonal Psychotherapy, Science and Behaviour Books, Stanford 1991
13. Boss, Medard; A psychiatrist discovers India, Oswald Wolff, London 1965.
14. Brahma, N. Kanta; Philosophy of Hindu Sadhana, Motilal Banarsidass, New-Delhi 1993.

15. Brammer L. M, E. L. Shostrom, P. J. Abrego; Fundamentals of Counseling and Psychotherapy, Prentice-Hall Int, New-Jersey 1989.
16. Brena, Steven F; Yoga and Medicine, The Merging of Yogic Concepts with Modern Medical Knowledge, Penguin Books, New-York, 1976.
17. Bromberg, Walter; From Shaman to Psychotherapist, Henry Regnery Comp, Chicago 1975.
18. Brown, D. J. Pedder; Introduction to Psychotherapy, Tavistock Publications Ltd, London 1979.
19. Brown, J. A. C; Freud and the Post-Freudians, Penguin Books, Middlesex 1969.
20. Bucke, R. M; Cosmic Consciousness, a Study in the Evolution of the Human Mind, Citadel Press, New-Jersey, 4th printing 1982.
21. Buhler, C. and M. Klein; Introduction to Humanistic Psychology, Brooks/Cole Publishing Comp, Monterey, 1972.
22. Chakravarti, S. J; The Philosophy of Sri Aurobindo, Sterling Publishers Ltd, New-Delhi 1991.
23. Chaudhuri, H; Sri Aurobindo; The Prophet of Life Divine, Sri Aurobindo Ashram Press, Pondicherry 1973.
24. Coan R. W; Human Consciousness and Its Evolution: A. Multidi-mensional view, Greenwood Press Inc, Connecticut 1987.
25. Cox, Harvey; Turning East, Penguin Books Ltd, London 1977.
26. Coxhead, Nanda; Beyond Psychology: The potential of Conscious Thinking, Mandala Press, London 1991.
27. Cramer, Duncan; Personality and Psychotherapy, Open University Press, Buckingham 1992.
28. Dalal, A. S; Psychology, Mental Health and Yoga, Sri Aurobindo Ashram Press, Pondicherry 1992.
29. Deikman, A. J; Mysticism and Psychotherapy, Beacon Press, Boston 1982.
30. Dobson, Keith, S, Edt; Handbook of Cognitive-Behavioural Therapies, Hutchinson, London 1988.
31. Dryden, W and C. Feltham, Edt; Psychotherapy and its Discontents, Open University Press, Buckingham 1992.
32. Edelson, Marshall; Psychoanalysis. A Theory in Crisis, University of Chicago Press, Chicago 1988.
33. Ellis, A; Reason and Emotion in Psychotherapy, Lyle Stuart Press, Secausus, New-Jersey 1962.

34. Ellis, A; Why Some Therapies Don't Work; The dangers of Transpersonal Psychotherapy, Prometheus Books, Buffalo 1989.
35. Ewing, Charles P; Crisis intervention as Psychotherapy, Oxford University Press, New-York 1978.
36. Erwin, Edwin; Behavior Therapy: Scientific, philosophical and moral foundations, Cambridge University Press, Cambridge 1978.
37. Eysenk, H; Decline and Fall of the Freudian Empire, Penguin Books Ltd, Middlesex 1985.
38. Fagan, J and I, Lee Shepherd, Edt; Gestalt Therapy Now, Penguin Books Ltd, Middlesex 1970.
39. Fontana, D; The Meditator's Handbook, Element Books Ltd, Rockport 1992
40. Frankl, Victor, E; The Unheard Cry for Meaning, Hodder and Stoughton, London 1979.
41. Freud, Anna; The Ego and the Mechanism of Defence, The Hogarth Press, London 1979.
42. Fromm, E; Zen Buddhism and Psychoanalysis, Harper and Brothers, New-york 1960.
43. Grof. C and S. Grof; The Stormy Search for the Self, Jeremy Tarcher Books, New-York 1992.
44. Grof, S; Beyond the Brain: Birth, Death and Transcendence in Psychotherapy, State University of N-York Press, New-York 1985.
45. Grof, S; The Holotropic Mind, Harper Collins, San Fransisco 1993.
46. Grof, S; The adventure of self-discovery, Sunny Press, Albany 1988.
47. Hardy, J; A psychology with a soul; Psychosynthesis in evolutionary context, Routledge and Kegan Paul, London 1987.
48. Hillman, James; Re-visioning Psychology, Harper Perennial, New-York 1992.
49. Hendricks, G, and B. Weinhold; Transpersonal approaches to counceling and psychotherapy, Love Publishing Comp, Denver 1982.
50. Ivey A. E, M Bradford Ivey, L. Simek-Morgan; Counseling and Psychotherapy: a Multicultural Perspective, Allyn and Bacon, Needham Heights 1993.
51. Jahoda, Marie; Freud and the Dilemmas of Psychology, The Hogarth Press, London 1977.

52. Jacobs, Hans; Western Psychotherapy and Hindu Sadhana, George Allen and Urwin Ltd, London 1961.
53. Kakar, Sudir; the Analyst and the Mystic, Viking, N-Delhi 1991.
54. Kopp, Sheldon; All God's Children are lost, but only a few can play the piano, Prentice Hall Press, N-York 1991.
55. Kovel, Joel; A complete guide to Therapy, Penguin Books, London 1991.
56. Lomas, Peter; Personal Psychotherapy, Oxford University Press, Oxford 1981.
57. Madison, P; Freud's Concept of Repression and Defense, its Theoretical and Observational Language, University of Minnesota Press, Minneapolis 1961.
58. Marmor, J. and S. M. Woods Edt; The Interface Between Psychodynamic and Behavioral Therapies, Plenum Medical Book Comp, New-York 1972.
59. Maslow, A; Eupsychian Management: A Journal, Irwin Press, Illinois, 1971.
60. Maslow, A; Motivation and Personality, Harper and Row Publishers, N-York 2nd ed, 1954.
61. Maslow, A; Psychology of Science; A reconnaissance, Regnery, Chicago 1969.
62. Maslow, A; Religions, Values and Peak-Experiences, The Viking Press, New-York 1970.
63. Maslow, A; The Farther Reaches of Human Nature, The Viking Press, New-York 1971.
64. Maslow, A; Towards a Psychology of Being, Van Nostrand Reinhold Comp, New-York, 2nd ed 1968.
65. May, Robert, M; Cosmic Consciousness Revisited, Element Inc, Rockport 1993.
66. Misiak, H and V Standt Sexton; Phenomenological, Existential and Humanistic Psychologies. A Historical Survey, Grune and Stratton, New-York 1973.
67. Needleman, J, and D. Lewis Edt; On the way to self-knowledge, Alfred A. Konpf Inc, N-York 1976.
68. Nelson, John E; Healing the Split; Integrating Spirit Into Our Understanding of the Mentality Ill, State University of New-York Press, Albany 1993.
69. Okun, B. F; Seeking Connections in Psychotherapy, Jossey-Bass Publishers, San Fransisco 1990.

70. Parfitt, W; The Elements of Psychosynthesis, Element Books, Longmead 1990.
71. Perls F; The Gestalt Approach and Eye Witness to Therapy Bentam Books, New-York 1976.
72. Van Praag . D; Gestalt therapy, Academische Uitgevery, Amersfoort 1987.
73. Prochaska, James. O; Systems of psychotherapy. A Transactional Analysis, Brooks/Cole Publ Comp, Pacific Grove, California 2nd ed 1984.
74. Rama, Swami; Yoga and Psychotherapy; The Evolution of consciousness, The Himalayan Int Inst, Honesdale 1981.
75. Reddy, Madhusudan. V; Integral Yoga Psychology, Institute of Human Study, Hyderabad 1990.
76. Rischabhchand; The integral Yoga of Sri Aurobindo, Sri Aurobindo Memorial Fund Society, Pondicherry 1974.
77. Royce, J. R and L. P. Moss; Humanistic Psychology; Concepts and Criticisms, Plenum Press, New-York 1981.
78. Rowan, John; The transpersonal; Psychotherapy and councelling, Routledge, London 1993.
79. Sanders, C, H. de Wit and H. L. de Jonge; De Congitieve Revolutie in de Psychologie, Kok Agora, Kampen 1989.
80. Sasz T; The Myth of Psychotherapy; Mental Healing as Religion, Rethoric and Repression, Oxford University Press, Oxford 1979.
81. Schaef, Wilson, A; Beyond Therapy, Beyond Science, Harper Collins Publ, New-York 1992.
82. Schur, E; The Awareness Trapp; Self-Absorption Instead of Social Change, Quadrangle/The New York Times Book Comp, New-York 1976.
83. Sharma, Sohan Lal; The Therapeutic Dialogue. A Theoretical and Practical Guide to Psychotherapy, University of New Mexico Press, Albuquerque 1986.
84. Singh, Prakash S; Sri Aurobindo and Jung, Madhucchandas Publications, Aligarh 1986.
85. Smail, D. J; Psychotherapy; A Personal Approach, J. M. Dent and Sons Ltd, London 1978.
86. Sticker, George and Martin Fisher, Edt; Self-disclosure in the therapeutic relationship, Plenum Press, New-York 1990.
87. Storr, A; The Art of Psychotherapy, Routledge, New-York 1990.
88. Strupp, Hans. H, S. W. Hadley, Beverly Comes-Schwartz; Psychotherapy For Better or Worse; The Problem of Negative Effects, Jason Aronson Inc, New-York 1977.

89. Tart, C, Edt; Transpersonal Psychologies, Psychological Processes Inc, El Cerrito 1983
90. Underhill, E; Mysticism, Methum and Co Ltd, London 1911.
91. Vaughan F; The Inward Arc; Healing and Wholeness in Psychotherapy and Spirituality, Shambhala Publ, Boston 1985.
92. Vrinte, Joseph; The concept of Personality in Sri Aurobindo's Integral Yoga and A. Maslow's Humanistic/Transpersonal Psychology, Munshiram Manoharlal, New-Delhi 1995.
93. Walsh R, and F. Vaughan, Edt; Beyond Ego: Transpersonal Dimensions in Psychology, Jeremy Tharcher Inc, Los Angeles 1980.
94. Walsh, R, and F. Vaughan, Edt; Paths Beyond Ego, Jeremy Tharcher, Los Angeles 1993.
95. Washburn, M; the Ego and the Dynamic Ground; A Transpersonal Theory of Human Development, State University of New York Press, Albany 1988.
96. Watts, A; Psychotherapy East and West, Penguin Books, Middle-sex 1973.
97. Wedding, Denny and J. Corsini; Current Psychotherapies, F. E. Peacock Publ Inc, Illinois 1989.
98. Weiner, Irvin B; Principles of Psychotherapy, John Willey and Sons Inc, New-York 1979.
99. Welwood, John, Edt; Explorations in East/West Psychology; The Meeting of the Ways, Stocken Books, New-York 1979.
100. Whitmore, D; Psychosynthesis. Counselling in Action, Sage Publications, London 1991.
101. Wilber, Ken; The Atman Project, Quest Book, Illinois 1980.
102. Wilber, Ken; Eye to Eye; The Quest for the New Paradigm, Anchor Press, New-York 1983.
103. Wilber, Ken; No Boundary: Eastern and Western Approaches to Personal Growth, Shambhala, Boston 1985.
104. Wilber, Ken; Spectrum of Consciousness, Theosophical Publishing House, Illinois 1982.
105. Wilber, Ken and J, Engler, D. P. Brown; Transformation of Consciousness, Shambhala, Boston 1986.
106. Wilber Ken: Up from Eden; A Transpersonal View of Human Evolution, Routledge and Kegan Paul, London 1983.
107. Zeig, J. K. and M. Munion Edt; What is Psychotherapy? Contemporary perspectives, Jossey-Bass Inc Publ, San Fransisco 1990.

INDEX